The Interdisciplinary Future of Engineering Education

The Interdisciplinary Future of Engineering Education discusses the current state of engineering education and addresses the daily challenges of those working in this sector. The topics of how to do a better job of teaching a specific audience, how to facilitate learning, and how to prepare students for their future careers are extensively covered, and innovative solutions are proposed throughout. This unique book brings together a breadth of expertise, attested by the broad backgrounds of the experts and educational practitioners contributing to this volume, to lay the foundations for the future direction with the improvement of education of engineers in mind.

This collaborative effort by a group of uniquely placed educational practitioners provides guidance on the status of current engineering education and lays the foundations for its future direction. The reasons 'why we teach,' 'what we teach,' 'how we teach,' 'when we teach,' 'where we teach,' and 'who teaches' are all re-examined in a new light and ideas and solutions are proposed and evidentially supported. The book sets out ideas for the need to develop a systemic and interdisciplinary approach to the education of future engineers on a model of student-based learning.

This book will be of great interest to academics and educational researchers in the fields of engineering education and higher education. It will also appeal to higher education policymakers, educators, and university teachers.

Plato Kapranos is a Senior University Teacher at the Department of Materials Science & Engineering, The University of Sheffield. He teaches Personal & Professional Skills, Innovative Approaches in Teaching and Learning, and Creativity, Innovation, Enterprise, and Ethics for Engineers for both undergraduates and postgraduates.

The Interdisciplinary Future of Engineering Education

Breaking Through Boundaries in Teaching and Learning

Edited by Plato Kapranos

LONDON AND NEW YORK

First published 2019
by Routledge
2 Park Square, Milton Park, Abingdon, Oxon OX14 4RN

and by Routledge
52 Vanderbilt Avenue, New York, NY 10017

First issued in paperback 2020

Routledge is an imprint of the Taylor & Francis Group, an informa business

© 2019 selection and editorial matter, Plato Kapranos; individual chapters, the contributors

The right of Plato Kapranos to be identified as the author of the editorial material, and of the authors for their individual chapters, has been asserted in accordance with sections 77 and 78 of the Copyright, Designs and Patents Act 1988.

All rights reserved. No part of this book may be reprinted or reproduced or utilised in any form or by any electronic, mechanical, or other means, now known or hereafter invented, including photocopying and recording, or in any information storage or retrieval system, without permission in writing from the publishers.

Trademark notice: Product or corporate names may be trademarks or registered trademarks, and are used only for identification and explanation without intent to infringe.

British Library Cataloguing-in-Publication Data
A catalogue record for this book is available from the British Library

Library of Congress Cataloging-in-Publication Data
Names: Kapranos, Plato, editor.
Title: The interdisciplinary future of engineering education : breaking through boundaries in teaching and learning / edited by Plato Kapranos.
Description: New York : Routledge, [2019]
Identifiers: LCCN 2018038778 (print) | LCCN 2018050835 (ebook) | ISBN 9781351060790 (eBook) | ISBN 9781138481213 (hardback) | ISBN 9781351060790 (ebk)
Subjects: LCSH: Engineering—Study and teaching. | Interdisciplinary approach in education.
Classification: LCC T65.3 (ebook) | LCC T65.3 .I495 2019 (print) | DDC 620.0071—dc23
LC record available at https://lccn.loc.gov/2018038778

ISBN 13: 978-0-367-58251-7 (pbk)
ISBN 13: 978-1-138-48121-3 (hbk)

Typeset in Bembo
by Apex CoVantage, LLC

For Soori/Artemis, Roxanne, Alexia and all others who have enriched my own life journey ...

ITHAKA

When you set sail for Ithaka,
Wish that your voyage is a long one,
one full of adventures, full of discoveries and new understandings.
The Laistrygonians and Cyclopes, angry Poseidon,
do not let them frighten you.
You won't encounter them on your travels
as long as you keep your thoughts and dreams aloft,
and allow your body and spirit to roam on higher planes.
The Laistrygonians and Cyclopes, angry Poseidon,
you will not confront,
as long as you don't carry them inside your soul,
as it's from within your soul they materialize in front of you.
Wish that your voyage is a long one,
May there be many a summer morning when,
with what pleasure and what joy,
you sail into harbours seen for the first time;
arriving at Phoenician trading stations to buy their fine wares,
mother of pearl and coral, amber and ebony,
all kinds of sensual perfumes,
as many sensual perfumes as you can;
and may you visit many an Egyptian city
to gather stores of knowledge from their scholars.
But never lose sight of Ithaka,
for to arrive there is your destination.
Do not hurry the journey,
it's better it lasts many a year,
so that when you finally pull on the island's shores,
you are old, enriched by all the experiences
that you've gathered on your long voyage.
Do not expect Ithaka to make you rich,
Ithaka afforded you the amazing journey;
without her you would not have set sail,
she has no more to give.
And
if you find her impoverished, diminished,
drained by the passage of time,
Ithaka has not deceived you,
you are wiser, full of experiences,
and you should have come to appreciate
the real meaning of Ithakas.

A poem by Constantine P. Kavafy
Translated by P. Kapranos (June 2018)

Contents

List of contributing authors xiv
Acknowledgements xx
Foreword xxi

SUMMARY 1
Part 1 Setting the scene 3

1 **The case for new pedagogies in engineering education** 5
   RHYS MORGAN

   The challenges for engineering in the 21st century 6
   A fundamental misunderstanding 7
      GCSEs 8
      Post-16 education pathways 9
      Higher education 10
   Shortfall 11
   Addressing the skills challenge 11
   Visualization 15
   References 16

2 **Why go to university? The past and future of engineering education** 17
   MARTIN PITT

   Introduction 17
      Open University and others 17
      Open resources and MOOCs 18
      Distance learning and physical attendance 18
   What makes engineering special? 19

Science and engineering 19
Engineering is not science 20
Lectures and other university activities 20
   The lecture – real and virtual 20
   Problem-based learning 21
   Interactions with staff 21
   The timetable 22
   Laboratories 22
   Other practical skills 23
Back to the future 24
Conclusions and recommendations 24
   Conclusions 24
   Recommendations 25
References 26

SUMMARY 28

Part 2 Recent innovations in delivering effective engineering education 31

3 Pedagogical and cost advantages of a multidisciplinary approach to delivering practical teaching 33
ANDREW GARRARD AND STEPHEN BECK

Introduction 33
Costing model and operations 35
Academic liaisons and communication structure 37
Design of the teaching spaces 38
Oversight of the practical teaching in a degree programme 38
   Timeliness of activity 38
   Progressive practical curriculum 39
Commonality of student experience and expectations 40
   Induction labs 41
   Teaching sandwich 41
   Health and safety 42
   Lab books 43
Efficiency through commonality of business processes and utilization 43
   Utilization 45
Concluding remarks 45
References 48

4   **Engineering with a human face**   49
    PETER GOODHEW FRENG

    Introduction 49
    Current practice 50
    Potential future programmes 52
        Question 1: Why? 53
        Question 2: How could this experience be improved? 53
        Question 3: How many? 54
        Question 4: Cost? 54
        Question 5: Who pays? 54
        Question 6: What will be the impact? 55
        Question 7: What are the risks? 55
        Question 8: What happens afterwards? 55
        Question 9: Which language/country? 56
    Discussion 56
    References 57

5   **Interdisciplinary project weeks**   59
    PATRICIA B. MURRAY AND RACHEL HORN

    Introduction 59
    Two weeks and a spiral curriculum 60
        Enabling PBL at scale 60
        Features of both weeks 61
            Inspiration and context 61
            The problems and learning 61
            Alumni/industry 61
            Team outputs 62
            Marking and feedback 62
            Celebration of success 62
    The core learning 62
    Progression: the spiral 62
    Facilitator recruitment 63
    Successes 63
        For the undergraduates 66
        For the postgraduate student facilitators 66
        For the organizers 67
        For the faculty 68
    Challenges and changes 68
        Challenges and changes: student motivation 68
            Subject interest 68

Valuing skills development 69
   The challenge 69
   Changes 69
Team working 70
   The challenge 70
   Changes 70
Depth of investigation 71
   The challenge 71
   Changes 72
No-credit 72
   The challenge 72
   Changes 73
Challenges and changes: delivery 73
   Cascade teaching 73
      The challenge 73
      Changes 74
   Staff engagement 74
      The challenge 74
      Changes 74
Challenges and changes: the impact 74
The future 75
References 76

6 Towards improved engineering education in the United Kingdom 77
WAYNE SEAMES

Introduction 77
Active learning concepts 77
Course design 79
   The learning unit method 79
   The flipped class method 80
Active learning techniques 82
   Problem-based learning 82
   Case studies 83
   In-class reflections 84
   Working in groups 84
The Engagement Teaching Methods for Engineers workshop 85
Workshop assessment 86
In conclusion 88
References 89

SUMMARY	90
Part 3 Linking education to employability	**93**

7 Efficiency of teaching core knowledge and
    employability competencies in chemical engineering
    education   95
    JARKA GLASSEY

   Introduction 95
   Methodology 96
       Exploration of the significance of learning outcomes 96
       Framework development and testing 97
   Results 98
       Learning outcomes 98
       Framework development and testing 103
   Conclusions 110
   References 111

8 Personal and professional skills: something they do
    teach you at university   113
    PLATO KAPRANOS

   Introduction 113
   Current state of affairs 115
   What should the engineer of the future look like? 119
   Challenges and solutions in delivering the engineer of the future 122
   Diploma in personal and professional skills 124
       Learning outcomes of the PG diploma course 125
       Personal Development Planning (PDP) 125
       Course structure 126
   In conclusion 128
   References 129

9 Breaking boundaries with liberal studies in engineering   133
    LOUIS BUCCIARELLI AND DAVID DREW

   Introduction 133
   Engineering practice changed, engineering education challenged 133
   Two design challenges 135
   Two design requirements 136
   Rooted in the liberal arts 137
   Four modules illustrate "infusion" 139

Possible venues, strategies for implementation 142
Reflections 143
References 145

SUMMARY 147
Part 4 The affective side of education 149

10 Through the lenses of the two I's: implement or innovate? 151
ANDY PENALUNA

Purpose 151
Design/methodology/approach 151
Findings 151
Practical implications 151
Social implications 152
Originality/value 152
Introduction and context 152
   Discussion – where are we now? 152
   Discussion – where could we go next? 153
   Thinking deeper and deeper or thinking wider and wider? 154
   The role of the educator, guide-on-the-side, meddler-in-the middle, or simply sage-on-the-stage? 155
   Tell, conspire, or support: the contrasting roles of pedagogy, andragogy, and heutagogy 156
   Mind matters 157
From complexity to pragmatism, introducing the two I's model 160
Summary and conclusions 161
References 161

11 Enterprise education: outside classrooms, inside students' hearts 165
COLIN JONES

Introduction 165
Enterprising engineering graduates 166
Contemplating enterprise education 167
Signature pedagogy for enterprise education 169
Integrating enterprise and engineering education 170
Tools of integration 171
Conclusions 174
References 174

12 Enhancing and managing group creativity through off-task breaks 177
DERMOT BRESLIN

Introduction 177
Individual creativity and off-task breaks 178
  The unconscious and off-task breaks 178
  Mind wandering and off-task breaks 178
Group creativity and off-task breaks 179
  Group creativity and social-cognitive factors 179
  Individual versus group breaks 180
  Group processes and naturally occurring breaks 181
The time of the day effect 182
  Individual creativity and time-of-day 182
  Group creativity and time-of-day 183
Managing off-task breaks 184
  The nature of the off-task break 185
  The duration and frequency of off-task breaks 185
  Individual or group off-task breaks 186
  The timing of off-task breaks 186
Conclusions 187
References 187

Part 5 Concluding remarks: the way ahead 191

Index 194

Contributing authors

Prof. Stephen Beck
s.beck@sheffield.ac.uk

He is interested in quality enhancement of teaching and has served as Director of Undergraduate Studies and the Director of Learning and Teaching Development for the Faculty of Engineering. He was Faculty Director of Learning and Teaching, coordinating learning throughout the Engineering Faculty from 2008 to 2014, during which time he oversaw the implementation of a number of major changes to the teaching such as reducing Winter exams, the introduction of activity weeks, and a CPD scheme for teachers and lecturers. In May 2014, he was appointed to the Headship of Multidisciplinary Engineering Education. This involves ensuring that the practical engineering teaching in The Diamond, a new teaching facility at Sheffield University, is ready for September 2015.

Dr. Dermot Breslin
d.breslin@sheffield.ac.uk

Drawing on his commercial experience and ongoing research activities, Dermot is strongly committed to the continual development of learning and teaching within the undergraduate business management programs at the University of Sheffield. In recognition he was awarded a Senate Award for Sustained Excellence in Learning and Teaching in 2015.

Contributing authors xv

He was Director of MIT's Technology Studies Program, and has been a Curator of Science and Technology at the Smithsonian. He has received the Baker Award for Excellence in Undergraduate Teaching, has consulted for a wide range of industries, and has helped lead a coalition of engineering schools (ECSEL) in the renovation of undergraduate education. He is the author of "Designing Engineers" (MIT Press, 1994); "Engineering Philosophy" (Delft Univ. Press, IOS Press, 2003; Chinese Translation, 2008); and is currently working on a book tentatively titled "Re-envisioning Engineering Education" with Arne Jakobsen of the Danish Technical University.

Prof. Louis (Larry) Bucciarelli, *llbjr@mit.edu*

Holds the Joseph B. Platt Chair in the Management of Technology at The Claremont Graduate University. He is the author of 200 publications, including nine books, about a) the improvement of mathematics and science instruction at all levels of education, b) the development and evaluation of effective undergraduate programs, and c) building strong university research programs. These publications include a book reporting an evaluation he directed of a billion-dollar National Science Foundation program, a RAND report for the White House about federal funding of biomedical research, and a book about how to increase research productivity in the nation's universities.

Prof. David Drew
profdaviddrew@gmail.com

He is a senior university teacher and Director of Academic Operations for Multidisciplinary Engineering Education in Sheffield University's new flagship teaching facility, The Diamond. The focus of his research was modelling fluid flow, experience of which he brings to leading the teaching of experiments in The Diamond's Fluids Engineering lab. At Sheffield he created and led a new Energy Engineering degree programme and won the University's inspirational teacher award.

Dr. Andrew Garrard
a.garrard@sheffield.ac.uk

Contributing authors

Prof. Peter Goodhew Freng
goodhew@liverpool.ac.uk

No longer teaches regularly but remains fascinated by learning and teaching at university level. He is very active within the Royal Academy of Engineering, as chair of their Visiting Professors Steering Committee and a longstanding member of the Education Committee, a STEM Ambassador frequently visiting schools to talk about Engineering. He was the leader of the UK SuperSTEM project at the STFC Daresbury Laboratory for ten years and has been Dean of Engineering and Pro-Vice-Chancellor of the University of Liverpool. During his career at the Universities of Surrey and Liverpool he established the MATTER computer-based learning project and was the founding Director of the UK Centre for Materials Education (UKCME), one of the Subject Centres of the Higher Education Academy. He is the author of the 2010 book "Teaching Engineering."

Prof. Jarka Glassey
jarka.glassey@newcastle.ac.uk

Executive Member of the Education and Accreditation Forum of IChemE with responsibility for Educational Development; Executive Vice President of the European Society of Biochemical Engineering Sciences and Secretary of Working Party on Education, EFCE. Prof Jarka Glassey's interests in chemical engineering education centres around the efficiency of delivering core knowledge and employability competencies to students in increasingly larger classes.

Prof. Rachel Horn
R.HORN@sheffield.ac.uk

Rachel is currently the Director of Learning and Teaching in the Faculty of Engineering, and contributes to numerous Faculty and University committees. In addition to departmental teaching, Rachel is also a leading member of the faculty team who have developed and run the annual faculty-wide project weeks for all first and second year engineering students (Global Engineering Challenge ~900 first year engineering students, and Engineering, You're Hired ~900 second year engineering students).

Contributing authors   xvii

He joined the University of Queensland from Tasmania's School of Management in 2017, having previously been a small business operator, with extensive experience in the franchising of home services. He is a latecomer to the world of academia; he has owned and operated many service-related businesses. In the early eighties, Colin gained a trade qualification working as a Diesel Fitter. During the late eighties, a move into the financial investments sector provided another outlet for his passion of helping people. This was followed by his development of the VIP Home Services franchise group throughout Tasmania. He also created and took to market a unique educational product, imported tractors for resale, and worked as a business consultant in a diverse range of industries.

Dr. Colin Jones
c81.jones@qut.edu.au

His approach to teaching is based on personal continuous improvement through reflection and on student-centred learning. He is involved in the teaching of 'Personal & Professional Skills,' distance learning, research into 'Innovative Approaches in Teaching and Learning' such as online assessment and feedback, use of classroom electronic response systems, active learning, problem-based learning (PBL), and the teaching of 'Creativity, Innovation, Enterprise, and Ethics for Engineers' for both UG and PG levels.

Dr. Plato Kapranos
p.kapranos@sheffield.ac.uk

Rhys has a leading role to co-ordinate the work of the engineering community in ensuring the education system is appropriate at all levels for developing the next generation of engineers. He leads a team whose work includes teacher CPD and curriculum resource materials, research into learning and teaching in engineering education, curriculum and qualification development, and improving diversity in engineering. He advises the Government and devolved assemblies of the UK on all aspects of education policy that affect the formation of engineers.

Dr. Rhys Morgan
rhys.morgan@raeng.org.uk

xviii Contributing authors

Dr. Patricia B. Murray
p.b.murray@sheffield.ac.uk

Started teaching and developing the Postgraduate Certificate in Teaching and Learning at the University of Sheffield. Currently a Faculty University Teacher specializing in Teaching and Learning at the Faculty of Engineering. Currently manages and develops the two cross-faculty project weeks, runs a Continual Professional Development programme in teaching and learning, manages and develops interactive teaching using students' personal devices, and represents the faculty on teaching and learning issues.

Prof. Andy Penaluna
andy.penaluna@uwtsd.ac.uk

The UK's first Professor of Creative Entrepreneurship. Andy chaired the UK's Quality Assurance Agency's Graduate Enterprise and Entrepreneurship Group, putting together expert guidance for the UK University sector. In October 2014, the UK sector skills organization for small business mentoring ('SFEDI') awarded Andy their prestigious enterprise educator award in the House of Lords at Westminster. This followed his co-authorship of the All Party Parliamentary Group for Micro Business's policy paper, "An Education System fit for an Entrepreneur."

Dr. Martin Pitt
m.j.pitt@sheffield.ac.uk

Recently received an ExxonMobil Excellence in Teaching Award from the Royal Academy of Engineering, he is currently the Chairman of the Working Party on Education of the European Federation of Chemical Engineering and Secretary of the Royal Society of Chemistry Tertiary Education Group. Member of the Management Committee of the Engineering Subject Centre of the Higher Education Academy from its beginnings in 2000 to the present day.

Prof. Wayne Seames
wayne.seames@engr.und.edu

Chester Fritz Distinguished Professor, Department of Chemical Engineering, University of North Dakota, School of Engineering. 2013 Faculty Scholar Award for Excellence in Scholarship, Teaching, and Service; 2012 Award for Interdisciplinary Collaboration in Research or Creative Work; 2012 Faculty Spirit of Achievement Award; 2011 Chester Fritz Distinguished Professor for sustained excellence as a tenured faculty member (UND's highest faculty award); 2007 Foundation/Thomas Clifford Faculty Achievement Award for Individual Excellence in Research; 2006 "Professor of the Year" award from UND School of Engineering and Mines. Fulbright Distinguished Chair and a Visiting Professor at the University of Leeds, UK (2014–15).

Acknowledgements

The editor would like to thank his co-authors who contributed their knowledge and expertise in making the idea of this publication a reality.

Thanks are also due to Stephen Birch for his assistance with generating the 'Index' of this publication and Zarah Hill for help with some of the figures.

The author of section 2.4, 'Towards improved engineering education in the United Kingdom,' would like to thank the UK Fulbright Commission and the University of North Dakota's Office of Instructional Development for sponsoring this work. Thanks are also due to the Faculty of Engineering University of Leeds, School of Chemical and Process Engineering, and the Energy Research Institute for supporting this effort. Special thanks to William Gale, Collin Poole, and Robert Cochrane of the University of Leeds for their thorough review of the workshop contents and for helping me to translate from "American Academic English" to "British Academic English."

The author of section 3.1, 'Efficiency of teaching core knowledge and employability competencies in chemical engineering education,' would like to thank colleagues at partner institutions (Université de Lorraine, International Balkan University, University of Porto, Slovak University of Technology, and TU Dortmund) for their contribution to the project "Improving of Teaching Effectiveness in Chemical Engineering" (ITEACH), Project No. 539959-LLP-1–2013–1-UK-ERASMUS-EQR, funded by the Life Long Learning Programme Erasmus Multilateral projects programme.

Thanks are also due to all the participants who provided their opinions through the completed questionnaires.

Foreword

It is frequently heard that the world is becoming more complex and more connected and that our daily lives are being continuously assailed by the effects of increasing globalization and unrelenting rates of scientific, technological, social, and environmental changes.

CP Snow commented that "Technology brings you great gifts with one hand and stabs you in the back with the other," whilst Carl Sagan sounded a warning bell with

> We've arranged a civilization in which most crucial elements profoundly depend on science and technology. We have also arranged so that almost no one understands science and technology. This is a prescription for disaster! We might get away with it for a while, but sooner or later this combustible mixture of ignorance and power is going to blow-up in our faces.

Looking at the world through discipline-based lenses, we can discern that on one hand social scientists study our cultural world and practitioners of the arts help to create and enrich it, and on the other, scientists study our physical world and how it operates, whilst engineers contribute in creating and shaping it. Our world is full of both challenges and opportunities and we need educated graduates of all disciplines that can face up to these challenges and at the same time grasp the opportunities that are being offered.

Education has always been multidisciplinary and interdisciplinary in nature. However, as the complexity of our world became more and more intense, especially since the Industrial Revolution, differentiation of specializations evolved to what appears to be today's norm. However, one has only to look at major developments and projects that have been and are happening around the world, as well all the major challenges we face as a species, to realize that they all have the hallmarks of multidisciplinarity and interdisciplinarity. It is equally evident that in order for these to be successfully realized, skills and know-how from across many disciplines have to be brought to bearing. The connectivity of the world dictates a holistic approach by humanity to the challenges we face and to the developmental direction we take as we move forward into this still young century.

At the University of Sheffield, an institution that is rooted in the legacy of the Industrial Revolution, we have invested substantial resources and effort in the development of teaching and learning. We believe that over recent years there is a lot of good practice we can share with educationalists, educators, policymakers, decision makers, or anyone around the world who has an interest in contributing to the future direction of education. We are also a civic institution, firmly connected to our city, but with an international outlook, and we want to improve not only our city and the lives of our citizens, but we also want to influence the way the world looks and moves into the future beyond our immediate surroundings. Of course we are neither the first nor the only institution that has such ideals but we remain confident that we are out there with the best of them working towards the common good of humanity in providing solutions to key global challenges facing all of us wherever we happen to be.

We provide inclusive education and we are working towards removing artificial barriers wherever and whatever these might be. The only way to deliver the future we want for ourselves and the generations that follow is to have a vision of it and direct our efforts to turn this vision into reality.

Our educational vision is that the Future of Engineering Education is Interdisciplinary, and that Teaching and Learning is more effective when it is Breaking Boundaries; the theme of our most recent conference on Education of Engineers had the very appropriate motto: Μνήσθητε ότι το πεπρωμένον πάντων έστιν απόρροια της συμπεριφοράς εκάστου – "Remember, upon the conduct of each depends the fate of all," Alexander the Great (356–323 BC); working together, building bridges across boundaries, or removing them altogether.

This volume is put together by an international group of educators with a common vision; that of continuously improving education by being innovative and experimenting with new ideas and practices in our world of flux: Τὰ πάντα ρεῖ καὶ οὐδὲν μένει – "Everything flows and nothing remains the same," Heraclitus (535 BC – 475 BC).

In Part 1, we examine issues such as the importance of engineering skills to the future of society, the supply of engineers, and the skills they have to have to meet global grand challenges, how engineering education has been changing over the last ten to twenty years and whether the current education system is fit to meet future challenges. The rise of distance learning for university-level courses is reviewed and answers to the question 'Can education be achieved and a degree awarded purely by distance learning?' are sought.

In Part 2, the pedagogical and cost advantages of a multidisciplinary approach to delivering practical teaching are critically analysed. Together with the practical aspects of Multidisciplinary Engineering Education (MEE), the challenges, along with strategies and solutions to overcome them, are discussed.

We explore what might be meant by Liberal Engineering, and what such an undergraduate programme might comprise, and the inter-relationship between engineering and the whole of society. This is done through a New Model in Technology and Engineering – nmite.org.uk, where a team of visionaries in the UK is developing university-level programmes with several unusual features; this will be explored through content, learning outcomes, and a pedagogic approach.

We recognize that professional engineers operate in an increasingly sophisticated, global world, often working on international projects or in international locations. To do so, they must be agile team players, adept communicators, reflective, and able to operate effectively within interdisciplinary and multi-cultural working environments. To address the need for transferable skills needed by tomorrow's professional engineers, the Faculty of Engineering at the University of Sheffield introduced project weeks, one for all first year students and one for all second year students, where they work in interdisciplinary and multi-cultural teams challenged with real-world problems. These weeks constitute a spiral approach to learning where in the first week the core is open-ended project working and soft-skills development, and the second week builds on the first one, albeit with less scaffolding. The spiral continues into the individual project working that all students undertake in their final year. These weeks offer numerous opportunities for students in their teams to receive feedback from different sources.

While some active learning techniques (instructional methods that require students to do meaningful learning activities and to think about what they are doing, whereas in a traditional lecture, students passively receive information from the instructor) have been used for decades, there is a growing understanding in educational pedagogy that introducing active learning activities into the classroom to replace and/or supplement traditional lecture improves student learning.

Active learning is being revisited, to introduce academic staff to many of the common engagement techniques that are used to replace lectures as the only means of instruction, including student collaborative activities, case studies, and problem-based learning.

In Part 3, the teaching of core knowledge and employability competencies are examined through the development of a robust and objective framework for assessing the efficiency of various pedagogical methodologies. In particular, those methodologies that facilitate the development of important core competencies related to employability. The validity for a range of pedagogical methodologies used in chemical engineering in a range of geographical and educational contexts is evaluated.

Developing the professional industrial leaders of tomorrow is examined through the development of a Diploma in Personal and Professional Skills at the doctoral training level. This approach aims to achieve the creation of the academically sound, ethically minded, enterprising individuals capable of driving our industries of the future.

Continuing with the theme of global challenges, a diverse group of teachers of history, literature, philosophy, anthropology, economics, and other domains in the humanities, arts, and social sciences came together with teachers of engineering at a workshop in Washington D.C to explore possibilities for establishing an innovative undergraduate degree programme – a Bachelor of Arts in Liberal Studies in Engineering that would infuse exemplary and substantive engineering content throughout a sequence of core courses rooted in the liberal arts, aiming to provide a smoother pathway into engineering and better prepare students for the grand challenges they might face in an uncertain future. We explain why such a programme is needed, the boundaries that challenge implementation, and the problems encountered in attempting to break with tradition in both the liberal arts and engineering to fuse new and needed connections.

In the final Part 4, we highlight the need for further support as educators around the world are being challenged to enhance the abilities of their learners, to make them creative and innovative, in order to be able to respond positively to change and to better meet the challenges that tomorrow's world of work will bring. However, most educational environments predict student outcomes so that they can be carefully measured and assessed against prior expectation. Learning is carefully contrived within step-by-step stages that predict and schedule learning sessions for each successive topic – based on the content that the educator is expected to deliver and the curriculum is therefore content-led, and has to be delivered within carefully pre-designed packages that can be evaluated by peers and experts. To compound this approach, new course development and evaluation usually occurs some time ahead of the course delivery through validation exercises in the programme, and this can further compound the predictability aspects of the process.

Behind innovation and its development lies creativity. Creative thinking is dependent on the development of divergent thinking strategies – ways of assisting enlightenment through the production of as many alternative solutions as possible, which requires 'visioning skills' where learners are required to create 'multiple and intangible mental constructions.' This requires breadth as well as depth of thinking. The type of insights needed to be innovative require the ability to see things in different ways, and the preparatory brain state influences the type of thinking needed. Through the lenses of the two I's – asking if we ask students to *implement* or do we ask students to *innovate*? – we consider what happens beyond the threshold of human consciousness, and challenge the way we educate and prepare our students, and offer potential new ways forward.

The world of tomorrow needs enterprising individuals, so the case is made for enfolding enterprise education into the lives of every university graduate by unfolding enterprise education from the formal curriculum. The primary claim is that enterprise resides within the lives of each individual student and not in the curriculum of learning institutions, and that the challenge for learning institutions is to work with what each student naturally brings to the table.

There is a need to develop a holistic and interdisciplinary approach to enterprise education and a new model of enterprise learning is offered that is student-based, not institution-based. This new approach has many implications for all key stakeholders. The key changes required for all participants and the need to elevate such planning above other discipline-based norms and planning procedures are highlighted and discussed.

Moments of insight have played a key role in the evolution of technology over the decades. But can these ephemeral and enigmatic *eureka* events be managed?

The role played by off-task breaks in triggering the unconscious processing of ideas is explored, as is the possibility of breaking up the working day with low effort routine tasks and breaks, to significantly enhance the creativity of individuals. Taking time away from the job becomes a key link in the creativity process, but this requires careful management of the off-task breaks during the innovation process and suggestions how this can be successfully done are put forward.

This book aspires to link together as many facets of educational development as possible, that we perceive as being important to the needs of a rapidly changing world, into a coherent whole that the reader can appreciate in its entirety or as individual themes.

The reasons 'why we teach,' 'what we teach,' 'how we teach,' 'when we teach,' 'where we teach,' and 'who teaches' are all re-examined in a new light and ideas and solutions are proposed and evidentially supported.

This book is neither an 'instruction manual' nor a 'set of recipes' to be followed: it is the 'vision,' experiences, and good practice of a group of individuals from around the world that the readers have to critically examine and interact with, and hopefully adapt to their own needs and requirements.

It has been my pleasure and honour to have worked with my highly esteemed colleagues who have contributed their vast knowledge and experiences on the various topics presented in this volume and I hope that you will find our work fascinating and valuable in equal measures.

I will finish with this sentiment by quoting Richard Feynman: "For a successful technology, reality must take precedence over public relations, for Nature cannot be fooled"; in our case interchanging 'education' for 'technology.'

This is not a public relations exercise; this is our vision of what education ought to be in the 21st century.

Plato Kapranos
Sheffield 2018

Summary of Part I

The 20th century saw many engineering achievements that have without a doubt improved virtually every single aspect of human life. The new century presents us with many challenges that stem from the past and many others that are the result of population growth and the need to continue in supporting their lives at least at the same standard of living of the current generation in a sustainable manner that does not undermine the living standards of future generations.

In 2016, the United Nations launched 17 Sustainable Development Goals (SDGs) of the 2030 Agenda for Sustainable Development, and there is little doubt that engineering will play a crucially important role in achieving many of these goals. The education systems across the world must address not only the need for training the many more engineers that will be necessary to tackle these challenges, but also take steps to provide the pedagogies that will give these engineers the appropriate knowledge, thinking, and doing skills they will need to carry out these tasks. Education must move with the relentless pace of change and nurture the attributes and professional traits in our future engineers by inspired approaches that excite their curiosity, their creativity, and their engagement with their world; we cannot find solutions to our problems with the same mindset that created them in the first place. To facilitate the necessary changes in our educational systems we will need teachers who will take the role of the 'guide-on-the-side' rather than the traditional lecturing role of 'sage-on-the-stage.'

The exponential growth of information being available at our fingertips and the means of instant electronic communication over vast distances has afforded us educational opportunities as never before. Educators must make use of such tools to complement, and not to the detriment of, traditional ways of teaching and learning. With the online facilities now available, one may ask if attending a traditional university is worthwhile. Can the education be achieved and a degree awarded purely by distance learning? This would provide a great savings for international students and a potential disaster for many traditional universities. For engineering, the answer appears to be 'no' (with some provisos), but there is a strong need for a rethink of how an engineering degree should be delivered.

The rise of distance learning for university-level courses is reviewed, and the sort of subjects offered. Some kind of attendance (at least at a local centre) is generally required for assessment, and perhaps for laboratory work or other exercises. Most engineering first degrees generally require a significant practical element, often with large, expensive equipment. There are many introductory level courses online, and a few master's degrees of a theoretical type, where the student will normally have had the necessary practical experience in a traditional bachelor degree.

The often overlooked pedagogic advantages of having students physically present and the burden on staff of managing distance learning are discussed. Engineering is a special case, because it is about doing. While virtual systems have some use, actual operation of physical equipment should be a motivating factor for students (and thus a selling point for a university) as well as providing educational advantages. Many universities are now investing in both physical resources and in staff and administration in order to give a greater number of students a greater number of hours of practical experience and effective feedback. Meanwhile, online systems can provide some automation of standard learning of support subjects to allow more time for design and group work appropriate to real engineering.

The development of the engineering habits of mind must start with young people, from school age onwards; it may help them to understand the role of engineers better and also give them the confidence and the self-efficacy to take on engineering challenges themselves. In doing so, we may find a more fruitful mechanism for addressing the engineering skills shortage challenge.

Part I

Setting the scene

Part I

Setting the scene

Chapter 1

The case for new pedagogies in engineering education

Rhys Morgan

Throughout history humankind has managed to overcome the many barriers it has faced in order to prolong life and improve our existence on the planet. These engineering achievements are well documented. The earliest examples can be identified as primitive stone tools for hunting and preparation of food to the control of the elements; in particular the direction of water for irrigation, farming, and sewerage and the creation of monuments and other early infrastructure. Later followed the ability to harness heat energy that led to basic working of metals, and casting and shaping for creation of tools, weapons, and ornaments.

Skipping forward several thousand years, it is worth reflecting on just a few just profoundly impactful innovations from the 20th century; electrification, the automobile, the aeroplane, radio and television, integrated circuits and computing, rockets, and spacecraft. There are of course many more, but the extraordinary impact on humanity from just these few alone has changed life for billions of people that inhabit our tiny fraction of the universe.

Many advancements in engineering have had unexpected and unintended consequences on our lives in ways we could never have imagined. The laser, for example, first created in 1960 by Theodore Maiman at Hughes Research Laboratories in the USA, which has had such profound impact on so many aspects of life, from telecommunications to advanced manufacturing to entertainment, was initially mockingly described as a solution waiting for a problem! Another surprising example is the advent of air conditioning, which has transformed our world in a way well beyond its immediate intention. The air conditioner was developed in 1902 by an inventor named Willis Carrier and was created to prevent paper wrinkling in the heat and humidity of the printing and lithography company in which he worked in Brooklyn, New York. Some years later, after air conditioning units had spread throughout industry, they became popular in movie theatres and cinemas, and the cool environment of the theatres became an attraction in themselves to allows the masses to cool down in the summer heat. Various commentators argue that it is not a coincidence that the Golden Age of Hollywood began around the same time. But perhaps most fascinating is the fact that because of the advent of home air conditioning, many Republican

Americans were able to migrate to southern and western states which were previously too hot and humid to comfortably inhabit in the summer months. This migration brought affluent pensioners to the southern states, which in turn skewed the US Electoral College system in favour of the Republican Party in the 1980s and led to the election of Ronald Reagan and several subsequent Republican presidents, including Donald Trump today. I allow the reader to judge for themselves whether they believe air conditioning has therefore had a worthwhile impact on humanity!

The challenges for engineering in the 21st century

The 20th century saw the greatest engineering achievements that humankind has created, and have arguably improved virtually every single aspect of human life. This new century holds as many challenges as those in the past and, as the population continues to grow, the challenge of sustaining civilization's continuing advancement, while continuing to improve the quality of life for the expanding global population, will become ever more pressing.

In 2008, the National Academy of Engineering in the United States of America published the Grand Challenges for Engineering. Drawing on input from leading engineers and technological thinkers from around the world, 14 goals for improving life on the planet were identified. The vision of the grand challenges called for "Continuation of life on the planet, making our world more sustainable, secure, healthy and joyful."

The global grand challenges idea captured the imagination of the profession, engineers and academics, policymakers, and students across the globe. Since the publication of the initial Grand Challenges report, there have been three international summits held in London (2013), Beijing (2015), and Washington (2017). An undergraduate student programme has been developed and momentum continues to build as more young people beginning their engineering careers recognize the role that engineering serves to society and people

Table 1.1 Grand Challenges for Engineering (NAE, 2008)

Make solar energy economical	Reverse-engineer the brain	Secure cyberspace	Restore and improve urban infrastructure
Provide access to clean water	Engineer better medicines	Prevent nuclear terror	Enhance virtual reality
Develop carbon sequestration methods	Advance health informatics	Engineer the tools of scientific discovery	Advance personalized learning
Provide energy from fusion	Manage the nitrogen cycle		

Table 1.2 UN Sustainable Development Goals (2016)

1. No poverty	2. Zero hunger	3. Good health and wellbeing	4. Quality education
5. Gender equality	6. Clean water and sanitation	7. Affordable and clean energy	8. Decent work and economic growth
9. Industry, innovation, and infrastructure	10. Reduced inequalities	11. Sustainable cities and communities	12. Responsible consumption and production
13. Climate action	14. Life below water	15. Life on land	16. Peace, justice, and strong institutions
17. Partnership for the goals			

and the need for a global mindset to work and engage with engineers anywhere in the world in the 21st century.

More recently, in 2016, the United Nations launched the 17 Sustainable Development Goals (SDGs) of the 2030 Agenda for Sustainable Development (see Table 1.2). The SDGs, call for actions across all countries to end all forms of poverty, fight inequalities, and tackle climate change, while ensuring no one is left behind.

Again, engineering will play a crucially important role in achieving many of these goals. Clearly, addressing issues such as clean water and sanitation, sustainable cities and communities, and affordable clean energy require engineering domain knowledge and skills. But the role of technology in reducing poverty, improving opportunities for education, increasing access to better healthcare, and many others will also rely on engineers to address these challenges.

A fundamental misunderstanding

Despite this role that engineers have had in shaping humanity's life on the planet and the key part they will play in addressing the 21st century's challenges, society still appears to misunderstand the profession. The definition from the Oxford English Dictionary provides an excellent illustration:

Engineering: Noun: The branch of science and technology concerned with the design, building, and use of engines, machines, and structures.

It is worth reflecting at this point on the etymological root of the word, engineer. It comes from the Latin, *ingenium*, which means 'genius' or more generally, talent, natural capacity, clever, and problem solver (McCarthy, 2009). It leads to well-known derivatives such as ingenious and ingenuity – words that we often associate with engineering solutions. In many European countries, the name engineer is still spelt with an *i*, such as *ingenier* (French), or *ingegnere*

(Italian), reflecting the Latin root more precisely. The word engine with an 'e' itself appears around c. 1300 and has its origins in the creation of instruments of war, specifically armaments that were developed in the middle ages. The use of the word engine for a mechanical device converting energy to mechanical power (in particular steam) did not come about until the early 19th century and the beginning of the Industrial Revolution.

We might say – oh, how different the discipline might be viewed then but for a single letter! One might imagine young people engaged in feverish competition to gain places to study how to become ingenious at university!

But why does this matter? Today, in the UK certainly, where we discarded the letter 'i' in favour of 'e,' we find the public more generally associating engineering with the grease, oil, and tools that are synonymous with machines that transfer energy to power – notably reciprocating engines found in vehicles and other forms of transport. This has been exacerbated by a number of other skilled trades identifying themselves as engineering, and while exhibiting some aspects of engineering knowledge and skills, many in the engineering community argue the occupation of the name engineer by technical workers has done irreparable damage to the status of the profession and undoubtedly has been a contributing factor to the UK suffering from an engineering skills shortage.

Engineering UK, the body which analyses engineering skills demand and supply data for the engineering profession, highlights in its 2018 annual report a demand of 124,000 engineers and technicians over a ten year period between 2014 and 2024. Assuming a flat annual demand profile, this means 124,000 engineers and technicians each year (The State of Engineering, 2018).

While this figure appears extraordinary at first glance, it is actually not as unreasonable as it might appear. Engineering in the UK is substantial. Around half of the UK's exports come from manufactured goods and the sector accounts for around 25% of GDP (RAE, 2015). According to national statistics data, there are some 4.5 million people working in engineering occupations in the UK (The State of Engineering, 2018). Assuming an average 40-year working life, this would require the replacement of around 112,500 engineers and technicians each year just from retirements alone. Add to that any additional demand due to expansion of particular sectors, such as software and digital engineering, and it becomes apparent how quickly the demand figure can be reached.

The question therefore is how does the education system meet this demand? The graph in Figure 1.1 illustrates the typical annual supply of people into engineering.

GCSEs

Each year, there are around 650,000 students taking GCSEs – the first formal assessment in the education system across England, Wales, and Northern Ireland. Scotland has a different qualifications system and while not presented here, the

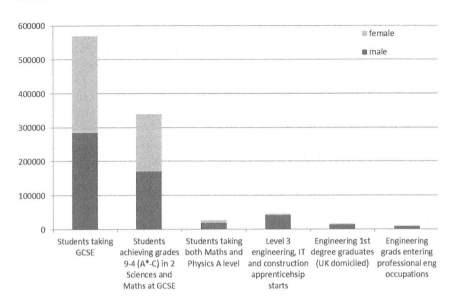

Figure 1.1 Key transition points in engineering education skills supply

Source: UK Department for Education, Higher Education Statistics Agency, Engineering UK, State of Engineering, 2018 report.

pattern of progression is similar. Of those students taking GCSE qualifications, around half will achieve good grades A★-C (or in the new grading system 9–4), which allows them to readily progress to some form of study towards engineering in their post-16 education, although many schools will require at least a B grade to continue studying mathematics and physics on an academic pathway.

Due to the compulsory nature of GCSE qualifications, the cohort achieving good grades is fairly representative of the student population in terms of gender and ethnicity but is under-represented by those from lower socio-economic groups (SEEdash). Computing and Design & Technology, two other important enabling subjects, are not compulsory at Key Stage 4. These have participation of 65,000 and 165,000, respectively. There is increasing concern at the gender profile of the computing cohort with only 20% of young women choosing the subject at GCSE.

Post-16 education pathways

After GCSEs, there is a significant decrease in the skills supply to engineering as students are given their first opportunity to choose future subjects and pathways (academic or vocational/technical) of study.

'A levels' are the academic pathway for study after the age of 16 across schools in England, Wales, and Northern Ireland (with Scotland continuing its separate qualifications system). At A level, encouragingly mathematics is now the most popular subject, with around 95,000 students, of which 40% of are female (JCQ). Maths is seen by many students as an 'open' subject leading to a wide range of destinations. As such it is studied with a broad combination of other subjects such as history, economics, geography, music, computing, and the sciences. Physics, by contrast, has a significantly lower number of students at around 35,000, with only 20% of the cohort female. Participation of A level maths and physics by ethnic groups also remains fairly constant with the proportions of the cohort at GCSE level.

The number of students taking maths and physics, often pre-requisites for engineering degrees, is slightly lower at around 30,000. In stark terms, this means that 95% of the annual cohort of students opts out of following an academic route towards engineering at the age of 16. For girls, the figure is even worse, with only 2% of the cohort choosing to study subjects leading to engineering.

For vocational and technical pathways at age 16, students may opt to follow a work-based training route (apprenticeships), or continue with full-time college based vocational education. The popularity of apprenticeships has been increasing steadily in the UK over the last ten years, and latest data shows that approximately 110,000 people started apprenticeships in engineering and associated subjects in 2015/16 (The State of Engineering, 2018).

This highlights the criticisms of many commentators that employers are using apprenticeships to reskill or upskill their current workforce, which is welcome for addressing the UK's productivity challenge, but is not contributing to increasing the number of engineers and technicians to meet current and future skills demand. Female participation in apprenticeships in engineering is very low, at around 5–6% of the annual cohort.

For full-time college based provision, it is currently difficult to accurately calculate the size of the cohort because of the way the data is currently collected. However, estimates based on qualification data and the scale of the FE sector in the UK suggest an annual cohort of between 20,000 and 25,000 students. It is worth noting however, that the majority of young people taking apprenticeships and full-time vocational qualifications in colleges are taking programmes of study that are equivalent to GCSE qualification level, rather than progressing to advanced qualifications equivalent to A level.

Higher education

At age 18, many young people in the UK will leave education and enter the world of work. However, record-breaking numbers of students continue to study in higher education. In 2017, the proportion of young people undertaking undergraduate degree programmes reached 49%. For engineering, around

25,000 graduates are produced each year, of which approximately 15,000 are UK domiciled. Within the UK cohort, around 10% are female, while ethnic minority students continue to reflect their proportions in the wider UK population (FE). As an interesting comparison, it is worth noting that the entire UK domiciled output of engineering first degree graduates over the past four or five years is around the equivalent of the student cohort at the University of New South Wales in Australia!

The Royal Academy of Engineering has undertaken detailed analysis of graduate employment in the UK, looking at destinations and factors affecting outcomes for graduates (RAEng, 2016). Overall, around 65% of engineering graduates enter the workplace within six months of graduation. Of these, 56% find work in professional engineering occupations. This means that 80% of those graduates entering work are going into engineering roles. Also encouragingly, the transition into engineering employment is very similar for both males and females, although graduates from minority ethnic backgrounds are significantly less likely to find engineering employment and indeed are more likely to find themselves unemployed.

Shortfall

The number of students taking apprenticeships, vocational/technical qualifications, and engineering degrees amounts to around 60,000–80,000 per annum (depending on accuracy of technical pathway data). This suggests an overall yearly shortfall of somewhere between 30,000 and 50,000. The lack of accuracy of this figure is compounded by the fact that graduates from related disciplines, such as mathematics, physics, and computer science might also enter engineering occupations, thus increasing the talent pool and reducing the shortfall.

Despite the relatively straightforward supply and demand analysis presented here, there are members of the engineering community that question the skills shortage, citing limited salary increases of engineers and anecdotal stories of graduate engineers struggling to find work. In addition, companies such as Rolls Royce, National Grid, and Jaguar Land Rover apparently have little difficulty attracting many thousands of high calibre applicants. The globally competitive nature of engineering resulting in small margin businesses, and the current ability of blue chip UK companies to attract talent from around the world, largely answers these questions. However, organizations such as EEF (the manufacturers association) and the IET (The Institution of Engineering & Technology) continue to highlight critical skills shortages in employer surveys (EEF Skills report, 2016; IET Skills survey, 2017).

Addressing the skills challenge

The Royal Academy of Engineering has been pursuing a new approach over the past four years to address the engineering skills challenge. What if at least part of the reason that we do not have enough engineers is because we just don't know enough about how great engineers actually think? Or at least if we do know this, we do not make enough use of what we know? And what if schools, colleges, and universities are actually teaching engineering in ways that do not cultivate the kinds of engineering minds we need? Re-present the issue like this and it moves away from economics and market forces towards psychology and pedagogy.

With the support of a community of academics and engineers led by Professor Bill Lucas, Director of the Centre for Real World Learning at the University of Winchester, UK, the study has provided new insights into the ways engineers think and act and explores ways in which the education system might be redesigned, in all phases, to develop more effective engineers. Using an education psychology approach called habits of mind, the work has identified key characteristics or attributes that engineers exhibit, and has explored pedagogies and approaches to nurture these thinking and doing skills.

The notion of habits of mind was first used by psychologist Al Cuoco and colleagues to describe the thinking skills demonstrated by students for mathematics, as shown in Table 1.3.

Later, researchers applied the same approach to scientists, with the resulting habits of mind identified in Table 1.4.

In 2014, the Royal Academy of Engineering gathered a group of engineers, academics, and educators to explore those professional traits that are common to engineers. These are presented in Figure 1.2, which one might think of as the cross-section of an engineer's brain!

At the core of the engineering mindset is the determination to 'make things work' or make them work better. One might argue about terminology – should it be create rather than make? Things might immediately suggest physical objects, while many would argue engineers develop systems, solutions, processes, and software that are not physical, but the principle that engineers make things is strong – it is not curiosity driven, like science, but rather solutions driven; an important difference.

In order to achieve the 'made' outcome, there are a series of supporting habits of mind. They do not exist in any particular order, but a natural pattern based around the engineering design process does begin to emerge.

The first is Problem Identification. Engineers need to be able to articulate and specify a problem to arrive at a solution. Take the following example:

> A simple problem might be the need for a person to cross a river. As an immediate answer to this, one might suggest a boat. But further specification of the problem might include frequency of crossings, the necessary speed of travel, and the loads to be carried. One might then come to the conclusion that a bridge might be better. Then more detailed information will be required; the width of the river (perhaps necessitating multiple spans), the ground conditions and geo-technical considerations on either

Table 1.3 Mathematical habits of mind (Cuoco et al., 2015)

Pattern sniffer	Always on the lookout for patterns and the delight to be derived from finding hidden patterns and then using shortcuts arising from them in their daily lives
Experimenter	Performing experiments, playing with problems, performing thought experiments allied to a healthy scepticism for experimental results
Describer	Able to play the maths language game, for example, giving precise descriptions of the steps in a process, inventing notation, convincing others, and writing out proofs, questions, opinions, and more polished presentations
Tinkerer	Taking ideas apart and putting them back together again
Inventor	Always inventing things – rules for a game, algorithms for doing things, explanations of how things work, or axioms for a mathematical structure
Visualizer	Being able to visualize things that are inherently visual such as working out how many windows there are on the front of a house by imagining them, or using visualization to solve more theoretical tasks
Conjecturer	Making plausible conjectures, initially using data and increasingly using more experimental evidence
Guesser	Using guessing as a research strategy, starting with a possible solution to a problem and working backward to achieve the answer.

Table 1.4 Scientific habits of mind (Calik & Coll, 2015)

Open-mindedness	Being receptive to new ideas, prepared to consider the possibility that something is true, and willing to change ideas in the light of evidence
Scepticism	Using critical questioning, adopting a critical appraisal approach, only according provisional status to claims until proved otherwise
Rationality	Appealing to good reason and logical arguments as well as a need to revise arguments in the light of evidence and argument
Objectivity	Adhering to accepted modes of inquiry in different disciplines and recognizing the need to reduce the idiosyncratic contributions of the investigator to a minimum and always looking for peer scrutiny and replication of findings
Mistrust of arguments from authority	Treating arguments sceptically irrespective of the status of the originator
Suspension of belief	Not making immediate judgements if evidence is insufficient
Curiosity	Demonstrating a desire to learn, inquisitiveness and a passion for discovery

14 Rhys Morgan

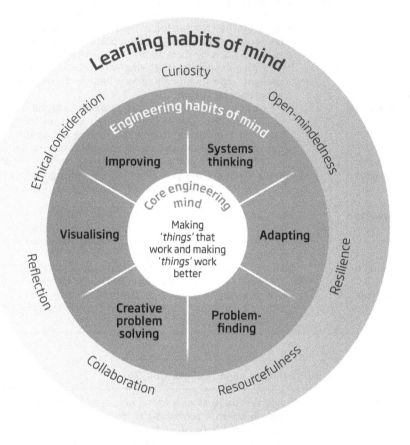

Figure 1.2 Engineering Habits of Mind (Royal Academy of Engineering, Thinking like an engineer, 2015).

side of the river, and indeed under the river bed itself. Perhaps on answering these questions one might find a tunnel is required.

The purpose of this example is to highlight the careful articulation and specification of the problem that is a key skill for engineers, and one that, as educators, we do not spend sufficient time developing in our students.

The second engineering habit of mind is creative problem solving. I have often heard members of the engineering profession say that engineering is about creativity. That may be true, but on its own it is not specific enough. How does engineering differ from other forms of creativity – art, music, sculpture, dance, poetry, and so on? The specific nature of creativity in engineering is for addressing specific problems.

Those problems again need to be defined as above, including physical constraints, understanding user needs and wants, aesthetics, ergonomics, and a whole range of other factors. The development of idea generation and creativity skills is therefore essential in the formation of engineers.

Visualization

The third engineering habit of mind is visualization. I cannot think of an engineer I know who doesn't sketch out a diagram as they think – be it an engineering sketch or a production diagram or even a process flow around engineering education.

Visualizing is a key component of the engineer's skill set and it builds in sophistication during the lifecycle of an engineering project – from 2D sketches to 3D CAD, to physical models and functional prototypes. All are forms of visualization. Yet in engineering education, little time is spent on the early stage of visualization, and on understanding how to sketch as part of the idea generation process and to use it as a form of rapid communication among team members.

Adapting is a further trait exhibited by engineers, who will apply solutions from different contexts, rather than developing solutions from first principles each time. It is the application of ideas and knowledge that is a key attribute of engineers.

Improving and a relentless drive to make products better is another attribute of engineers. It is the result of constant tinkering and experimenting, testing new ideas, and evaluating against pre-determined criteria to find better solutions. However, again there is little opportunity for multiple iterations of designs and solutions in the engineering education system because of limited time available, and as such this is not developed as much as it could be in future engineers.

Systems thinking is the final trait of engineers, who recognize that their work is only a subset of a larger system and that their designs and solutions may have unintended consequences on the wider system. The iterative improvement cycle therefore plays a key role in the systems approach.

Clearly the traditional method of designing curricula that produce only specialists in their disciplines no longer adequately represents the reality of the ever increasingly varied employment market and societal needs. The interdisciplinary nature of science and engineering dictates a new approach that re-examines our conventional structures and focuses on developing the diverse, multi-skilled, complete graduates of the future.

The development of the engineering habits of mind in young people, from school age onwards, may help them to understand the role of engineers better and also give them the confidence and the self-efficacy to take on engineering challenges themselves. In doing so, we may find a more fruitful mechanism for addressing the engineering skills challenge.

References

Calik M & Coll R (2015) *Thinking Like an Engineer*. Royal Academy of Engineering Url:www.raeng.org.uk

Cuoco A et al. (2015) *Thinking Like an Engineer*. Royal Academy of Engineering Url:www.raeng.org.uk

EEF Skills report (2016) An upskill battle Url:www.eef.org.uk

FE Data library Url:www.gov.uk/government/collections/fe-data-library

IET (2017) Skills survey Url:www.theiet.org

JCQ Joint Council for Qualifications Url:www.jcq.org.uk

McCarthy N (2009) *Engineering: A Beginner's Guide*. Oxford: Oneworld Publications

NAE USA (2008) *Grand Challenges for Engineering* Url:www.engineeringchallenges.org/

RAEng (2016) *Employment Outcomes of Engineering Graduates: Key Factors and Diversity Characteristics* Url:www.raeng.org.uk

Royal Academy of Engineering (2015) *Engineering for a Successful Nation* Url:www.raeng.org.uk

SEEdash – the Science and Engineering Education Dashboard, Established by the Royal Academy of Engineering, Institute of Physics and Gatsby Foundation Url:www.seedash.org

The State of Engineering (2018) Url:www.engineeringuk.com

Thinking like an Engineer (2015) *Royal Academy of Engineering* Url:www.raeng.org.uk

UN Sustainable Development Goals (2016) Url:www.un.org/sustainabledevelopment/

Chapter 2

Why go to university? The past and future of engineering education

Martin Pitt

Introduction

Open University and others

In the days before the Internet, the Open University (OU) was a remarkable innovation (Kaye, 1973), which showed that education up to full degrees could be achieved by people who studied away from the campus via television and postal work. The development of computers and the Internet has vastly increased the possibilities and ease of access. A great many universities now offer some courses online, though those offering full degrees are many fewer. The Universidad Nacional de Educación a Distancia (UNED) (National Distance Learning University) in Spain was launched in 1976 (UNED, 2016) and is probably the first major success after the OU. In 1995 the Universitat Oberte de Catalunya (UOC) (Open University of Catalonia) was launched and claims to be the first purely online university offering full degrees (UOC, 2016). A notable feature of these two is that the courses are taught in Spanish and Catalan. (Most online courses are in English.) By the year 2000, substantial offerings were available in Europe, Australia, North and South America, China, India, and Bangladesh (Harry, 1999). Because of the distances involved and scattered population, Australia has an obvious demand for online courses as well as a tradition of schooling by radio and television, and so has been particularly active. However the first year dropout rate for online degrees was found to be nearly twice (28%) that of traditional degrees (15%) (Ben-Naim, 2015). A recent review found that business qualifications predominated in online university courses (Kumar et al., 2017).

At present, and apart from those mentioned above, most online courses seem to be a small offering from traditional universities, making use of current trends in preparing course material online. However corporate training by large international companies is substantially aligned to as much online activity as possible, though their work is not generally reported in the academic literature.

Open resources and MOOCs

A further development has been putting material online that can be accessed by anybody. MIT was notable in putting videoed lectures and other material on the Internet. However, this was material designed for standard students. By contrast, the OU has material for lone learners and made some of this openly available since 2006 (Gourley & Lane, 2009). Interestingly it provides facilities for others to set up projects and effectively provide online open courses via the Moodle VLE (OpenLearn, 2018). In practice, YouTube is now hosting a great many videos including instruction and demonstrations in science and engineering, and many university lecturers make use of them in their teaching, either during lectures or as preparatory or support material.

The difference between such open material and a MOOC is that a student has to enrol. At the simplest level, a certificate may be given for completion of content (watching a video, completing a quiz) or there may be some interaction between students in groups and/or students with staff. With staff being (currently) real rather than virtual, there are time, and thus money, costs for the institution and usually for the student. Harvard limits its enrolment on a copyright course to 500 so that 21 staff can manage it, because "high-quality legal education depends, at least in part, upon supervised small-group discussions of difficult issues" (Laurillard, 2014).

Several institutions in the USA have been offering online degree courses in engineering since 1993, though these are mostly master's for those with a bachelor degree.

Distance learning and physical attendance

It should be noted that the Open University requires some attendance at its main campus or an increasing number of other centres for its qualifications. This is particularly important for science and engineering courses to allow hands-on laboratory work. The UOC does not require any attendance but is limited to subjects not requiring hands-on activity: it does not offer science or engineering. The OU has always been strong on science, and has developed experiments which can be carried out in the home, along with small items such as a compact microscope which can be sent by post (Kay, 1973). However, it remains very limited in engineering, and this is generally true of the online offerings at all levels. A commercial equivalent, RDI, focuses on subjects such as law and business and offers no engineering and no science apart from healthcare (RDI, 2016). UNED provides the possibility of attending laboratories at its main site or associated centres, but these appear to be complementary rather than essential. Experiments can be done on virtual laboratories, but it does not appear to have the home experiment kits of the OU.

There have been examples of engineering laboratory courses where some students are distance learning (typically by viewing a video) and where they are found to be equally successful (e.g. Abdel-Salam, Kauffman & Crossman, 2006, 2007; Stefanovic, 2013). However, these students generally had a qualification (e.g. associate degree) in the subject and worked in industry, so their education had already included practical work. They were thus not fully educated in engineering online.

Software engineering can of course be done online, and it is feasible to have electronic components supplied or bought locally for exercises, but some of the lab work traditionally found in other engineering subjects requires large and often expensive equipment. (Though as the OU and some other providers demonstrate, a certain amount can be done with household items.)

An increasing number of things can of course be simulated, so students can collapse bridges or make aeroplanes crash online, but I believe that a wish for some degree of actual contact with serious engineering limits the provision of engineering courses purely by distance learning, very probably influenced by the professional institutions in their accreditation.

A notable exception is a degree programme in chemical engineering at the University of Strathclyde, which is accredited by the Institution of Chemical Engineers (Strathclyde, 2016). However, this is for people working in the industry (such as operators, technicians, chemists) who have the practical experience but need the theoretical background. This model would not work for students straight from school. Likewise, a number of USA colleges offer online master's courses in engineering topics, but not generally the full bachelor course, though a first year certificate can be done (Bourne et al., 2005). Students are also required to attend exams in person, avoiding many of the issues associated with coursework or online assessment (i.e. that the work is not being done by someone else). UNED also requires personal attendance at exams. The Open University of China offers engineering degrees, but is not fully online, and includes face-to-face and laboratory work at local centres (Freear, 2016).

What makes engineering special?

Science and engineering

In practice, a motivated person with access to a good library has always had the capability to study and achieve knowledge up to degree level in many subjects, and there are many examples of self-taught people achieving considerable eminence. This includes some academics that have moved into fields substantially different from their first qualification. By careful reading and increasingly by use of resources such as videos on the Internet, individuals can gain a good knowledge of many humanities and science fields, and perhaps even a fairly deep understanding.

However, it is the general practice that degrees in science and engineering include some practical work in laboratories. The OU has been particularly ingenious in devising experiments which can be carried out in the home, using small, relatively cheap equipment which can be provided, and this has been used from the outset for science foundation courses (Kaye, 1973). It is notable that a recent book on open and distance learning includes very little about these techniques for engineering, and is mainly restricted to video (Lockwood, 2013). The literature tends to describe virtual machines and experiments, with very few cases of actual (and very simple) equipment which can be accessed remotely. The Technical University of Berlin (TUB, 2016) has several solid state physics experiments, and the University of Cambridge has two experiments based on a "stirred tank" (essentially a beaker) for chemical engineers (Botero et al., 2016).

Accreditation by professional institutions such as Engineers UK, ABET, or EUR-ACE is usually conditional on some demonstrated ability to devise and carry out experiments, which has been one limit. The potential advantages of student remote access to equipment has often been recognized, but the costs and practical difficulties for timetabling are also clear (Bourne et al., 2005) and its use at present seems infinitesimal.

Engineering is not science

The Finniston Report (Finniston, 1980) complained of the "misleading tendency to regard engineering as a subordinate branch of science," which unfortunately remains widespread, including in academic institutions. (This error was again made in the forward to a UNESCO report in 2007, though the content of the report is very valuable.) To put it simply, science is about finding out, by experiment and observation; engineering is about designing new things and processes. Science and mathematics are merely tools, but not the only ones. The scientist may need to design apparatus and experiments and the engineer may need to find out, but these are means not ends, which are quite different. Engineering is about doing, so it is important that the degree experience includes as much of this as possible; it is not about receiving and uncritical acceptance of information. Engineering also requires appreciation of the limits of the real world, which will not be found by ideal mathematical models or perfect simulators.

In the 1980s there was movement in the UK called "Education for Capability" – the idea that graduates should not be mere repositories of knowledge, but should be actually able to do something with it, an aim particularly appropriate for engineers (Pratt, 1986). Sadly, this had no discernible effect.

Lectures and other university activities

The lecture – real and virtual

Much of the literature on higher education is basically about ways to mitigate the inherent and long-known defects of the lecture as a teaching method (Bligh, 1972; Regmi, 2012; Pritchard, 2017; Illeris, 2016, 2018; Smith & Firth, 2018).

For example: that students cannot pay attention just listening for more than about 20 minutes without a break, so a real lecture should adopt some structure or change of pace (Bligh, 1972, 2008; Buzan, 1995; Pickford & Clothier, 2003; Perrin & Laing, 2014). Unfortunately the design of lecture theatres generally makes a change to some group activity difficult. As Bligh said "The architecture of many lecture theatres makes the use of any other teaching method extremely difficult. Heads of departments commit their teaching staff to decades of inappropriate teaching methods when they accept an architect's plans." There has been little change, and it is rare for a new building to start by an appraisal of what would be the desirable educational method.

The advantage of a video lecture is that the student can, of course, pause and rewind. Those academics using the flipped lecture technique also tend to limit the video to no more than 20 minutes. Of course, the whole point of a flipped lecture is that the students can then experience some activity, typically including interaction with staff, one of the reasons to attend university.

The work of Hake (1998) is a key study of the unsurprising fact that passive lecturing is much less effective than methods in which students are more engaged, and has been widely replicated. One of these is of course problem-based learning.

Problem-based learning

This has been an area of some interest and enthusiasm, since its initial use in medical schools, but has found significant use in engineering, commonly as part of "blended learning," that is, as a minor part of a mixture with conventional lectures, etc. A few exceptions include engineering at Alborg University (AAU) in Denmark, where 50% of the students' time is given to project work, compared with 20% at many other institutions which utilize PBL (De Graaf & Kolmos, 2003). An interesting comparison was made between engineering graduates from the Technical University of Denmark (TDU) with a traditional programme and AAU (UNESCO, 2007). This found a virtually identical level of achievement in quality of engineering skills, but some considerable advantage in project and people management and in innovative and creative skills. A review for MIT on UK practice in this area identified good practice, but concluded that it was particularly resource intensive, and in most cases operated as isolated modules rather than a major learning method (Graham, 2009). There has been enthusiasm for online methods of doing this, though some subject areas are more easily adapted (Savin-Baden & Wilke, 2006). However, it remains to be seen if purely online students would get the same benefit as groups who actually meet.

Interactions with staff

The interaction with academics who are experts in their fields has long been one of the purported benefits of attending university, with the small group tutorial in an Oxbridge college being the television standard. However with class sizes of hundreds in many engineering courses in a lecture, it is common experience that only a small number of students do all the asking and answering of questions. Thus a student watching via a video link is not greatly disadvantaged. The use of 'clickers'(Electronic Voting Devices) does provide a useful method of both engaging the students and showing how the learning is progressing, so that the academic can move on, or spend time perhaps with some board explanation when required. This seems entirely possible to carry out with a virtual community.

Students do already engage with staff via email, and some academics use Twitter. However, there is a limit to how many technical questions can be dealt with in a day, and students sometimes have unrealistic expectations of the speed of response, which is now quite a burden for many teachers. In principle, forums are more effective since earlier questions and the answers can be preserved to save the same answer being given.

It is one thing to deal with standard questions for an exam, another to deal with group issues in projects. There is already an issue with students in group work where one student says they will not attend, but will go home and communicate electronically with the group and academic.

The timetable

While one of the virtues of virtual learning is commonly said to be the possibility of the student learning at their own pace at times of their choosing, this is again poor preparation for most of the jobs a graduate will seek. People who work for themselves at home, such as writers, often get up and dress as if going to work and frequently have a separate workplace, even a shed away from the house so that they are 'at work.' Thus, for the student to get out of bed and go to the university will probably increase the chance that some studying may take place. In addition, there is much to be said for habit. Good habits of regular work are only attained by practice, and the transition to university offers an exceptional chance to achieve this (Wood et al., 2005).

Laboratories

In conventional universities, the intended learning outcomes for laboratories are often unclear to staff and students, both dealing with them as a chore, and going through a fixed process based on detailed instructions. I suggest it is plausible that any serious virtual laboratory might of necessity do better in instructing students than many traditional ones.

Das and Hough (1986) described what they called a crisis in engineering laboratory instruction; according to them,

> The problem (in the laboratory manual) is already defined and the solution methodology is clearly stated. This is a contradiction to the real-life

situation in industry. The laboratory instruction performed in this manner provides little challenge and initiative on the part of the student. Obviously the students find the laboratory experience dull and they have developed apathy towards such experience.

Unfortunately, the solution for some universities seems to have been not to change the experience, but simply to reduce time on practicals even more (Bhathal, 2011).

A major reason (though an often unstated one) is the generation of observations and data on which a report can be written. This can be achieved by video recordings, simulations (though the fact that they are not real must have some negative psychological impact), or by the remote actual experiment. It is my view that there should be some interaction with the real world and a reason to use safety equipment. A virtual world where nothing can go wrong and no one can get hurt is poor preparation for an engineer's responsibility.

Other practical skills

Fifty years ago in the UK, students entering engineering degree courses were almost, but not quite, entirely male, and had a number of practical skills from ordinary life (Pitt, 2018). A typical student could service a bicycle (many a motorcycle), carry out basic carpentry tasks, and had designed and built items using nuts and bolts and metal parts using a popular constructional toy called Meccano. A student entering electrical/electronic engineering would certainly have built many circuits. A chemical engineering student would have from school the basic lab skills now expected of a second year university chemist, and had handled dangerous substances in significant quantities. Summer work on a building site was easy to obtain, and very common, giving practical knowledge of civil engineering and understanding of concepts such as mass, weight, force, gravitational potential, work, and energy. Only the most unfortunate (and generally the richest) students entered without these experiences. There were many engineering degree programmes where all students had a guaranteed industrial placement in a sandwich year. It was therefore not necessary for universities to attempt to teach such matters. Though part of the education of the engineer, it was provided by others. (Sadly, industrial placements are now rare, and education must proceed for students who do not have this experience.)

By the 1980s, and particularly following Finniston (1980), students were often lacking these practical skills. The Engineering Council stressed that engineering should be "taught as a vocational subject, from the basis of real applications in a business world, rather than being an exercise in engineering science" (Chapman & Levy, 2004), and introduced the requirement for "Engineering Applications" 1 and 2, which typically included hands-on experience of appropriate technology such as welding, machining, and assembly. Universities had to provide these as well as their more scientific laboratory work. However, the current requirement is much vaguer in this area and stresses scientific experiments

(Engineering Council, 2014), as does ABET (Crawley et al., 2007). It is worth noting that the Royal Society of Chemistry (RSC) is less specific in syllabus content but requires 300 hours of practical work for BSc and 400 for MChem (RSC, 2016). That is, students should spend a lot of time doing chemistry.

The CDIO initiative in engineering proposes Conceive, Design, Implement, Operate (Crawley et al., 2007, 2011). It is commonly reported in exercises where actual groups of students make actual products. Fairly obviously, it is well suited to software and is a common feature of computer engineering. It can also be applied to electronic engineering at modest cost. Civil engineers often have small "design and build model" exercises which can well give a good feel, and now 3D printing gives possibilities in mechanical engineering. Apart from software, it does suggest the creation and operation of something tangible, which would limit the experience of totally online student.

Back to the future

Universities founded in the 19th and early 20th centuries often were specifically concerned with practical engineering, including MIT (founded as part of the Morrill Land-Grant Colleges Act to fund institutions "to promote the liberal and practical education of the industrial classes"), Northern universities such as Sheffield in the UK (as Sheffield Technical School for the steel, chemical, and textile industries), the Technical Universities in Germany, and many in Australia (Bhathal, 2011).

Returning to this idea with 21st century technology and educational methods should appeal to both students and employers. Fortunately a number of institutions are investing in buildings, equipment, and dedicated staff to make access possible for large numbers of students to carry out practical operations as a significant part of their studies. An example is The Diamond engineering building at the University of Sheffield. This includes having multiple sets of equipment and some practicals common to several departments (though with tailored instructions), with the same room being periodically re-equipped during the year as the students work through their syllabus. (Heavy equipment such as lathes remains throughout, but has been selected to get maximum use.) It is important that all students get this experience, not just a few on advanced projects. A major factor has been the dedicated staff and organization to ensure that student work is marked and quickly returned, so that the students get feedback from which they can progress. The building also has study facilities and computing available 24/7.

Conclusions and recommendations

Conclusions

Successful distance learning has in the past been achieved by mainly older students with sufficient self-discipline. For greater numbers, the fact of actually being present in a place in a group has some advantages which must not be overlooked in terms of getting them to do work by the timetable and with a peer-group. It is readily observed that though students today demand much more to be put online for their access at a convenient time of the day or night, they do not necessarily make good use of it (Pitt, 2018).

The traditional requirement of hands-on work in engineering limits what can be done with no attendance at all. Much can be done online, and it is feasible that some virtual practicals could be as good (or better) than many traditional ones in terms of learning outcomes. There is some blending of the two types in that many laboratory courses in science use online material including videos or simulations to prepare students for an actual class. However, for various reasons some universities seem to have reduced practicals and could potentially go on to replace them with virtual ones for all students. This is particularly so for institutions which still take the view that engineering is just science with some lectures on applications.

Engineering is about doing, not the passive receipt of knowledge or the process of finding out of science, and engineering students should be 'doing' as much as possible during their degrees. This goes along with the current view of active learning and also the initiatives of Education for Capability and CDIO. Classical science-based teaching promoting formal derivations and learning of 'right' answers needs to move to a method more aligned with design and creation, including work that is literally 'hands-on.' Part of this 'doing' can only be achieved by students who are physically present, and much else can be better done if they are. Failure to do this will lead to graduates unprepared for industry, and may lead to the students moving to universities which are found more satisfactory by employers.

While learning technologies can and should be used, they do not of themselves achieve education, which depends on recognizing the objectives and understanding the processes needed. These must be the ones which are appropriate to the subject, not those suited to arts degrees. Forming effective work habits and solving problems are possibly as important as the syllabus.

Recommendations

Traditional universities with engineering need to move (carefully) away from the traditional model of passive lectures as the main activity and the emphasis on science. In order to be attractive to students and effective in producing engineering graduates, as much practical work as possible should be done, and this must be for every student, not just a favoured few. This should be accompanied by as much design work as possible with students in teams or groups, with the basic theory and mathematics immediately recognized by the students as support, not a separate chore. New buildings should be considered as a means to facilitate practical and project work, and this could give immense advantages if done well.

References

Abdel-Salam T, Kauffman PJ & Crossman G (2006) Does the lack of hands-on experience in a remotely delivered laboratory course affect student learning? *European Journal of Engineering Education*, Vol. 31, pp. 747–756

Abdel-Salam T, Kauffman PJ & Crossman G (2007) Are distance laboratories effective tools for technology education? *The American Journal of Distance Education*, Vol. 21, No. 2, pp. 77–91

Ben-Naim D (2015) Online learning can work if universities just rethink the design of their courses, *The Conversation* Url:https://theconversation.com/online-learning-can-work-if-universities-just-rethink-the-design-of-their-courses-50848

Bhathal R (2011) Retrospective perceptions and views of engineering students about physics and engineering practicals, *European Journal of Engineering Education*, Vol. 36, No. 4 pp. 403–411

Bligh DA (1972) *What's the Use of Lectures?* London: Penguin

Bligh DA (2008) *Evidence of What Lectures Achieve*, San Francisco: Jossey-Bass Publisher

Botero ML, Selmer A, Watsond R, Mukta B & Kraft M (2016) Cambridge weblabs: A process control system using industrial standard SIMATIC PCS 7, *Education for Chemical Engineers*, Vol. 16, pp. 1–8

Bourne J, Harris D & Mayadas F (2005) Online engineering education: Learning anywhere, Anytime *Journal of Engineering Education*, Vol. 94, No. 1, pp. 111–146

Buzan T (1995) *Use Your Head*, London: BBC Books

Chapman CR & Levy J (2004) *An Engine for Change: A Chronicle of the Engineering Council*, London: The Engineering Council.

Crawley EF, Malmqvist J, Lucas WA & Brodeur, DR (2011) *The CDIO Syllabus v2.0 An Updated Statement of Goals for Engineering Education*, Proceedings of the 7th International CDIO Conference, Technical University of Denmark, Copenhagen, June 20–23rd Url:www.cdio.org/files/project/file/cdio_syllabus_v2.pdf

Crawley EF, Malmqvist J, Östlund S & Brodeur DR (2007) *Rethinking Engineering Education: The CDIO Approach*, New York: Springer

Das B & Hough CL Jr. (1986) A solution to the current crisis in engineering laboratory instruction, *European Journal of Engineering Education*, Vol. 11, No. 4, pp. 423–427

De Graaf E & Kolmos A (2003) Characteristics of problem-based learning, *International Journal of Engineering Education*, Vol. 19, No. 5, pp. 657–662

Engineering Council (2014) *The Accreditation of Higher Education Programmes UK Standard for Professional Engineering Competence*, 3rd Edition, UK: Engineering Council

Finniston M (1980) *Engineering Our Future, Report of the Committee of Inquiry into the Engineering Profession*, London: HMSO

Freear G (2016) Open University Personal Communication

Graham R (2009) *UK Approaches to Engineering Project-Based Learning*, MIT White Paper Url:www.rhgraham.org/RHG/Recent_publications_files/MIT%20White%20Paper%20-%20UK%20PjBL%20April%202010.pdf

Gourley B & Lane A (2009) Re-invigorating openness at The Open University: The role of open educational resources, *Open Learning*, Vol. 24, No. 1, pp. 57–75

Hake RR (1998) Interactive-engagement versus traditional methods: A six-thousand-student survey of mechanics test data for introductory physics courses, *American Journal of Physics*, Vol. 66, pp. 64–74

Harry K (1999) *Higher Education Through Open and Distance Learning*, London: Routledge

Illeris K (2016) *How We Learn-Learning and Non-Learning in School and Beyond*, 2nd Edition, Abingdon, Oxon: Routledge

Illeris K (2018) *Contemporary Theories of Learning-Learning Theorists . . . in Their Own Words*, 2nd Edition, Abingdon, Oxon: Routledge

Kaye AR (1973) The design and evaluation of science courses at the Open University, *Instructional Science*, Vol. 2, pp. 119–191

Kumar A, Kumar P, Palvia SCJ & Verma S (2017) Online education worldwide: Current status and emerging trends, *Journal of Information Technology Case and Application Research*, Vol. 19, No. 1, pp. 3–9

Laurillard D (2014) Five Myths about MOOCs, *Times Higher Education*, January 16th

Lockwood F (2013) *Open and Distance Learning Today*, Abingdon, Oxon: Routledge

OpenLearn (2018) *The Open University* Url:www.open.edu/openlearn/

Perrin RW & Laing GK (2014) The lecture: A teaching strategy through the looking glass, *e-Journal of Business Education & Scholarship of Teaching*, Vol. 8, No. 1, pp. 67–77. Url:www.ejbest.org

Pickford R & Clothier H (2003) Ask the audience: A simple teaching method to improve the learning experience in large lectures, *Teaching, Learning and Assessment in Databases* Url:www.ics.ltsn.ac.uk/pub/databases03/PICKFORD.pdf

Pitt MJ (2018) *Author's Recollection*, unpublished

Pratt J (1986) *Engineering for capability* chapter 9, in Burgess T (Ed.), *Education for Capability* (pp. 97–106), Windsor: Royal Society of Arts

Pritchard A (2017) *Ways of Learning-Learning Theories for the Classroom*, 4th Edition, Abingdon, Oxon: Routledge

RDI (2016) *Arden University* Url:www.rdi.co.uk/

Regmi K (2012) A review of teaching methods – lecturing and facilitation in Higher Education (HE): A summary of the published evidence, *The Journal of Effective Teaching*, Vol. 12, No. 3, pp. 61–76

RSC Royal Society of Chemistry (2016) *A Student Guide to Accreditation of Chemistry Degrees* Url:www.rsc.org/careers/future/sites/futureinchemistry/files/file_uploads/031539_Student%20Accreditation_Guide_WEB.pdf

Savin-Baden M & Wilkie K (2006) *Problem-Based Learning Online*, New York: McGraw-Hill Education

Smith M & Firth J (2018) *Psychology in the Classroom – A Teacher's Guide to What Works*, Abingdon, Oxon: Routledge

Stefanovic M (2013) The objectives, architectures and effects of distance learning laboratories for industrial engineering education, *Computers & Education*, Vol. 69, pp. 250–262 https://doi.org/10.1016/j.compedu.2013.07.011

Strathclyde (2016) *University of Strathclyde Chemical Engineering BEng Distance Learning* Url:www.strath.ac.uk/courses/undergraduate/chemicalengineeringbengdistancelearning/

(TUB) Technical University of Berlin (2016) *Remote Farm* Url:http://remote.physik.tu-berlin.de/

(UNED) Universidad Nacional de Educación a Distancia (2016) Url:http://portal.uned.es/

UNESCO (2007) *Engineering: Issues, Challenges and Opportunities for Development* Url:http://unesdoc.unesco.org/images/0018/001897/189753e.pdf

(UOC) Universitat Oberta de Catalunya (2016) Url:www.uoc.edu/portal/en/

Wood W, Tam L & Witt MG (2005) Changing circumstances, disrupting habits, *Journal of Personality and Social Psychology*, Vol. 88, No. 6, pp. 918–933

Summary of Part 2

As suggested in chapters 1 and 2, educationalists will have to make substantial changes in order to address the educational needs of our future engineers. These will be changes that are reflected in the delivered curricula, the way of their delivery, and the spaces that are used for teaching, real or virtual. These changes will have to take place in a background of increasing student numbers as well as educational costs, both to the students as well as the providing institutions.

Professional engineers operate in an increasingly sophisticated, global world. Often working on international projects or in international locations, engineers must be agile team players, adept communicators, reflective, and able to operate effectively within an interdisciplinary and multi-cultural working environment (Bourn & Neale, 2008; Royal Academy of Engineering, 2007).

Part 2 looks into these factors that have necessitated the development of innovative strategies for delivering teaching at scale with targeted resources in order to provide effective methods of education.

The multidisciplinary approach adopted at the Faculty of Engineering at the University of Sheffield considered in chapter 3 provides an alternative to reducing practical teaching due to cost constraints, while increasing the potential to leverage greater learning from activity with further pedagogic benefits achieved as a result of a single department having an overarching responsibility for the delivery of practical activities. The described approach is generally efficient, but it is not cheap in terms of either money or effort.

The driver has been to try to enhance the student experience and to ensure that Sheffield University Engineers graduate with a good skill set in terms of experimental capabilities and an understanding of experimental limitations and experimental design and of safe and professional behaviour in practical work. The theme of ensuring that our future engineers are appropriately equipped to deal with a rapidly changing, globalized world is considered through examples of changing pedagogies.

Professional engineers operate in an environment where non-technical issues are important – and sometimes are paramount – therefore we explore the potential content of liberal studies topics and how they might be integrated into a programme for professional engineers as the means of educating our future engineers in the context of the development of a totally new engineering programme, provisionally called Liberal Engineering, by NMiTE in Hereford. We want to train the complete engineer, a creative critical thinker, versed not only in the knowledge of his particular field but also aware of aesthetics, architecture, ethics, public health, sociology, politics and political protest, noise pollution, finance, the profit motive, pedagogy, management, marketing, charity, and any other topic afforded by our imaginations. This, as is suggested in chapter 4, is to be achieved through the "guide-on-the-side" support and it will require teachers learning together with their students.

Successive governments have highlighted the "skills agenda," the need for workforce skills to match those required by employers, since this is highly associated with economic growth. Universities are considered paramount in delivering on this, by producing graduates who are both academically capable but also equipped with an array of soft (or work) skills.

In order to enable cross-disciplinary working, understanding of the global dimensions of our major challenges, awareness of sustainable development, the human aspects of engineering design, as well as delivering a raft of employability skills, the Faculty of Engineering at the University of Sheffield developed two cross-faculty project weeks: The Global Engineering Challenge (GEC) for all first year students, and Engineering You're Hired (EYH) for all second year students, described in detail in chapter 5, expanding on the challenges of their delivery as well as proposed solutions. The second part concludes with chapter 6 on the theme of changing pedagogies with a workshop focused on how to design modules (courses) that improve student engagement through active learning. The workshop was used to introduce academic staff to many of the common engagement techniques that are used to replace lecture during instruction. Pre- and post-workshop quizzes were used to assess the effectiveness of the workshop and the assessment results are provided.

Part 2

Recent innovations in delivering effective engineering education

Chapter 3

Pedagogical and cost advantages of a multidisciplinary approach to delivering practical teaching

Andrew Garrard and Stephen Beck

Introduction

Faced with a need to expand the space available for teaching beyond the limits of their existing, grade II listed, Victorian building, the Faculty of Engineering at the University of Sheffield decided to commission a new facility, The Diamond. Initial specification produced a list of requirements for this which led to the unexpected and radical conclusion that it was necessary to create a new department to deliver the practical teaching for engineering students. This department would hold a faculty-wide perspective, dedicated to the design, operation, and delivery of all first and second year practical teaching to the other seven, existing engineering departments and three interdisciplinary programmes, using a novel multidisciplinary approach. Discussed here are the efficiency gains and pedagogical advantages of this multidisciplinary approach adopted by the new department to deliver the practical, hands-on portion of all engineering students' overall education.

The background to this was based on previous University learning and teaching grants. When the University moved to a stronger faculty system, the new Faculty Director of Learning and Teaching obtained £250k from the faculty to build a shared fluids laboratory between Mechanical and Civil Engineering. The successful project, called 'Lab in a box,' was a laboratory about flow-down pipes (Rossiter et al., 2010). This was collaboration between the Faculty's Mechanical, Civil, and Chemical Engineering departments. In this, the participants shared teaching equipment, notes, and presentations. The finances allowed them to buy multiples of matched equipment which were shared between twice as many students. This got a much higher use out of both equipment and space. It also showed that departments could profitably work together to share space and that there was a lot of commonality in teaching across the faculty.

While this was happening, the University was obtaining financing for a new building to accommodate teaching of increased numbers of engineering students that the faculty's plans for expansion required. Inspired by the 'Lab in a box' project, it was decided to design the teaching laboratories in the new building around principles of engineering science, rather than departmental disciplines. For example, the fluids laboratory would be shared by students from five different Engineering courses. In order to get the all of these students through the laboratory, it had to be of a large scale. It was therefore decided to create each large laboratory space and its main experiments to be able to cope with 80 students in groups of four doing the same activity at the same time (Hillman, 2014).

During this period, it was necessary to specify the laboratory equipment and also how the various labs were to be set out. So, for each of the 17 labs, a lab lead and a list of all of the interested parties were assembled to decide what equipment was needed and how the lab was to work. The main task for this meeting was to ensure that everyone understood how the labs were to operate, and the shared nature of the equipment and spaces. Outcomes from the meetings were reported back to the architects and were able to ensure that the equipment and configurations of the laboratories were academically-led. This avoided the potential for problems to arise from a building being designed and delivered, ready for occupancy for engineering teaching, by the central university and architects, who would have less understanding of its particular requirements. The people with the experience in Learning and Teaching, and in the student experience, designed the building for their own purposes. Therefore, labs were acquired with infrastructure and services in the right quantity and where they were needed. The number of late (and expensive) changes were therefore minimized by these carefully organized processes.

In addition to equipment and space, teaching academics and techniques are required to design, maintain, organize, and deliver the activities students will be performing. Individual departments making use of the space and equipment, by assigning staff to develop teaching and technicians to set up equipment, order consumables, etc., results in numerous people performing similar tasks, which reduces efficiency. With a shared, multidisciplinary approach to creating a practical teaching environment for engineers, it becomes justifiable to create appointments dedicated to running each laboratory.

The faculty therefore decided to set up a new department, with teachers, technicians, and administration staff to put on the laboratories and practical teaching in the new building. This new department was called Multidisciplinary Engineering Education (MEE). MEE was built from scratch and now has 50 staff and a budget of over £3M.

As a separate initiative, the idea of creating a new department, separated from the departments into which students enrol, to service teaching a portion of their degree programme, appears unwise. However, after the model of sharing equipment and resources has been embraced, the decision to separate the delivery of practical teaching to a new department becomes logical. Furthermore, with careful planning and consideration, the multidisciplinary approach to practical engineering can be both more efficient with resource and better for students' learning.

The adoption of a multidisciplinary approach to delivering practical education has numerous advantages over a traditional discipline-specific approach. These advantages can be placed into one of three categories.

- Oversight of the practical teaching in a degree programme
- Commonality of student experience and expectations
- Efficiency through commonality of business processes and utilization

Each of these categories is discussed. There are also potential problems associated with "service teaching," where one department delivers teaching for another. When setting up the new department, these problems have been anticipated and mechanisms to mitigate this have been put into place and are also discussed.

Costing model and operations

In the traditional approach, adopted by the Faculty of Engineering at the University of Sheffield before the construction of The Diamond, delivery of practical teaching was resourced by individual engineering departments. For example, in this approach, the Department of Civil and Structural Engineering is responsible for resourcing and delivering the hydraulics laboratories to Civil and Structural Engineering students. The resource required to deliver practical teaching includes academic staff development and contact time, technical staff time, laboratory space provision, demonstrator recruitment and training, consumables, administration, and assessment. All of this is a large cost, but apart from demonstrator costs, departments do not actually visibly account for this as a cost, as staff salaries are already paid for, and space is a de facto cost.

As much of the undergraduate practical teaching was moved from the departments into The Diamond, there was a need for a transfer of funds to support this activity. A number of costing models were contemplated when considering how to fund the creation and operation of the new department.

MEE staffing is currently about 11 academics, 33 technicians, and five admin staff. There is also the cost of Graduate Teaching Assistant support (PG demonstrating). Along with a consumables budget and a replacement scheme, this requires a steady state budget of around £3M, which needed to be funded from the departments in the faculty. Three possible charging models were offered and considered (Table 3.1).

The first one, termed the "Alton Towers" model, divides the total cost of running The Diamond by the number of students using it. This will give a cost per student. Departments would then be charged proportionally to the number of their students. There may need to be some fine tuning to ensure that this is fair to departments. A first order costing for this model indicated a requirement of about £500 per student.

Table 3.1 Costing models

Name	1) Alton Towers	2) CentreParks	3) Funfair
Costings	Per student	Per student + Per activity	Per activity
Advantages	• Simple • Activities are cheap • Encourages use • Easy to plan	• Cost follows activity • Cost per activity is low • Expensive activity could cost more • Can drive use by cost • Can ration by cost • Could in effect charge consumables separately	• Cost follows activity • Expensive activity could cost more • Hard to plan
Drawbacks	• May need to ration access • More activity is more expensive • Differential costing per department may be needed • How to account for low usage students (PGT/FY projects)	• Costing more complicated • Needs more negotiation • Possible PYA situation • How to account for low usage students (PGT/FY projects)	• Costing more complicated • Less activity is cheaper, may compromise the building • Needs more negotiation • Possible PYA situation
Notes	Probably the simplest, but is it the fairest?	Hybrid, and thus more flexible, but more complicated.	Similar to current practice. Cost of activity is clear.

The third model, the "Funfair" model, charges departments per activity. This will need to be costed, based on timetabling. It would be possible to charge different activities at different costs to reflect the expense of putting on certain laboratories. This was predicted to come out at about £25 per student activity.

The middle option, the "CentreParks", model is a hybrid of these two. The cost of running the large, heavily used, multidisciplinary laboratories would come from a per student cost, based on cohort size, with an extra subvention to cover a particularly esoteric or specialized activity that would be applicable to only a small number of departments. This was of the order of between £300 per student and £10 per activity. For each one, we have set out the advantages and disadvantages, though there may be some more issues and variations possible.

At a theme park, the ticket price allows you entry to the premises and as much utilization of the rides as you wish. Some rides are more popular than others, and waiting in line means you can do fewer activities. As a customer, you make the decision about what you wish to use and attempt to maximize the value of the price you have paid by doing as much activity as possible. It was decided the "Alton Towers" model would be selected, at least in the first instance, as it simple to administer but, crucially, it encourages departments to maximize use of the building, staff, and facilities.

In addition to driving utilization, multidisciplinary cross fertilization will also be encouraged. In the "Alton Towers" model, no department has priority over specific laboratories or equipment, but pays equally for the totality of the resource. Therefore it is in the interest of the departments to make use of resources not typically associated with a particular degree programme. For example, fluid flow and heat transfer are important topics in a chemical engineering curriculum, but it difficult for a chemical engineering department working in isolation to justify owning a dedicated thermodynamics and fluid mechanics laboratory. In a multidisciplinary approach, accommodating students into these laboratories is routine and straightforward, with relativity minimal additional cost, as the resources are justified for other cohorts. Also, by allowing students access to laboratories not normally associated with their degree program, there is the opportunity to broaden their range of skills for all students in the faculty to understand other engineering disciplines.

Academic liaisons and communication structure

MEE as a department has no students, but delivers a small portion of teaching to all students in the faculty. One of MEE's aims is to ensure that students do not feel as if the teaching delivered by MEE is separated from their teaching delivered by their home department and the experience of their programme is a coherent and connected set of activities. To overcome the potential for MEE's practical teaching and departments' theoretical teaching to become disconnected, a deliberate communications structure was embedded into the MEE departmental model. This communications structure includes:

- Academic leads – Module leads: All MEE activities are part of a departmentally owned module. Each module has a module leader assigned in their home department, and each MEE activity has an MEE academic. MEE's business processes require negotiation and discussions between these two parties to ensure joined up delivery.
- Academic liaisons – Departments: All departments and interdisciplinary programmes are assigned and MEE academic liaison. This role is to ensure coordination of activities at a programme level and to act as a point of contact for departments. For example, a student studying Civil and Structural Engineering may undertake activities with the fluids lab lead, the material lab lead, and the structures lab lead. The liaison has academic oversight of these activities. Academic liaisons are required as members of departmental staff-student committee.

Design of the teaching spaces

When the initial scoping of the laboratories was conducted, a spreadsheet of laboratory scopes and sizes was devised by one of the authors and Professor Mike Hounslow, the Pro-Vice Chancellor for Engineering. This was created by collecting the number and duration of each of the labs for each student cohort and multiplying this by the predicted 2020 cohort of students. These were then divided up by topic and laboratory. It became obvious as part of this exercise that it was possible to move many experiments from one lab to another. We decided on a quantum of 80 students, and to design the building on this multiple. All of the large labs in the building were conceived for 80 students, though there turned out to be variants in this. Additionally, the lecture theatres in The Diamond were specified in multiples of 80 (there is one 400 seater, two 240 seaters, four 160 seaters, and two 80 seaters). The three workrooms in the building are each capable of holding 80 people too.

Having labs of a unitary size means, that when timetabling is being done, each course can be divided into large groups of less than 80 which can then be moved around the labs as a cohort.

Oversight of the practical teaching in a degree programme

Timeliness of activity

Normally in engineering courses, the labs are set out with one or two sets of equipment of each type, and students rotate around activities throughout the course of a teaching period. This is known as a 'round robin' approach. While it may be efficient in terms of equipment and space use, it does not necessarily support student learning for two main reasons. Firstly, a given experiment may occur either well before or after the topic is covered in the course. This means that the students may either have not covered the material, or will have done it in the past. Secondly, the students will have been provided with the same laboratory sheet, so that each experiment must be designed as free standing, with the same student expectations.

Using the model implemented in The Diamond, this is different. Pooling resources between departments allows for a greater potential to purchase larger amounts of shared teaching equipment, facilitating large class sizes to conduct the same activity simultaneously. In a multidisciplinary approach with the provision of sufficient equipment, practical activities can be designed to coincide in a timely way with material delivered simultaneously in theory and practice, reinforcing student learning, understanding, and engagement. Because of the size and the number of sets of equipment, it is possible to get even the biggest cohort of students (320 second year Mechanical Engineers, for example) through the laboratories in groups of 80. If the lab sessions are each two hours, then in four sessions all of this cohort can do the lab; this could be one morning and one afternoon with two groups in each. This means that it is possible to, say, introduce a topic on a Monday, get all the students to conduct an associated experiment on the Tuesday and Thursday, and then use their experience to better illuminate a subsequent lecture on the Friday.

Progressive practical curriculum

The MEE approach results in students on a programme doing the same activity at a specific point in their curriculum and requires that a dedicated team be assigned to delivering only and all the practical teaching for a faculty. The combination of these factors presents the opportunity to carefully curate and manage the students' practical curriculum.

In a traditional approach to engineering teaching, laboratory and classroom activities associated with a specific topic are traditionally taught by the same academic. There is often both horizontal and vertical coordination between different academics for theoretical content (for example, it is planned that students will have completed fundamental thermodynamics before starting advanced thermodynamics). However, it is less common for the same coordination in the level of rigour and expectation of the capabilities of the students to perform practical activities to be applied. Some programmes of study include dedicated lab modules that attempt to iteratively increase the experimental capabilities of students as they progress, which can be problematic for two reasons. Firstly, as mentioned above, unless large multiples of the same equipment is available, large cohorts will inevitably experience their activities in a random order, making the coordination of increasing laboratory complexity difficult. Secondly, engineering courses are traditionally intensive and the creation of dedicated laboratory modules can result in the reduction of the module credits available when designing programmes.

The department of MEE has oversight of all the practical activities undertaken by students. From this viewpoint, the diet of practical activities, regardless of the module they belong to, the theoretical topic they are considering, the laboratory they are working in, or the semester they are delivered, can be considered as a continuum, with a mapped and progressive increase in the level of expectation for experimental competencies.

The team of academic staff in MEE are dedicated to delivering practical teaching. This resource provides the capacity to carefully consider what skills an engineering experimentalist should possess and how many steps students should perform in order to obtain these learning outcomes. So that students keep moving from one laboratory to another, run by a different academic specialist, work has been done to identify, agree, and articulate various types of experimentation that can be performed (demonstration of a principle, validation of a theory, investigation of an open-ended problem) and the range of laboratory competencies required. For each of these items, levels of attainment, from novice to expert, have been described, in order to ensure agreement between teaching staff and coherence in the student experience. This approach gradually builds the students' capabilities as independent experimentalists so they can begin their final year's investigative projects with sufficient capability to tackle problems. In addition, it provides a programme level view of assessment to ensure experimental capabilities are not over or under assessed.

Commonality of student experience and expectations

Students often, and quite justifiably, become deeply dissatisfied with their university experience when there is a lack of clarity or failure in administrative processes. In addition, making the effort to become familiar with administrative processes is tangential to learning their taught curriculum and arguably a waste of effort they could be otherwise expending on their studies. When practical teaching is distributed between numerous departments or modules, there is the potential for the numerous rules and conventions to confuse students. Before the opening of The Diamond, fragmentation of laboratory rules and processes were a particular problem for interdisciplinary programmes that are created by obtaining portions of their teaching from other departments. Students on these programmes had to accommodate differing sets of rules dependent on the department they happened to be receiving their teaching from. It is of course possible to standardize the professional expectations on students if all of the laboratory experiences fall under the same team.

For example, MEE has implemented a standardized approach to students being late. Simply, after the start time, when all of the waiting students are admitted, the doors shut and further admittance is not allowed. If in the first few years, a number of staff were less strict about this, students therefore expected the whole system to be less strict. This led to some "discussions" with certain students who pointed out that a different lecturer had let them in late. We therefore had to tighten up on the process, and now students make an effort to be there on time. This means that it is possible to start the laboratory at the required time, which increases the experimental time for each student and increases the professionalism of the students. Other lab policies, such as forgetting lab books, use of mobile phones, students using alternative languages, etc., have all been identified and agreed. The creation of a lab policy may not seem significant, but its consistent application to all practical activities, for all students within a faculty, provides students with a definitive set of rules and allows focus to be paid to the more important theme – engaging with the learning and teaching in the laboratory. It has been found that, once communicated clearly, students quickly adapt to the rules and working to them quickly forms part of their culture (@sheffengmemes, 2017).

Induction labs

Before the move to The Diamond building was contemplated, a group of technical and academic staff had developed the "Danger Lab" to introduce students to the concept of risk. This was originally developed for use in the Materials Science & Engineering department for their students, but was soon rolled out to cover other cohorts, such as Mechanical Engineers. Inspired by this, it was decided to ensure that all of the students entering into The Diamond for their labs would have this induction. After establishing the requirement that all students would need to safely and effectively use the facilities in the laboratories, two other areas were identified. The first was that of workshop safety, and generally how to behave in a lab, and the second was the collecting of data and identifying and handling uncertainty in measurements. So, two additional induction labs were developed to ensure these issues were covered.

One of these labs was to enable students to safely use the workshop. This built on the view of risk introduced in the Danger Lab to get students to look at the dangers in the workshop and safely use hand and power tools.

The other, called the "Measurement Lab" introduced students to lab procedure and the taking of the same data using a variety of instruments. They would then begin to understand that there were errors in all readings and that uncertainty would play a role in all of their subsequent lab experiences. They were also introduced to yet another form of risk by performing a risk assessment of this laboratory. All later laboratory introductions contain compulsory questions on Health and Safety, so students know that this is their responsibility when they go into a lab or workshop.

The induction labs are mandatory for all first year students in the faculty and delivered within the first two weeks of starting their degree programmes. This provides a common foundation of core practical skills onto which discipline-specific skills can be built. The numbers of students enrolled on these activities justifies the significant effort in developing high-quality teaching material, enhancing the student experience with an effective use of resources.

Teaching sandwich

For all activities delivered by MEE, students are required to complete a pre-lab activity before they arrive, preparing them for their practical experience, and a post lab activity, designed to encourage reflection about the work they have performed. Pre-lab activities include, as a minimum, an automatically marked test students must complete with 100% pass rate, or they are not permitted into the laboratory to take part in the activity. As with many aspects of the initiatives set up in MEE, the inclusion of pre-activity working or post-activity reflection has been done elsewhere and is considered pedagogical good practice. The approach of MEE is to take the pockets of good practice and apply them with ubiquity across a faculty.

Traditional laboratory teaching activity would involve having students arrive and providing them with an induction to the basic concepts under investigation, the equipment/procedures, and the necessary health and safety. A typical pre-lab activity in MEE would consist of flipping this teaching online to the University's VLE and checking engagement with a multiple-choice test. As with other MEE process, a culture of completing the pre-labs quickly develops amongst the student cohort, individuals refused entry to a laboratory rarely repeat the error, and compliance is generally extremely high.

The result of the pre-lab activity is several efficiency gains. Firstly, without the need to provide didactic instructions at the start of the session, students are able to spend considerably more time with equipment – which is the principal purpose of being in a laboratory. Coupled with late entry rules, in a class of 80 it typically takes between five and ten minutes to register all students' attendance, ensure completion of the pre-lab activity, and provide a short welcoming address, after which, practical work begins. Secondly, the introduction of the pre-labs has dramatically reduced the number of routine questions from students that don't contribute to their fundamental learning. For example, "Which dial do I turn to make the equipment perform a particular function?" As the activities are run year on year, the common questions that require algorithmic answers are identified and embedded into the pre-lab activity. This frees academics' and demonstrators' time to answer more interesting questions and engage students in higher level discussion about the work they are conducting.

One disadvantage of the MEE approach is the potential for the separation of classroom and practical teaching due to different staff in different departments creating a disconnection in how the theory and application are taught. It is critical that students consider the laboratory activities an extension of the concepts learned as part of their class learning in their home departments. The careful design of pre- and post-lab activities can be used to help students to bridge the gaps between the deliveries of the two different departments and reconnect theoretical and practical teaching. An example of applying this concept is discussed in Garrard & Nichols (2017).

Health and safety

Because the experiments and other activities that take place in The Diamond that are delivered by MEE are among the most dangerous and risky on the engineering programmes, it is necessary to have a very clear culture of safety in the department. This also provides an opportunity to inculcate an understanding of safety and risk in all the students. This starts off with the "Danger Lab" which all students do early on in their courses. Then, every pre-lab has a section on Health and Safety which the students need to complete before they are allowed entry. Then, as the courses progress, students are expected to be more aware of H&S. If appropriate for their courses, they will be expected to fill in their own risk assessments and COSHH forms. Naturally, they are trained to be able to do this and hopefully will understand why it needs to be done. This means that when they become independent workers and researchers, they will be risk capable, and aware of the rules and practices of safe practical work.

Lab books

With dedicated academics creating teaching material for multiple groups of students, it is justifiable to create high-quality resources. MEE has lab sheet templates that all staff use to create instructional material for each experiment. This includes pre-lab information, for example the equipment students will be using and the procedure they will adopt, basic recaps of required theory, and health and safety information. It contains information on the method and also guides the students through the mechanics of keeping a good record of what happened in the lab. These can also be progressive, with the earlier experiments being explicit in their instructions and the later ones being blank with graph paper, letting the students plan their recording, based on the experiences passed down to them by the academics in the earlier sessions.

It will be noted that even if the basic activity is offered to a number of different cohorts, the exact student requirements will be different between each group. For example, Chemical Engineers treat work into a system as positive, as they concentrate on stirring. However, Mechanical Engineers, who are interested in energy production, will treat power out of a system as positive. Likewise, the symbols, units, and equations used by different cohorts will need to be the same as they get on the associated courses. As well, even if these are the same, a laboratory delivered to second year students will have different requirements on them to those that a first year student will need. The second year lab will be more open ended, the experimental record keeping should be more detailed, and the experimental skills of each student should be greater. The basic lab-sheets will be similar, but what is actually delivered to each type of student will be subtly different. The outcome creates efficiency in reusing material that is generic to all students, but sufficiently bespoke to ensure students understand the applicability to their discipline. It also allows activities to be created for cohorts, to which is it currently not delivered, with relatively little effort.

All lab-sheets are combined into a single, professionally printed lab book, which is provided to students at the start of their studies. The template ensures the book is internally consistent. A different book is printed for each cohort specifically, based on the particular set of lab-sheets they require. As the experimental laboratory programme is planned and the order and timing of the activities fixed to coincide with lecture courses, it is therefore possible to correctly order the lab-sheets in the book.

Efficiency through commonality of business processes and utilization

Due to the overlap of taught material between different engineering disciplines, there is a lot of commonality in the delivery of laboratories. For example, a laboratory on flow-down pipes can be delivered, with minor changes in emphasis, to students in Mechanical, Aero, Civil, and Chemical Engineering. In a multidisciplinary approach, the commonality of resource requirements from different departments is identified and shared where possible to ensure maximum efficiency and utilization. To wit, a fluid dynamics laboratory for a Mechanical Engineering student will be only marginally different to a Civil and Structural Engineer's hydraulics laboratory. Where similar teaching to more than one cohort can be delivered by a single department, the resource required to deliver both with marginal differences is smaller than the sum of resources required for two individual departments to deliver the teaching independently. And the amount of resources required to learn to use equipment, to design and plan activities, and to complete assessment is considerable. With MEE staff, learning to use equipment, and buying multiple copies of the same equipment, means quick reusability and considerable efficiency gains through high utilization of staff, teaching material, equipment, and an optimized process compared to the more traditional approach of practical teaching.

As MEE was being developed from scratch, it was decided that a suitable digital system should be created to store and access all teaching and laboratory material. This common repository is set up with suitable permissions to edit and view so that all staff creating material can gain insight into the work of their colleagues, and so that senior staff and academic liaisons can gain oversight at a programme level and administrators can perform department wide processes, such as uploading to the VLE.

Alongside designing and delivering practical teaching, a number of administrative processes also are required for running laboratories. These include:

- Health and Safety compliance
- Procurement
- Demonstrator recruitment and payment
- Timetabling (including resits)
- Attendance monitoring and grade data input

When laboratories with similar administrative requirements are run individually by departments, these processes are repeated by different members of staff multiple times. By centralizing these processes at a faculty level, both efficiency and quality can be increased. When combined and centralized, the overall staff time cost becomes less opaque and the justification to streamline the process becomes apparent. In MEE, two processes, which were previously executed manually by numerous members of staff, have been optimized using a deliberate process improvement methodology.

The first is a lab demonstrator (referred to as graduate teaching assistants or GTAs) system. Each step in the process of registration, advertisement of post, candidate selection, invitation, training, and payment were identified and dissected. Where possible, automated systems have been developed and tools, such as Google calendar, are used to communicate between administration, demonstrators, technicians, and academic staff.

The second is an attendance and mark recording system. Laboratories, as compared to lectures, typically carry a requirement to have attendance of student monitored and often require a grade to be awarded to work conducted. Due to the weight of attendance and grade data from one department delivering this type of work, a bespoke, digital system was written to allow in-lab real time marking and attendance monitoring to take place. This uses student and GTA registration cards to record lab entry and the completion of the exercise. It will also accept and record feedback and intermediate marks.

The built-in QA of this system is such that it records what the GTA recorded, who recorded it, and when it was done. This means that marks can be changed and a record of this is preserved in the cloud. Pre-lab marks can be downloaded to it and checked to ensure that students have completed the online exercises prior to arrival. Afterwards, there are upload options to the University's VLE and attendance monitoring systems as required. Departments (who are responsible for student marks and performance) can thus be almost immediately informed of student attendance/grades once the laboratory has finished.

Both of these systems required an initial outlay of resources to develop and implement. However, the reduction in staff time to perform these administrative tasks and the reduction of number of errors has been substantial. And, of course, the outcome of a more efficient business process is the liberation of staff time to enhance quality in other areas of the department.

Utilization

One of the major drivers for the creation of MEE was the potential to maximize space utilization. Space is a resource that is often at a premium, especially in a city centre-based campus such as the UoS. Departmentally owned teaching labs can often sit empty for a large portion of the teaching semester. In the shared space resource model operated by MEE, driven by the Alton Towers costing model, high utilization of space can be achieved. The figures for teaching year 2016/17 are shown in Table 3.2, where large, highly multidisciplinary labs get utilization between approximately 20–45%. The smaller, less multidisciplinary labs obtain lower utilization figures, as they do not fit the MEE model to the same extent.

Concluding remarks

The uptake of this approach is timely for two reasons. Firstly, removal of student number controls in 2015 has resulted in a sharp increase in the cohort sizes for highly regarded HE institutes. Secondly, the introduction of higher tuition fees has increased student expectation. These factors have necessitated the development of innovative strategies for delivering teaching at scale and

Table 3.2 Utilization data for labs in The Diamond for teaching year 2016/17

Lab	No. of events	% used	% capacity	Utilization	Average lab length	No. of hours non-teaching use	Lab capacity
Project Space	207	69	65	45	3.2	100	160
Machine Shop	117	43	93	40	3.5	12	16
Structures	134	32	62	20	2.3	696	80
Jet	32	3	103	3	0.8	112	12
Clean Room	163	56	51	29	3.3	17	14
Analytics	124	30	78	23	2.3	302	40
Pilot Plant	42	10	82	8	2.2	108	12
E & C	221	73	49	36	3.2	157	144
Machine Room	71	26	72	18	3.5	96	21
Materials	187	51	46	23	2.6	319	80
Fluids	137	30	63	19	2.1	257	80
Thermo	175	40	54	22	2.2	258	80
VAR	4	1	100	1	2.0	39	20
Tissue	41	12	57	7	2.9	19	40
Bacterial	51	16	25	4	2.9	24	40

ensure resources are targeted at providing the most effective methods of education. Due to their expense and complexity, reduction of practical teaching is a convenient way to reduce costs and increase efficiency, which is detrimental to the breadth of the learning available to students. The multidisciplinary approach presented here provides an alternative to reducing practical teaching due to cost constraints, while increasing the potential to leverage greater learning from activity.

Further pedagogic benefits to the multidisciplinary approach are achieved as a result of a single department having an overarching responsibility for the delivery of practical activities. In a degree programme constructed as a collection of modules, laboratory activity associated with specific modules can suffer from being designed only to illuminate concepts delivered during classroom-based teaching. Ensuring a coherent laboratory programme, that develops sequentially from one laboratory activity to the next, independent of the module with which it is associated, through planning and negotiation, represents cost and complexity that goes beyond the teaching and other activities for often already overstretched academic staff. An alternative approach to overcome this problem is the introduction of a laboratory module within the programme. However, this approach has the significant disadvantages of decreasing the credits available for taught modules, traditionally at a premium in compressed engineering curricula. This can reduce the connection between theoretical concepts and experimental activities. The multidisciplinary approach presented here represents a hybrid approach, where the dedicated teachers of practical activities in a separate department take a programme-level view and interweave a meta-module of activities that incrementally develops transferable laboratory skills, as students progress through their course, while maintaining the association of the conceptual aspects with specific theoretical concepts delivered in the classroom. Described is an example of applying this approach to a general engineering undergraduate degree, where a variety of physical science concepts are taught and enhanced through associated experiments, and the need to conserve credits is paramount.

Even though what is described above is generally efficient, it is not cheap in terms of either money or effort. The driver has always been to try to enhance the student experience and to ensure that Sheffield University Engineers graduate with a good skill set in terms of experimental capabilities, including experimental design and professional behaviour in practical work, and an understanding of experimental limitations. The result of centralizing the delivery of all practical teaching into a single department is the ability for staff in that department to focus on only this task. This affords the time to improve 'stuff' by fine tuning and introducing new activities, which is the exact opposite of efficiency. Very rarely do staff in typical academic departments have the time to do this.

References

@sheffengmemes (2017) "When you don't complete the pre lab", *Engineering Memes for Diamond Teens Facebook Post*, May 8th, viewed April 30th 2018, Url:www.facebook.com/sheffengmemes/photos/a.321308304956144.1073741828.321272818293026/321309598289348/?type=3&theater

Garrard A & Nichols A (2017) *A Teaching Sandwich Approach to Integrating Classroom and Practical Teaching*, paper presented to Royal Academy of Engineering UK & IE Engineering Education Research Network-5th Annual Symposium, November 23rd and 24th

Hillman N (2014) The latest report from the *Higher Education Policy Institute*, A guide to the removal of student number controls, September 18th

Rossiter D, Beck S, Delbauve M, Hogg M & Priestman G (2010) Improving engagement and learning experience for students using lab-in-a-box concept, *Engineering Education 2010*: Inspiring the next generation of engineers, Aston University, EE2010, July

Chapter 4
Engineering with a human face
Peter Goodhew Freng

Liberal Arts colleges are commonplace in the USA, but recently programmes in Liberal Science and Liberal Engineering have begun to appear. In this contribution I will explore what we might mean by Liberal Engineering, and what such an undergraduate programme might comprise. The single most important aspect of what I mean by Liberal is the inter-relationship between engineering and the whole of society. This should be quintessentially important for a graduating engineer, but is difficult to deliver to a diverse undergraduate cohort with different backgrounds and different aspirations.

In the UK a team of visionaries at NMiTE (the New Model in Technology and Engineering – nmite.org.uk) is developing university-level programmes with several unusual features. These are likely to include: almost no lectures – focusing instead on student-centred learning by problem- and project-based techniques; student involvement, alongside industrial employers, with the development of the curriculum; 30% of non-engineering content; no terms, just three-week blocks of learning time; gender-equal admissions and staffing; unconventional admissions requirements, with energy, commitment, and experience trumping A-levels; close links with employers in work placements, mentoring, and curriculum development; academic staff with expertise beyond engineering – in art, design, human factors, ethics, and so on; and encouragement to fail creatively and positively.

I suggest one way to implement the Liberal curriculum, and report on several world-wide initiatives to achieve similar goals in other countries.

Introduction

There can be no doubt that professional engineers operate in an environment where non-technical issues are important – and sometimes are paramount. No bridge is designed and built without the money being raised, planning permission granted, environmental impact assessed, and traffic patterns analysed. No smartphone reaches the market without its aesthetics being judged, its price point established, its communications protocols agreed internationally, and its potential impact on the health of the user being evaluated.

At one level, an engineer can be modestly successful while being insulated from these non-technical considerations; she can get on designing the foundations of the bridge or the touch-screen of the smartphone. However, engineers at senior levels cannot avoid the need to engage with wider society, both inside and beyond their company or employer. A "senior level" engineer might be the owner of a start-up with three staff or the manager of 500 other engineers. To be successful, these engineers need to be knowledgeable about – and comfortable with – regulations, finance, the persuasive arts, marketing, ethics, and keeping their staff and customers happy.

While a cohort of educated citizens who had some familiarity with engineering would be welcome, this does not remove the need for practising engineers – with engineering degrees – who understand and empathize with the societal context of their work. We therefore need a new type of engineering degree that combines professional engineering with what I have called – for want of a better phrase – liberal studies. It is the primary purpose of this chapter to explore the potential content of the liberal studies topics and how they might be integrated into a programme for professional (i.e. in the UK, chartered) engineers.

A key word in what follows is "integrated." Many undergraduate engineering programmes contain modules on non-technical topics, for example "communication skills," "project management," or "ethics." These are usually taught as separate topics, sometimes by non-engineers, often based outside the school of engineering. Student resistance to these topics is – anecdotally, at least – high, with comments such as "this is not why I came here to study mechanical engineering." In an integrated approach, the student would encounter every non-technical topic in the context of a technical topic – that is, while learning about an aspect of engineering. Each topic would be seen as a part of engineering, not an add-on.

In this paper I will present some examples of current practice around the world and then move on to discuss the potential range of non-technical topics which could, and – I will argue – should, be experienced by an engineering student, together with some ideas as to how this can be achieved. I will do this in the context of the development of a totally new engineering programme, provisionally called Liberal Engineering, by NMiTE in Hereford.

Current practice

The inclusion of a limited amount of non-technical content within engineering degrees is encouraged by the bodies which regulate chartered or registered engineers (e.g. The Engineering Council in the UK or ABET in the USA). As an example, the most recent edition of UK-SPEC (2016) specifies (inter alia) that Chartered Engineers should be able to:

- Provide technical and commercial leadership
- Demonstrate effective interpersonal skills
- Demonstrate a personal commitment to professional standards, recognizing obligations to society, the profession, and the environment

These requirements include non-technical topics (commercial leadership, interpersonal skills, obligations to society, and the environment), but they fall a long way short of the set of skills which we should expect from an engineer who is fully sensitive to society's needs and who is capable of helping to deliver a better society. Significantly for educators, UK-SPEC specifies the desirable attributes of a Chartered Engineer some years after graduation (typically two years, but often more). Even the modest list above is not expected from a newly graduated engineer, although she will probably have had courses on communication skills and project management. I will examine whether we can do better than this.

The phrase "Liberal Engineering" has been used as a working title by the New Model in Technology and Engineering, NMiTE (2018) but has not otherwise featured as the title of a degree programme, although it has been used by Grasso (2015) in a recent polemic article.

The term "Liberal Science" has gained a little traction, with a few degree programmes carrying this or related titles (Laurentian University, Nipissing University, and University College London UCL). However, the objective of these programmes is quite different from what we are aspiring to. They do not aim to produce professional scientists, only graduates who are aware of science. The Liberal Sciences programme at Laurentian University in Canada "is geared to students who want to obtain a science related degree but who do not necessarily intend to become working scientists" (Laurentian University). Similarly, the Liberal Science program at Nipissing University (also in Canada) "is general in nature and will expose you to a range of scientific disciplines, and provide a broad-based understanding of science. You will study the basic concepts and approaches of modern science and consider its role in society today" (Nipissing University). As a third example, the Arts and Sciences degree (BASc) at UCL in London "is UCL's Liberal Arts course. The degree offers a great range of disciplines across UCL. Students combine science and humanities/social science courses according to their interests and take core modules designed to foster interdisciplinary thinking" (UCL). These degree programmes are undoubtedly fascinating, and will produce better-educated citizens, but none of them aspire to produce better-educated professional scientists or engineers. Study.com even says "The field of liberal science is synonymous with liberal arts, liberal studies and the humanities" (http://study.com/liberal_science_degree.html)!

A few institutions offer undergraduate science or engineering degrees which contain significant liberal elements, although their degree titles do not reveal this. Among these are Olin College, the Lassonde School of Engineering at York, Ontario, which uses the phrase "Renaissance Engineer," Quest University in British Columbia, which like UCL offers a degree in Arts and Science, and Harvey Mudd College, a US liberal arts college which claims to educate engineers, scientists, and mathematicians who become leaders in their fields and have a clear understanding of the impact their work has on society. It is interesting, but probably not very significant, that so many of my cited examples are based in Canada.

The world-wide CDIO movement also espouses a number of non-technical topics but offers no prescription on how they might be delivered.

Finally, harking back to the word "Human" in the title of this paper, there are a small number of degree programmes in Humanitarian Engineering. Two examples in the UK, at Coventry and Warwick Universities, are both at master's level. They both emphasize engineering applications in the developing world, which is not quite the same as liberal engineering designed for application in any field of engineering.

Potential future programmes

Very few of the existing programmes described in the previous section specify an engineering or science sub-discipline. Programmes which aspire to be liberal are usually based on general engineering or general science, perhaps better described as multidisciplinary rather than "general." They are not "Humanitarian Electronic Engineering" or "Liberal Chemistry" or "Arts and Mechanical Engineering." There is a good reason for this: the sub-disciplinary content does not define a graduate as a scientist or as an engineer. There is, for example, little overlap of curricular content between a civil engineer, a materials engineer, and a computer engineer. Their disciplinary knowledge is not what makes graduates of these sub-discipline engineers. Engineering (and science too) are attitudes of mind, exemplified by approaches to the world which transcend subject matter. This is captured in (admittedly over-simplified) descriptions such as "engineers design and make useful stuff" or "scientists work to discover how the world works." In order to become a liberal engineer – with a human face – it is not important what your field of expertise might be. In a general engineering or general science programme the student must acquire some knowledge and expertise in order to demonstrate their engineering (or science) approach, but it matters little what the subject matter is. In what follows I therefore omit almost all reference to engineering topics; any type of engineer can demonstrate a human face.

The following ideas about liberal engineering, producing professional engineers with human faces, have been developed in the context of the new programme being developed at NMiTE. This programme will be delivered by project-based-learning, with few or no lectures. Every student will therefore become involved in many projects – perhaps as many as 25. Each project will have technical "engineering" aspects but will also, in every case, involve contextual material which will enable students to experience the full range of non-technical interactions with other key players in society. Ensuring that every student has had an appropriate range of experiences after completing her projects is an outcome which will require careful planning and supervision. In order to help the curriculum team, and the students, to achieve these I have devised a set of questions which can be applied to any project. Although these were devised in the context of a project-based general engineering programme, they would translate without much modification to almost any science or engineering programme. It is on this basis that I use them as a lens through which to consider integrated "liberal" content.

The questions will be addressed in turn. They are all open-ended and I will present some of the topics which could potentially be opened up in response to each. Of course, I expect to be surprised and delighted by imaginative students whose responses far exceed my expectations.

Only the first two questions necessarily apply to every project (or design, or in principle any piece of work). The other seven questions are presented in no particular order, and not all of them will necessarily be applied to any particular project or piece of work – although I have tried to make them as widely applicable as possible.

Question 1: Why?

This is the fundamental question which we hope all students are asking themselves the whole time. In the context of a project, we could expect the student to address the reasons why the project is worthwhile; why its outcomes will be useful to society; why they are timely; why the opportunity for this work presents itself now. In the context of her own learning the student should be questioning what she is learning, and how it relates to other aspects of the programme; what it needs to be supplemented by; how it advances her own life and career aspirations. A more thoughtful student might question why the staff (and project sponsors, if any) chose this project; what they hoped to get out of it; why this particular project was chosen instead of other possible vehicles for the same learning outcomes; whether the published learning outcomes are appropriate; how well the technical and non-technical aspects fitted together.

Question 2: How could this experience be improved?

This question too should be constantly at the front of all students' minds. Reflection may be one of this decade's most over-used words, but here it has clear value. In terms of learning, the question has two aspects: how could my own behaviour have improved my own learning, and in what ways could the experience have been constructed or delivered differently to maximize both what was learned and the ease or speed of the learning process? The thoughtful student will also ask herself how the experience could be improved for other students, who may have different aptitudes or ambitions. She might even consult a book on the topic e.g. Goodhew (2010).

When the question applies to a project, particularly one in which something is made, the obvious implications may be more concrete: how could my product/design/outcome be better, cheaper, have lower impact on the environment, have higher impact on its intended users, be lighter, use less energy, and so on. And, as an important aside, what does "better" mean? Could I/we have carried out the project more effectively or efficiently, for instance if we had deployed proper project management tools? Students might need reminding of the definition I used earlier: "Engineers design and make useful stuff." How does this project relate to this definition?

A further lateral thought process leads to the question: could this have been done in a better space? This is an issue which arises almost daily when "newer" pedagogies are trialled in institutions which are replete with lecture theatres and fixed seating. Thoughtful students will follow this trail and consider issues of architecture and human group behaviour.

Question 3: How many?

Some explanation might be required for this question. For a project in which some artefact is designed and/or made, the question can be taken at face value: how many of these things are needed? How many could be sold? The student could present a market analysis, with proper consideration of market penetration, resource requirements for this number (materials, staff, training etc.), and delivery options, and so on.

Less obvious interpretations of the question might occur to some students, but might have to be suggested to others. For the set of activities associated with either a project or a conventional technical module, how many of them contribute directly to the intended learning outcomes? How many key concepts have been explored/revealed/explained in this activity? What are they? Should there have been more or fewer?

Question 4: Cost?

Again, the simple interpretation is appropriate for a project: what did/does/will your project outcome cost? This will involve consideration of materials, costings, manufacturing methods, transport, labour, economies of scale, etc. Additionally, for any exercise, the student should be able to deduce its cost (although few students do). What was the cost of mounting this course/module/project? What overheads are associated with teaching and learning? To what extent are there economies of scale; what is the difference between the base cost and the marginal cost of adding an extra student? Are there discontinuities associated with the filling of classrooms or labs? Does the fee you pay cover all this? For the more perceptive student: what would alternative pedagogical approaches cost? Can you perform a cost-benefit analysis for various teaching styles?

Question 5: Who pays?

This rather stark question can be unwrapped to reveal many societal issues. In terms of education, who pays for your learning and your degree? The answer will not simply be "my fees," but must include government, taxpayers, parents, and other family members or supporters. "Pays" may not imply only money.

In terms of a project (with its implication of making something) the question is: who will be prepared to pay for the thing you have made or designed? Will this be individuals, governments (presumably via taxation), businesses, or whom? Who will, or should, make a profit? If the thing you have made or designed is intended for charitable use – for example in a developing country – then how will the money be raised and by whom? Should anyone in the manufacturing and supply chain for a charitable product make a profit?

In all cases, what are the conditions under which money might be raised, lent, and paid back?

Question 6: What will be the impact?

For any manufactured article (or even design), we should obviously consider its potential impact on its users, on the environment, and on the use and depletion of resources. Slightly less obvious are its impacts on society via its aesthetic qualities, the noise it generates, the activities it encourages or displaces, and on the health of the user (for example if it replaces walking or cycling, there is a potential health deficit). It is not impossible that there could be political repercussions and/or public protests (think fracking). Are there ethical considerations which beg the further question "should we be doing this at all?"

Pedagogically, the obvious impacts of an activity are on the student's understanding of key concepts, on her progress towards a qualification, and on her ability to tackle more advanced ideas.

Question 7: What are the risks?

For a project, there will be potential risks associated with the final product, and with the execution of the project itself. Perceptive answers to this question will need to refer to health and safety legislation, to legislation associated with the product, and to laboratory working practices. For a project which involves making, there are likely to be workshop practice issues and there may be other hazards. Beyond these initial responses lie questions associated with the risk of the project not being completed successfully, of the learning outcomes not being met, or of human factors such as team breakdown, or just the loss of a team member. A full response would include a graded risk register, with mitigation plans for each contingency. In some cases a probabilistic analysis would be appropriate.

In terms of the educational development of the student, it would be appropriate to evaluate the impact on learning and degree progression of various outcomes, including recovery plans.

Question 8: What happens afterwards?

The educational issues should include an analysis of what next steps are needed: what learning or knowledge gaps have been revealed by the current activity?

Does the student's future programme need modification? Has she kept a sufficient record of progress to contribute convincingly to a CV or portfolio?

For a project the obvious considerations include: disposal of unused materials; disposal (if not to be used) of the manufactured article; the potential for recycling or re-use at the end of life; and maintenance during the product's lifetime. Possibly less obvious to the student might be: what changes could be expected in society if the product was widely adopted? What might be displaced? What current patterns of behaviour and use might change, with what impact on society?

Question 9: Which language/country?

Engineering (certainly) and education (to an increasing extent) are international activities. It would often be useful if engineering graduates could comfortably operate with a second or third language. This applies whether the graduate's career is in industry, commerce, or the third sector. Of course, many students whose first language is not English currently do this – demonstrating admirably that bilingual working is quite achievable. For those programmes which set fluency in a second language as a learning outcome, some way of achieving this has to be found.

A potential solution arises in the context of the nine questions. If each student is to answer 20 or more such questions during an undergraduate programme, then the answering of a subset – perhaps half a dozen – of the questions could be in a second language. Since most cohorts of engineering students contain individuals with a variety of first languages, it would usually be possible to select second languages which were spoken by some members of the cohort, thus providing internal support (from fellow students already familiar with engineering and its vocabulary) for each learner.

Other questions with similar potential, and a greater variety of suggested approaches to answering them, could easily be developed by a programme team.

Discussion

My nine questions, simple in themselves, raise a large number of "liberal" or "human" issues which are not conventionally regarded as engineering. They also demand critical thinking. Among the topics which every student will encounter are aesthetics, architecture, ethics, public health, sociology, politics and political protest, noise pollution, finance, the profit motive, pedagogy, management, marketing, and charity. This list is limited only by my own imagination, and will certainly be easily extended by colleagues and students. All these issues have been raised, however, in the firm context of engineering learning – whether via projects or any other pedagogy. Asking these (or similar) questions during technical modules ensures the integration I identified as desirable in the introduction.

Questions should be asked during every module, project, or other significant activity. In most undergraduate engineering programmes, students will undertake between 20 and 30 such activities. If, each time, they have to answer just one question, then by the time they graduate they will have answered each of the nine questions two or three times – in different contexts (and possibly, different languages). This should be enough to allow improvement but not too much to result in boredom. The questions can be answered, and communicated, in a number of ways, resulting in significant opportunities for the practice of communication skills. Essays, reports, web sites, blogs, and public presentations are all possible. If, say, one-third of the questions had to be answered in a second language, then language development would also be encouraged.

Clearly not every topic I have sketched above will occur to every student. The key role of staff in the process will probably be to nudge students in appropriate directions – making suggestions for avenues of exploration. One of the features of implementing the ideas in this paper will necessarily be collecting feedback on the level of intervention which proves necessary as students wrestle with the – initially unfamiliar – questions. This is classic "guide-on-the-side" support: I would not suggest that lectures should be given on any of the topics listed at the start of this section.

How long should all this take? That depends how "human" we want our graduates to be. My own view is that addressing these questions should comprise a significant component of the degree programme. Answering a question in degree-worthy depth cannot be done in an hour, but more realistically will take a day or two. The NMiTE programme which prompted this analysis will probably allocate one-third of student time to non-engineering activities typified by these questions. However, I understand that this might be considered too large a fraction of a dedicated sub-disciplinary programme, and in such cases 20% (one day a week) should suffice to ensure that an engineering graduate resembles a human being who is ready to take a leading place in society. Students in a number of universities over the next decade – not only at NMiTE – will test my analysis rigorously.

References

CDIO Url:www.cdio.org
Coventry University Url:www.coventry.ac.uk/course-structure/engineering-environment-and-computing/postgraduate/global-humanitarian-engineering-msc/
Franklin W, *Olin College*, Boston, USA Url:www.olin.edu
Goodhew P (2010) *Teaching Engineering* Url:http://core.materials.ac.uk/repository/teaching-engineering/teaching_engineering_goodhew.pdf

Grasso D (2015) *Journal of Engineering Studies* Url:http://dx.doi.org/10.1080/19378629.2015.1062500
Harvey Mudd College, CA Url:https://hmc.edu
Lassonde School of Engineering, York University, Toronto Url:http://lassonde.yorku.ca
Laurentian University, Ontario, Canada Url:www.laurentian.ca
Nipissing University, Ontario, Canada Url:www.nipissingu.ca
NMiTE (2018) Url:www.nmite.org.uk
Quest University, British Colombia, Canada Url:https://questu.ca
https://study.com/
UCL, London Url:www.ucl.ac.uk/basc
UK-SPEC (2016) 3rd Edition Url:www.engc.org.uk
Warwick University Url:http://www2.warwick.ac.uk/fac/sci/eng/research/grouplist/eerg/whec/

Chapter 5

Interdisciplinary project weeks

Patricia B. Murray and Rachel Horn

Introduction

Professional engineers operate in an increasingly sophisticated, global world. Often working on international projects or in international locations, engineers must be agile team players, adept communicators, reflective, and able to operate effectively within an interdisciplinary and multi-cultural working environment (Bourn & Neale, 2008; Royal Academy of Engineering, 2007). Engineering is a vocational subject, and most engineering undergraduates at the University of Sheffield intend to pursue an industry career. In 2011, recognizing that their student engineers worked largely within the traditional silos of their discipline areas; the Faculty of Engineering identified a strategic aim to make use of the newly formed faculty structure to enable cross-disciplinary working. Around the same time, other strategic aims were identified, in particular to bring a focus, early in student programmes, on global dimensions and considerations of sustainable and human aspects of engineering design. Furthermore, there was a growing recognition that many of our students were not good at identifying and articulating (to potential employers) the skills and experience that they had acquired within and beyond the curriculum, so we wanted to support students to reflect on their learning and to take ownership of their personal development (Royal Academy of Engineering, 2013). Finally, we identified that students spend much of their time focused on performing for assessment, providing little opportunity to learn and develop without risk of failure, so we wanted to offer a rare space in the curriculum in which students are encouraged to experiment and have fun with their learning without negative recourse – i.e. there is no contribution to overall grades.

A working party comprising academics from the nine departmental areas in the faculty was brought together and a project manager (the lead author) was appointed to deliver the outcome. Two cross-faculty project weeks were the result: the Global Engineering Challenge (GEC) for all first year students, and Engineering You're Hired (EYH) for all second year students.

In each week, the students work in interdisciplinary teams to address defined problems. Requisite engineering knowledge is taught, with skills sessions and skills practice throughout the weeks. The weeks occur in January/February, time released from a coincident move to 20 credit, year-long modules and the associated reduction in the number of mid-year exams. While time was freed, the decision was taken to make the two weeks non-credit bearing, in order to provide opportunities for students to experiment, reflect, learn, and develop from their experience, without the inhibition of credit acquisition. We also wanted all students to participate. Experience showed that if the weeks were optional, the strongest students with least need for skills development would be the most likely to opt in. The weeks were therefore compulsory to attend for all students, but without credit, which charged us with motivating the students by inspiring and engaging them (rather than assessing them). A final constraint was to avoid overburdening academic staff with significant extra work.

The cohort of 876 students who entered in academic year 2011/12 did GEC in 2012 and then EYH in 2013. There have now been seven GECs and six EYHs; the cohort size has risen to 1405 and a total of 8139 students have now completed GEC.

Since 2012, the public debate about industry needs and the role of higher education in delivering that need has broadened (University World News, 2013). Successive governments have highlighted the "skills agenda," the need for workforce skills to match those required by employers, since this is highly associated with economic growth. Universities are considered paramount in delivering on this, by producing graduates who are both academically capable but also equipped with an array of soft (or work) skills. The recent Wakeham Review (2016, p3) highlighted "the value that employers place on graduates being in possession of a strong set of soft or work ready skills" and suggested "the development of soft skills could be embedded more systematically and robustly in degree curricula." Also noted was graduates' lack of understanding of how their skills and knowledge map onto the jobs market. This supports the continuing relevance of our key drivers for the weeks.

What follows will first be a description of the two project weeks and what, from the outset, worked well. We will then spend time discussing the challenges we have identified over the years and changes we have made to address those challenges. Finally, we will note what our next steps will be.

Two weeks and a spiral curriculum

The weeks are based on a "problem-based learning" (PBL) approach within a spiral curriculum, whereby a core set of knowledge and skills are identified, and then revisited with increasing levels of sophistication. The spiral extends into the third and fourth years when students build on their core skills while undertaking their disciplinary group design projects.

Enabling PBL at scale

The students (876 in 2012 and rising to 1405 in 2018) are organized into teams of six. Each team has no more than two members from any one department and a home/international student mix that reflects the faculty as a whole (typically 1–2 international students per team). Six teams are then organized into "hubs" (36 students), and a hub has a dedicated trained PhD student facilitator, an attached staff member, and a base (hub) room for the week.

The week's schedule is divided between facilitator-led sessions addressing engineering topics and skills, and team project working time. As well as introducing new knowledge, activities within the facilitator-led sessions are focused around the projects the teams are working on, sustaining the momentum of progress.

All teaching materials are prepared in advance by the organizers, and the PhD student facilitators are trained in their use: cascade teaching (see later section on Facilitator recruitment).

Features of both weeks

Inspiration and context

Each week opens at 9am on the Monday with students in lecture theatres. Industrial speakers and the organizers give short presentations intended to provoke interest, set context in terms of the curriculum as a whole and their future careers, and give operational details. Students then go to their hub rooms where they meet their team members and facilitator, and under facilitator guidance they embark on the initial team-building activities.

The problems and learning

Open ended, real world engineering problems are the basis of both weeks. Teams first negotiate to decide which problem they want to work on. Engineering knowledge (design process, sustainability considerations, etc.), necessary to progress the problem, is introduced in the early part of each week, followed by sessions on skills (communication, reflection/skills review, etc.), timed to precede the practising of the skill. While the facilitators lead on the teaching, staff drop in for short periods, questioning and advising the student teams.

Alumni/industry

Practising engineers are invited to participate on the middle Wednesday of both weeks. They visit the hubs and talk about their career path, and work with the teams on their projects. They are encouraged to inject the "real world" into the students' considerations of their problems. This manifests as costs, the market, competition, and aspects of project management that most teams have not considered and may not be familiar with.

Team outputs

Teams produce a written report by the Friday morning (submitted to the university's virtual learning environment (VLE)) and then deliver a team presentation to their hub in the afternoon.

Marking and feedback

The facilitators mark and generate feedback for the reports in their own hub. They do this on the Friday morning (while students are preparing their presentations). In the afternoon, teams present to their hub, including the facilitator and staff member (and in the case of EYH, a Senior Engineer). Facilitators encourage competition between teams. Ability to ask questions is another valuable skill to develop, so students (and the staff/Engineer) are encouraged to ask questions to rival teams, simultaneously providing feedback to the presenting team. The presentation is scored by the audience in GEC, and by the facilitator/staff/industry board in EYH.

Celebration of success

Once presentations are finished, the students reconvene in the lecture theatres to celebrate their achievements. After showing a video featuring highlights of the week, the teams winning "Best Communicated Solution" in each hub are announced and awarded certificates.

Finally, after the weeks, the teams with the highest combined report/presentation mark in each hub are recognized.

The core learning

The core engineering knowledge and skills which are introduced in GEC and then developed further in EYH are:

- The engineering design process
- Sustainable design
- Engineering judgement
- Project management

- Multidisciplinary, multi-cultural team working
- Problem solving and creativity
- Communicating and defending ideas
- Reflecting on learning and articulating knowledge and skills

Progression: the spiral

Development from Y1-GEC to Y2-EYH includes the nature of the problems and the skills required to progress them, the level of support provided, and the level of technical content of the project.

The problems in GEC require technical aptitude and an engineering approach. By their second year, the students are equipped with more discipline-based knowledge, and the EYH problems require the teams to use and integrate that knowledge. Having followed a structured Engineering Design Process in GEC, students in EYH are expected to progress more rapidly to the conceptual design stage and produce a more developed proposal along with the management and marketing of their proposal. In terms of support, more specific engineering knowledge is provided by greater staff time and industrial input, but in recognition of expected greater learner autonomy, there are fewer facilitated sessions and more independent team working time. Peer assessment of the final presentations in GEC is succeeded by a boardroom scenario in EYH. Invited senior Engineers join the staff member and the facilitator on the board, which adds gravitas to the presentations. The two cross-faculty project weeks are summarized in Table 5.1.

Facilitator recruitment

From the outset, we have dedicated considerable effort to recruiting and training PhD students. Application forms ask questions about teaching and team working. Successful applicants are invited to practical "group" interviews where they are asked to facilitate a discussion around one of the actual slides used for teaching and to demonstrate how they would support students to progress one of the projects. When not facilitating, they are asked to act as students. These active interviews, and in particular the facilitation task, have proved illuminating. They both give us a clear indication of the PhD students' abilities in facilitation and give the students themselves a realistic insight into what the job entails. We have found this recruitment format highly effective.

We interview a large proportion of applicants and recruit about 50% of the students we interview. Once successful, we ask the PhD students to attend University of Sheffield half-day courses on teaching skills. We then organize training, one and a half days for GEC and one day for EYH, focused on teaching with the materials for the weeks; this is the process of cascade training. We pay students for the specific project week training, but not the generic teaching training.

In addition to its teaching effectiveness, the cascade teaching model has scaled well, coping with the 60% increase in student numbers over the seven years. For the first GEC, we had 876 students in 24 hubs and there were 26 different facilitators. In 2018, we had 1301 students doing GEC in 36 hubs and 1405 students doing EYH in 39 hubs; there were 52 different facilitators.

Successes

Numerous elements of both weeks worked well from the outset.

Table 5.1 Summary of the two project weeks

Aspect	Global Engineering Challenge (GEC)	Engineering You're Hired (EYH)
The problems	Problems based on the Engineers Without Borders (EWB) Engineering for People Design Challenge (Engineers Without Borders, 2018). These problems, which are based in developing countries, are categorized into water, sanitation, energy, waste, transport, built environment, and digital. Example problems include: "Alternative methods of electricity provision," "Water quality," and "Smart greenhouses."	Multidisciplinary problems suggested by staff and industry. Example problem titles are "Swarm robots for precision agriculture," "Autonomous road vehicles for high speed motorway travel," "Biomimetic domestic buildings," and "Commercial electric aircraft."
Engineering knowledge sessions	• The engineering design process • Sustainable design • Innovation and ideas creation • Risk and ethics	• Recap on the design process • Feasibility analysis • Industry consultations • Project planning including cost, risk, and intellectual property
Soft-skills sessions	• Team building • End of day team review • Receiving, using, and giving feedback • Effective communication • Reflecting on the weeks' learning	• Team building • End of day team review • Answering an employability question of the day
Structure of the week	More taught sessions. Extended boardroom on Wednesday only.	More independent team working time. Daily end of day boardrooms.
Facilitator role	Present most of the week to lead/facilitate taught sessions.	Present to "top and tail" the days.
Staff role	Ask questions on progress/give general design advice through four hours of drop-in time, and three hours for end of week presentations.	More focused support for subject knowledge. Five hours of drop-in time. Six hours in boardrooms Three hours for end of week pitch sessions.

Alumni/industry role	Visit the hubs to talk about "How I got my first job" and support teams' progress on their problem.	Consultation appointments which teams can book. Commercial and project management focus. Part of the hub board.
Team outputs	1. Report 2. Presentation	1. Proposed design and a plan to take the design to "proof of concept stage." 2. Pitch for funding of the proposal.
Assessment of the report/proposal	Who: Hub facilitator. How: Reports submitted through VLE, which is used for feedback and marking so all team members can access.	Who: Hub facilitator. How: Same as for GEC.
Assessment of the presentation/pitch	Who: Peer assessment. Everyone present in the hub (i.e. students apart from the presenting team, staff member, and facilitator) score the presentations. How: Feedback via questions followed by online voting against assessment criteria.	Who: The board (in each hub): Senior Industrial Engineer, staff member, and facilitator. How: Feedback via questions. Marking by a marking rubric. Marks are averaged and recorded.

For the undergraduates

- Student evaluation of the weeks show that they value the opportunity to work with students from outside their own department. Often reported as simply having made new friends, this is still the mechanism by which they experience a different perspective and are introduced to a different disciplinary vocabulary and viewpoints. Particularly marked was feedback from international students, who welcomed early opportunities in their undergraduate experience to work with home students.
- In terms of their learning, students cite team working, followed by working on real-world projects, as being the most beneficial. Opportunities to practise giving presentations are also prominent in the feedback.
- Early exposure to industry is invaluable. Involvement of alumni/industry lends credibility to the weeks and helps students see the relevance of what they are learning, both for job applications and work itself. We ensure we have sufficient alumni/industry representatives to visit all hubs, enabling many students to engage and ask questions. Involvement of Senior Engineers on the EYH Friday afternoon "pitch for funding" brings gravitas to the proceedings, with the students placing particular value on the Engineers' opinions.
- There are a variety of opportunities in both weeks for the teams to receive awards. In each hub, teams are awarded "Best Communicated Solution," "Best Overall Solution," and more recently, "Best Professional Behaviours." Together with the individual experiences, both positive and negative, students develop evidence they can cite in job applications and interview scenarios. We very quickly started hearing anecdotes about job interviews where questions revolved around the project weeks, sometimes couched by students recalling that they hadn't seen the value of the project weeks at the time. We later captured this in the module evaluations, and found that even for the very first GEC/EYH cohort (who were fourth years in 2014/15), almost 50% of responders hadcited project weeks in their applications (see Figure 5.1).

For the postgraduate student facilitators

- PhD facilitators are involved in innovative teaching weeks, giving them practical teaching and leadership experience significantly beyond those of the more common lab demonstrating. Facilitators work with a hub of 36 students for the whole week, gaining experience in small group teaching techniques including nurturing team working and team reflection/review. They use a number of teaching technologies including online marking with an assessment rubric and feedback in the VLE, voting systems, and collaborative online tools.

Interdisciplinary project weeks 67

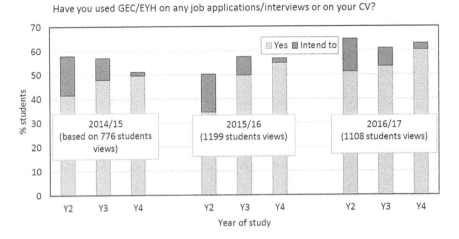

Figure 5.1 Year end student module evaluations.

- A number of PhD students have had their views of teaching transformed by the experience and have pursued teaching careers as a result. However, as for the undergraduates, they all acquire experiences and develop skills which will both help in future job applications and their future careers.

For the organizers

- Our implementation of a problem-based learning model, with teaching materials devised by the organizers and cascade teaching by a team of PhD students, has proved highly effective for student learning and skills development. The hub model means that irrespective of growth in student numbers, students experience small group teaching with 35 other students. This is best exemplified by the boardrooms, where each team gets the board's focused attention for consideration of their progress. This dialogue-format feedback, which in EYH happens daily, is exemplary for student learning.
- The hub model has proven highly scalable. From the initial 876 students in 2012, the cohort size peaked in 2017 at 1479 students. In spite of this near 70% rise in student numbers, we have sustained, and in fact evolved, a high quality and valuable experience for all students, and without placing an onerous burden on academic staff.
- Each year, more than 50% of our facilitators return, with a significant number returning for three years. The accrued wisdom they collectively amass, they willingly share with one another and the organizers to help evolve the week. They are a joy to work with.

For the faculty

- The weeks have become firmly established as a robust platform for skills development, experienced by all students across the faculty.
- The weeks are regularly used in the accreditation process and have been repeatedly highlighted as innovative teaching activities, highly beneficial to the students.
- A pool of 147 PhD students (over the seven years), trained and experienced in facilitating project weeks, are available for other teaching roles. Several have progressed into permanent academic roles within the faculty.
- An unforeseen outcome has been the regular contact with industry and alumni. Each year, we now attract about 100 engineers from all areas of practice, who both work with the students and assess them. This showcases our students, and also promotes wider links with faculty, staff, and activities.

Challenges and changes

Over the seven iterations of GEC and six of EYH, we have identified a number of challenges and made various changes. We discuss these under the heading of "student motivation," that is us attempting to develop students' motivation such that it matches our aims, and "delivery," in particular what we have learned from delivering at scale.

Challenges and changes: student motivation

Subject interest

THE CHALLENGE

While we recognize that much of the value of the week is about skills development, the students' focus is almost entirely on tackling the problems. In the first year of running, the method for team formation was based only on the student demographics (department and home/international), with each team then negotiating which problem they would solve. This meant that no-one necessarily worked on their preferred problem.

More generally, we thought that the EWB development problems, which require appropriate solutions within a context of sustainability, would be appropriate for first years that have little developed discipline knowledge. However, we hadn't appreciated how discipline-focused some students can be, with little interest in applying their knowledge in a different context. This is further compounded by a lack of appreciation of the importance of and therefore interest in social considerations and people-centred design, which may stem from the typical engineering student's background of sciences at school.

CHANGES

We now ask the students individually to rank their problem preferences and then feed that information, along with the demographic data, into an optimization routine. Most students now get their first problem choice, with about 10% getting their second or third. Those that don't choose are allocated projects popular with students from their department.

For GEC, we have widened the choice and nature of the problems by working with computer science academics at the University of Makerere in Uganda, and added a number of problems based on application of data science and AI to address problems in developing countries (University of Makerere School of Computing and IT, 2018). These data-based projects complement the EWB projects and have alleviated the discontent amongst students whose interest is limited to leading edge technologies, while still retaining the global sustainability and people-centred design focus.

Valuing skills development

The challenge

Many engineering students have studied mainly science subjects at school, focusing almost entirely on technical knowledge, and meaning they have "avoided" other, more discursive subjects. Some students also tell us they have "done" team working at school. The result is that some students' development of skills such as teamwork and communication is fairly rudimentary, and when they arrive at university to study engineering, they do not appreciate that further development of these skills is an important part of their programme and of their personal and professional development (Engineering Council, 2016).

Changes

In both project weeks, we give industry a platform to tell students what skills and attributes they are looking for when recruiting graduates, and what the students should do while at university in order to best position themselves for their future careers. This happens both in the opening plenaries and also, more intimately, when the alumni/industry visit the hubs on the Wednesdays. Alumni/industry are role models for the students, bringing credibility, endorsement, and an industrial perspective on the relevance of the project weeks. This, along with team dynamics reaching a productive stage, brings a discernible step change in the engagement of the student teams. In recognition of this injection of energy, we have, over the years, extended the time that alumni/industry spend with the students. In GEC, alumni are now invited for the whole day, and, following its success in EYH, we now have an extended boardroom presentation session on the Wednesday afternoon involving the alumni. For both weeks, in response to student comments, we now have a networking event. All industrial visitors' names, their degree subject (if alumni), and their role and company name are advertised in advance. Students are encouraged to attend, meet relevant alumni/industry, and practise their networking skills.

Team working

The challenge

Team working, highly effective for solving complex problems, can also be problematic. Students often think a single experience of working in a team makes them proficient team players, and yet may have never had any help in understanding how teams work and how they best contribute to the teamwork. In the student evaluation, "freeloading" is the most commonly cited team working difficulty. Other common issues are work division, role effectiveness, and communication.

Changes

We have implemented a number of changes to the way the student teams operate, guided by the five elements of co-operative learning (Johnson & Johnson, 1999).

1. The team size in GEC was reduced from six to five in order to promote "individual accountability." In EYH, the need for interdisciplinary knowledge was thought more important and the team size remains at six.
2. The role of team leader, rotated amongst team members on a daily basis, has been bolstered. In addition to the week's final outputs, there are now daily deliverables, and the day's team leader is responsible for ensuring that they are achieved. Since every team member is at some point the team leader, this should promote "positive interdependence."
3. Each day starts with a scheduled time slot when facilitators brief the team leaders who then lead team meetings, during which they are encouraged to set objectives for the day, divide tasks, and, if appropriate, allocate roles. This should promote "face-to-face promotive interaction."
4. Each day ends with a team review, again led by the team leaders. The team leaders are responsible for recording key points of the discussion, particularly any change recommendations; this helps the following day's team leader. Last year, this became a compulsory addendum to the team report and is assessed. This fulfils "group processing."
5. The fifth co-operative learning recommendation is for interpersonal skills and group skills, and is considered as part of the BIT project below.

Team leader-led meetings and review have always been part of both weeks. These changes are intended to ensure those meetings happen, to give greater responsibility to the team leader, with the intention of promoting better accountability and therefore team working.

A second change has been introduction of peer review, whereby team members are given the opportunity to mark the contributions of each of their peers. This is now part of the assessment and is discussed in the section titled 'No-Credit.'

Finally, students rarely get clear advice on the team working behaviours that will lead to the best outcomes for them and their team. In an engineering faculty, staff might not feel equipped to give such advice, so when we were approached by researchers from our Management School suggesting exactly that, we were keen to collaborate.

The "Behaviour in Teams" (BIT) research project is led by Professor Neil Rackham, whose career is based on working with teams in companies and researching the individual behaviours that give rise to the best team results. Applying his attention to student teams, a number of our hubs were part of the research study (University of Sheffield, 2018). Students in those hubs were shown videos introducing specific team behaviours. Observers for each team recorded team members' use of those behaviours, and students were intermittently shown the data on their own behaviour as a feedback mechanism for improvement.

Changes in students' behaviours through the week can then be compared to the team's success (as recorded in their team report and presentation mark) and the individual's success, as recorded by the peer review mark. This research is still ongoing, but if found to be positively impactful on student behaviour, then we would look to implement the aspects of the study that are possible at scale.

Depth of investigation

The challenge

Evaluation results from the first iteration showed that the students preferred working independently in teams, progressing their project and developing knowledge and skills in a facilitated session. However, the evaluation also contained comments such as "we could have solved the problem in three hours" and (for GEC) "these problems could be done by Geography 'A' level students." Furthermore, this shallow approach was reflected in the team outputs, with the reports and presentations showing lack of investigation and engineering approach.

The comments reveal that some students were not grasping the nature of open-ended problem solving, where the details and appropriateness of the solution is entirely limited by the research time. Furthermore, students were being impatient in wanting to problem solve without equipping themselves with the relevant engineering knowledge and, despite being introduced to the structured engineering design approach, were not following it. Particular areas of neglect were the initial context of the problem, consideration of more than one option, and quantification of both the problem itself and the conceptual design options. The students were indeed failing to think like an engineer.

Changes

We decided to give greater prominence to the engineering design process. We do this by briefly introducing the whole process at the beginning of the week, and then revealing the detail of each step of the process in a staged way over three days. We use a case study to illustrate the design process, thereby demonstrating the expected depth of contextual investigation as well as the process of estimating quantities and applying engineering judgement.

For our case study, we selected a UK-based scenario to help students see that sustainability and human centred design are equally relevant to a developed country. Ensuring the problem would be analogous to an EWB problem and also familiar to all our students, we decided on "Reducing energy use in terraced houses in Sheffield." We then created short videos, one for each step of the design process. Other engineering knowledge is still taught, but is now timed to support the considerations of the design process.

To further support this methodology, we now provide student teams with a report template that also maps to the design steps. These templates have pre-populated sections, prompt questions, and links to design tools.

No-credit

The challenge

Students are motivated by grades and with the aid of modularization, credit-definition, assessment criteria, and marking rubrics, are able to dedicate their effort to activities that contribute the most towards the grade. While understandable, such strategic behaviour suppresses creativity and experimentation in learning and conceptualizes learning as a linear reward process, which is not a realistic depiction of reward in the complex social environment of work. Motivating the students to engage in the week is however, crucial.

In the first few years, we didn't have a structured approach of recognizing engagement and rewarding quality of team outputs. Students were able to free-load with no mechanism for identifying or penalizing them. Having decided to make the weeks compulsory, but not graded, meant that students would either pass or fail, with no differentiation in the pass. It became evident that both "freeloading students" and "lack of recognition of excellence," were highly demotivating for the more engaged students.

Changes

We completely altered the way students were assessed in the weeks. This comprised three changes:

1. We introduced peer assessment, whereby students recognize the contributions of individuals in their team. Using "WebPA" (University of Loughborough, 2009), which is administered through the VLE, students are asked two questions about their team members: contribution to the team outputs and contribution to the process of team working. For each question, they weight the contributions by splitting 100 marks between their team members (including themselves).
2. We introduced a distinction level. The highest two team marks (report and presentation) in each hub are graded as distinction.
3. The individual mark is based on the team mark and the individual's peer assessment and attendance.

With these changes, students can achieve distinction, pass or fail, individuals can be promoted and demoted based on their peer-assessment score, and poor attendance can be mitigated by a positive peer-assessment score. While quite complicated, we believe that this is fairer to the students and they appear happier both with the power it affords them in influencing the assessment and in the differentiated result.

Challenges and changes: delivery

Cascade teaching

The challenge

While the facilitators performed an excellent job teaching with the pre-prepared materials, they were not themselves subject experts in the various knowledge areas. Our initial teaching strategy was to give subject detail within PowerPoint slides with comprehensive support notes for the facilitators. Student evaluation highlighted "death by PowerPoint," and we also became aware of the facilitators' inconsistent use of the support notes leading to a variable and sometimes stilted delivery, not ideal for the student experience.

Changes

We reviewed our teaching methodology and decided to deliver the engineering knowledge and design process case study through dedicated videos, delivered by knowledge experts. That way, we could reduce the reliance on PowerPoint, and at the same time ensure the content and quality of the delivery. There was a further benefit in that this process forced us to identify the salient knowledge for the short, focused videos.

With PowerPoint still forming the main teaching tool, the facilitators now introduce videos on "Sustainability," "Innovation and Ideas Creation," and each step of the design process. Each video is followed by discussion of a number of provocative questions and a summary of key points.

Staff engagement

The challenge

Many academic staff at Russell group universities such as Sheffield, even in a vocational discipline like engineering, have a research background and feel best placed and most interested in developing the students' academic knowledge and abilities. In spite of the accreditation need to empower the students with broad engineering/transferable skills and the political focus on universities to produce work-ready graduates, some members of staff are perhaps reluctant to recognize the importance of broad skills development and are not themselves motivated or equipped to support students to develop those skills.

Changes

As with the students, we attempt to engage staff in the importance of the breadth of skills development and the changing demands on the current generation of graduates. We have developed a short staff briefing session, which is delivered shortly before the weeks. This is supported by brief notes providing context and prompts for questioning groups on team and task progress. As a small focused team undertakes the overall teaching development and organization and the facilitators front-face the weeks, we keep the staff role to engaging directly with the student groups, making best use of their time for focused academic input.

Challenges and changes: the impact

The impact of the changes is summarized by our most recent (2017/18) end of week student evaluation, which shows very positive responses for questions covering a range of aspects of the two weeks:

Interdisciplinary project weeks 75

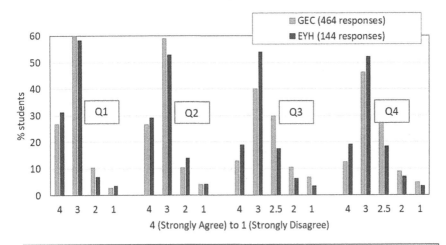

Figure 5.2 Week end student evaluation 2017/18.

Student responses to the range of questions appeared to be very positive in both weeks.

The future

This year, several of our students were offered placements after the EYH week as a result of the Senior Engineer seeing their work. This is the ultimate accolade for the weeks. We want to ensure that the weeks sustain this level of industry engagement and relevance, and that is exactly what the students want. We therefore need to continue listening to our stakeholders, and in particular industry, and evolve the weeks accordingly.

There is a recognition in the Wakeham Review (2016, p3) that "some students struggle in mapping their skills and knowledge to jobs," which confirms our own experience. GEC and EYH raise students' awareness of the importance of skills development, and have activities that promote reflection including explicit mapping of skills and knowledge against job specifications. However, the faculty has recognized that a more comprehensive and holistic, programme level approach is needed to help students fully recognize the breadth and depth of the requisite skills and attributes of "The Sheffield Graduate Engineer." Intended to act as a framework for programme development and skills reflection, students will evaluate their attributes and skills against this framework with the intention of raising students' aspirations and better informing them of their progress.

The BIT research study should soon provide us with evidence as to the impact of introducing the students to positive team working behaviours, and giving them immediate feedback on their own behaviours. It is hoped that the study will show clear benefits to the students, in which case we will explore which aspects of the study we can replicate at scale, for the good of all future students.

References

Bourn D & Neale I (2008) The Global Engineer: Incorporating global skills within UK higher education of engineers, in *Engineers Against Poverty and Development Education Research Centre, Institute of Education*, London: University of London

Engineering Council (2016) *The UK Standard for Professional Engineering Competence (UK-SPEC)* Url:www.engc.org.uk/ukspec

Engineers Without Borders (2018) *Engineering for People Design Challenge* Url:www.ewb-uk.org/engineering-for-people/

Johnson DW & Johnson RT (1999) Making cooperative learning work. *Theory into Practise*, No. 38, pp. 67–73

The Royal Academy of Engineering (2007) *Educating Engineers for the 21st Century* Url:www.raeng.org.uk/publications/reports/educating-engineers-21st-century

Royal Academy of Engineering (2013) *Skills for the Nation: Engineering Undergraduates in the UK* Url:www.raeng.org.uk/publications/reports/skills-for-the-nation-engineering

University of Loughborough (2009) WebPA Url:http://webpaproject.lboro.ac.uk/

University of Makerere School of Computing and IT (2018) *Artificial Intelligence in the Developed World* Url:http://cit.mak.ac.ug/cs/aigroup/

University of Sheffield (2018) *The Behaviour in Teams Project* Url:www.youtube.com/watch?v=z0HlEWaTiYQ

University World News (2013) *A Focus on Skills Increasingly Links Higher Education with Employment* Url:www.universityworldnews.com/article.php?story=20130103154436919

Wakeham Review of STEM Degree Provision and Graduate Employability (2016) Url:https://assets.publishing.service.gov.uk/government/uploads/system/uploads/attachment_data/file/518582/ind-16-6-wakeham-review-stem-graduate-employability.pdf

Chapter 6

Towards improved engineering education in the United Kingdom

Wayne Seames

Introduction

The usage frequency of active learning techniques in UK university engineering education lags behind many peer universities in the United States. Yet many studies have shown that these techniques lead to substantial improvements in student performance. To improve utilization, a three-hour workshop was developed and delivered to over 200 academic staff at seven different UK universities during the 2014/15 academic year. The first half of the workshop focused on how to design modules (courses) that improve student engagement through active learning. The second half of the workshop was used to introduce academic staff to many of the common engagement techniques that are used to replace lecture during instruction. Pre- and post-workshop quizzes were used to assess the effectiveness of the workshop. The following summarizes the key concepts from the workshop and presents the assessment results of the workshop's effectiveness.

Active learning concepts

Lecture-centric modules (classes, courses) are not the only way to teach university-level STEM (science, technology, engineering, and mathematics) topics. In fact, it has been well established that instruction that involves a significant degree of active learning activities increases student achievement and success (Freeman et al., 2014). Active learning, at its most general level, can be defined as any instructional method that requires students to do meaningful learning activities and to think about what they are doing (Prince, 2004). The core elements of active learning, namely student activity and engagement in the learning process, can be contrasted to the traditional lecture where students passively receive information from the instructor. Certain active learning techniques have been a part of university STEM education for decades, including practicals, tutorials, projects, and homework assignments. However, there has been a growing understanding in educational pedagogy that introducing active learning techniques into the classroom to replace and/or supplement traditional lecture improves student learning (Bonwell & Eison, 1991; Felder et al., 2000).

In their recent landmark work, Freedman and co-workers (Freeman et al., 2014) analysed 225 studies from published and unpublished literature that reported comparison data for examination scores and/or failure rates for university-level STEM modules taught under a traditional lecture-centric format versus those taught with at least some level of active learning replacing lecture during the primary Instructor-led class time. They found that on average, student performance on examinations and concept inventories were higher by 0.47 standard deviations from the active learning versions of the courses and that the odds of a student failing a module were 1.5 times more likely if they took the lecture-centric version of the module. These trends were seen irrespective of class size, STEM discipline, methodological rigour, student quality, or instructor.

In another of the many examples found in the literature, Hake (1998) collected pre- and post-test data for over 6000 students. Hake reported significant improvement in student performance in introductory physics modules with substantial use of interactive-engagement methods compared to modules relying on traditional lecture. Test scores measuring conceptual understanding were roughly twice as high in classes promoting engagement than in traditional courses. Statistically, this was an improvement of two standard deviations!

I have inserted active learning activities into my modules since I first began university instruction in 1997. In 2001 I designed my first module, a sophomore level course on fluid flow and heat transfer taught in a unit operations paradigm, with an active-learning centric structure. The structure I used required the students to learn the basic facts and figures from a textbook, while only a small portion of the in-class time was spent in lecture. This structure has since become known as a flipped class structure. The module was well received and I found that the fraction of enrolled students that showed up for class increased and student satisfaction, as measured by end-of-the-term student surveys, did as well.

However as more and more of my colleagues have begun using these techniques, I have begun to experience more initial resistance to the flipped module structure from students than previously. Exploring this resistance more fully, I found that the students disappointed to learn my module would be a "flipped class" had previously taken a poorly designed flipped module. This highlights an important point: while using more effective techniques can improve student performance from competent instructors, no technique can make up for an incompetent instructor. Instructors must master the art of designing and executing active-learning centric modules. And since very few current university instructors have ever taken an active-learning centric module themselves as a student, they cannot use their past experiences to guide them in how to successfully use these methods.

Course design

Effective teachers understand that module design is the single most important factor in whether that module meets the university's learning objectives for its students (Wiggins & McTighe, 1998). This is true no matter what instruction methods are employed. However, in my experience, good module design is even more important when incorporating active learning methods into instruction than with traditional lecture. Incorporating active learning methods into a poorly designed module will most likely still result in a disappointing outcome. Therefore, efforts to improve student outcomes need to start with good, well thought-out module design. If this process is accomplished early and correctly, incorporating active learning methods into the module can then enable the vast majority of students to reach deeper levels of understanding than will be achieved with a traditional lecture-based module.

The learning unit method

One common technique that most effective teachers use when planning their modules is to develop a schedule and outline of the module's desired content. If you are directly following a single textbook, you can organize your class by book chapters. But, the textbook was written by someone else. It organizes the material based on the author's priorities and in the way that makes sense to them. In essence, organizing by chapter means that you are teaching someone else's module. Most effective teachers develop their own outline and schedule of material and then find the resources that match their paradigm. So instead of organizing by book chapter, you might want to organize by learning unit.

A learning unit (LU) is a subset of the entire module that fits within a given key concept or principle. For example, in my Unit Operations module referenced previously, I had learning units for fluid statics, the Bernoulli equation, heat conduction, etc. No learning unit should be longer than three weeks or nine in-class sessions, as this is about the maximum amount of new information that a university-level student can learn at one time. If you need more than three weeks, split up the LU into multiple subset LUs.

To increase your effectiveness, you can design all of the activities for that LU as a cohesive unit. First, develop specific learning objectives. Felder and Brent (2009) define learning objectives as "explicit statements of what students should be able to do if they have learned what the Instructor wants them to learn." Objectives should be reasonable and measureable. In addition to making the topic more coherent to the student, objectives also make it easier to write fair tests. If you write measureable objectives, you can write test questions to measure whether the students have achieved the objectives you have written.

Next, determine the resources you want the students to use to learn the basic facts and knowledge about the subject. These resources could include material in one or more textbooks, online videos, posted lecture notes, in-class lectures, and so forth. There will be a temptation to include extra information that would be "useful" for the students to know that goes beyond the learning objectives you developed. Avoid this temptation! They will have enough trouble getting through the required material without the confusion of "extras."

In order to motivate students to study the material, you might want to develop a quiz on the material you have asked them to study. Make sure you quiz them on all of the material you have asked them to study. For most classes you can use multiple-choice quizzes. If using an online quiz, impose a challenging time limit that forces the students to either: 1) index the readings for easy reference, or 2) prepare a summary sheet from readings and videos.

At this point in the LU planning process, I suggest you identify the topics that need clarification beyond the initial resources you identified above. You will have to use your best judgement about this the first time you cover the learning unit. However, I have found that seeking feedback from students on material they want to cover in more depth allows me to identify concept reviews and/or webinars/YouTube videos to supplement the original resources so that in future course offerings, the material is clearer.

Next, you might want to decide how to make the learning unit topic "real" for the students. This can be accomplished by using a case study, and/or demonstrations, and/or laboratory experiments. The goal is to answer the question, "Why is it important that I learn this?" for the students.

To drive student comprehension beyond the basic level, design in-class problems and identify homework problems where the information is applied in progressively different/complicated ways. In-class problems should be simplified examples of how to apply the material, while the homework problems can be more extensive and time-consuming.

Once the learning unit is fully planned, I suggest you perform a quality check. To do this, map the material/activities you have identified and see if all of the learning objectives have been addressed. If not, reassess if the missing objective is important. If not, remove the learning objective. If it is important, add additional content. During your review you may also find that some of your content does not directly address any of your learning objectives. Again, you need to determine if the content is important. If yes, then add one or more additional learning objectives related to that material. If not, remove this content.

The flipped class method

In a flipped module, the student is responsible for assigned reading(s) or watching pre-recorded videos to obtain the basic facts and information on the topic being considered. It is assumed that students coming to class will already have read and studied the material from the reading. The use of webinars, FAQs, and other supplemental material can enrich this experience. A more formal definition of the flipped instruction paradigm is provided by the Flipped Learning Network (2016):

> Flipped Learning is a pedagogical approach in which direct instruction moves from the group learning space to the individual learning space, and the resulting group space is transformed into a dynamic, interactive learning environment where the educator guides students as they apply concepts and engage creatively in the subject matter.

However, numerous studies around the globe have shown that the only effective way to get students to study readings prior to class is to test them on their knowledge of the material *before* you begin to address the topic in class. There are multiple ways this can be done: online quizzes, in class quizzes, early homework assignments, etc. The key is to get students to understand that *they* are now accountable for learning the basic facts.

To understand this better, we can put this in the context of cognitive learning theory. A common qualitative method of defining the levels of student learning is with Anderson and Krathwohl's (Anderson et al., 2001) revised edition of Bloom et al. (1956) cognitive taxonomy, which is shown in Figure 6.1. When the basic concepts, facts, and ideas are provided by lecture, students will typically only advance through levels 1 (remembering) and 2 (understanding). Lecture-style tutorials (instructor walks through examples of how to apply

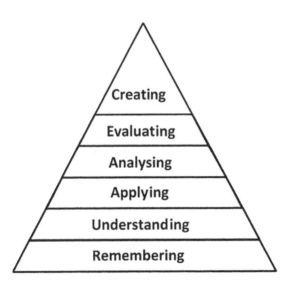

Figure 6.1 A visual representation of Bloom's cognitive taxonomy (after Bloom et al., 1956).

the applications) may allow students to advance to level 3, although interactive tutorials (students individually or in groups work through examples under instructor guidance) are more effective in achieving this level, and may also deepen learning into level 4 (analysing).

Tutorials can be considered a venue for active learning. However, because the sessions are decoupled from the lectures rather than integrated together, students sometimes miss the connection between lecture content and tutorial exercises. Integrating active learning methods with lecture can improve these connections.

One effective way to utilize this approach is to follow a "present-show-try" paradigm. A concept, or suite of concepts, is introduced by the instructor in a traditional lecture format. The instructor then walks through an example of how to apply the concept(s). Finally, the students work through a separate example, either individually or in small groups, during the class session. The instructor then moves to the next concept. This paradigm can often result in learning at levels 4 (analysing) and 5 (evaluating) in lower division modules and may allow learning all the way through level 6 (creating) in upper division and post-graduate level modules.

The next logical extension of the "present-show-try" paradigm is the flipped class paradigm. The students are expected to obtain their introduction to the concept from reading material, such as a textbook, prior to the start of the class session. This replaces the lecture-formatted "present" step. Formal class time is spent on the "show" and "try" steps. For simpler concepts, the "show" step may be skipped, and the entire formal class session devoted to the "try" step. An excellent summary of case studies evaluating the effectiveness of the flipped class paradigm along with the challenges associated with the method is provided by Aronson and Arfstrom (2013).

Employing the flipped instruction paradigm allows teachers who have mastered active learning techniques to routinely reach Bloom levels 5 and 6 for the majority of the material in their modules for the majority of the students actively participating in the module. Perhaps more than any other method, flipped instruction requires careful module design and up-front planning to ensure success. Instructors using this method also need to be fluent in the active learning techniques they will be using during formal class time to maximize student learning.

Active learning techniques

There are numerous ways to get students to engage with the topic. Presented here is a brief overview of some of the more common methods used.

Problem-based learning

Problem-based learning (PBL) is a student-centred pedagogy in which students learn about a subject through the experience of solving an open-ended problem (Cornell, 2017). PBL presents the concept to the student in the context of a problem, where the concept must be used in order to obtain a solution. This is the most common active learning technique used in engineering and has been widely applied for decades. When introducing a new concept, it is important that the PBL problem used during in-class sessions is simple enough that the concept is obvious to the student. Further, in-class PBL exercises must be short enough that all students can complete them in a reasonable amount of time. You have to be careful to ensure that the quicker students are not always sitting around bored waiting for the slower students. Simpler problems can help alleviate this, as the total time, even for the slower students, is relatively short.

For longer, more complex problems, you can start the problem in the classroom and have students finish them independently as a homework assignment.

Case studies

In the context of educational pedagogy, a case study is "a particular instance of something used or analysed in order to illustrate a thesis or principle" (Oxford, 2017). I use case studies for two separate learning objectives:

1) to provide context for a concept or topic and
2) as an extension of a PBL where the "story" provides the narrative framework within which the "problem" is presented. The vast majority of case studies are of the second kind, and there are hundreds of examples of these cases.

If the instructor is creative, they might develop their own case studies. However, there are also many case studies available in collections, most of which are accessible online. Examples include the collection of engineering ethics case studies at the Ethics Engineering library; the case collection at the National Center for Case Study Teaching in Science,; the collection of engineering failures case studies published by Alexander Street,; and probably the largest collection, the Open Educational Resources (OER) Commons.[1]

In addition to simple versions, case studies can be executed sequentially. The basic story narrative is presented along with one or more concepts. These are discussed and then additional concepts are presented. I have one version of this type of case study dealing with engineering ethics that includes up to seven sequences. Another way to use case studies is to embed a PBL activity within the case study narrative. Other cases may require a laboratory experiment or a simulation to provide the information necessary to reach the conclusions suggested by the case study. The variations and possibilities are limited only by the inventiveness of the case study author.

In-class reflections

This is a simple technique that is especially useful in very large classes. After a period of lecture, the instructor stops and asks the students to "reflect" on what they have learned. The reflection time can be very short – 30 seconds is usually enough for individual reflection. It is usually best to give the reflection some focus. For example, the instructor could ask the students to try to recall the three key points from the last 15 minutes. Or the instructor could ask the students to identify one topic from the last ten minutes that they still do not understand.

There are many variations on the method. For example, the instructor could ask the students to turn to the person next to them, or to the person in front of/behind them, and ask the other person to explain a topic to them that they do not understand. This is an example of the "think-pair-share" technique. Or, after trying to recall three key points, the students could be asked to share their lists with those around them until all of them have three key points. Again, the number and types of variations are limited only by the inventiveness of the instructor. The point of this method is to break up large blocks of lecture so that the students can refresh their attention rate. I have heard of at least one former master teacher of engineering who set a timer on his podium that rang after five minutes of lecture. He would then stop, even in mid-sentence, and do a reflection activity!

Personally, I prefer to interject in-class small group problems. The students divide themselves into groups of two to four and solve a problem that uses the material that was just presented. This is the "try" component of "present," "show," "try."

Working in groups

Almost every engineering programme stakeholder group recommends that teaching students to work in groups is a high priority. As a consequence, it is considered a routine part of most engineering curricula to include group projects, reports, experiments, etc. However, the way group activities are planned and executed has a substantial impact on the effectiveness of the "teaming" part of group activities.

Almost all active learning techniques can be used in group settings. Even if instruction is in a traditional tiered lecture hall, students can work in groups of two or three with the people sitting next to them.

To be effective at group work, students have to practice group work. One way is to use a seating chart, where you assign students to specific seats in the classroom or to a specific group with a designated area within the classroom. You can simply put the seating chart on a slide and post it in the room before class starts so that students can move to their seats before you even start class.

I suggest that you rearrange the groups around three times each semester. This ensures that students learn to work with a variety of different people. It also reduces student friction. If two students do not get along very well, they only have to put up with the other party for around three or four weeks!

Instructors can also assign homework and projects to groups of students. I suggest you limit these groups to no more than four students. Otherwise, some of the students will not actually work on the material. It is also recommended that peer evaluation forms be used when the instructor selects the group.

Rather than just putting students in groups and expecting them to know how groups work, it might be wise to actually provide the students with learning content on how to work in groups. Teach them the basic roles in a group (facilitator, scribe, data gatherers, questioners, etc.) and how to plan and run a group meeting.

The Engagement Teaching Methods for Engineers workshop

In the 2014/15 academic year, the author spent seven months in residence at the University of Leeds under a Fulbright fellowship. One of the author's projects was to develop and execute a three-hour workshop to assist university-level engineering instructors to increase student engagement in their modules and thereby improve student learning success.

The workshop was divided into two parts:

I. Module design and
II. Engagement techniques

The workshop outline is shown in Figure 6.2. During the introduction, the participants were provided data showing that undergraduate students do not always learn the same way as those who instruct them. As such, instructors

---

I. Introduction
II. Module Design

    A. Engaging Students – Flipped Classes
    B. The Learning Unit Method

        1. Integrated Units
        2. Learning Guides

III. Engagement Techniques

    A. Collaborative Learning
    B. Problem-Based Learning
    C. Case Study-Based Teaching Methods
    D. Using Technology

IV. Summary and Feedback

Figure 6.2 The Engagement Teaching Methods for Engineers workshop outline.

should not use their own remembered learning experiences as a good model for how their students learn.

In the module design portion of the workshop, participants were introduced to the flipped learning method and how to design learning units. Learning units, described above, facilitate the flipped learning method but are also an effective way to design and organize more traditionally configured modules.

The "Engagement Techniques" portion of the workshop focused on how to effectively employ collaborative (group) learning techniques and on the primary active learning methods utilized in engineering – problem-based learning and case studies. A brief introduction to utilizing technology within active learning techniques was included.

The workshop was conducted ten times during the period between November 2014 through March 2015, at seven different UK universities, with a total attendance of 233 participants. Further details are shown in Table 6.1. The workshop has also been delivered around half a dozen times in the USA, including at the American Society for Engineering Education's Summer School for New Chemical Engineering Academic Staff, which was held in July 2017 at North Carolina State University.

Workshop assessment

Pre- and post-workshop quizzes were completed by attendees during the 2014/15 UK workshops shown in Table 6.1. There were 203 pre-quiz responses and 167 post-quiz responses for most of the questions (some attendees arrived late or left early). One participant only answered two of the post-quiz questions, so most of the post-quiz data is based on 166 responses. Eleven identical questions were asked in both the pre- and post-workshop quizzes. The results are shown in Table 6.2.

After starting the process, it was found that some of the questions were poorly phrased, namely questions 3 and 5. Questions 9 and 10 were included as a check on participant comprehension and the care they were taking in completing the quiz. For example, it was expected that every participant would either answer "no" or "I don't know" to question 9 and "yes" or "I don't know" to question 10.

Table 6.1 A summary of the workshops conducted in the UK during the 2014/15 academic year

Date	Venue	No. of participants
19 Nov 14	Univ. of Leeds	12
25 Nov 14	Univ. of Leeds	12
3 Dec 14	Univ. of Leeds	13
12 Jan 15	Queens Univ. Belfast	20
22 Jan 15	Univ. of Leeds	7

Table 6.2 Quantitative assessment results from pre- and post-workshop responses from the participants in the 2014/15 workshops

Question	Answer	TRUE	FALSE	Don't know	TRUE	FALSE	Don't know
1 The way that faculty members learned as students is typical of the general population of undergraduates and postgraduates.	FALSE	30%	53%	17%	11%	87%	2%
2 Including engagement activities during recitation periods will reduce the number of topics that can be covered in a course.	FALSE	27%	58%	15%	7%	89%	4%
3 The traditional university paradigm of readings, recitation, and homework with/without accompanying laboratory sessions is still a relevant and effective method for learning engineering topics at the undergraduate level.	TRUE, but not the most effective	60%	22%	18%	49%	40%	11%
4 Engagement methods can be effectively employed in class sizes of over 100 students.	TRUE	58%	16%	26%	86%	10%	4%
5 Engagement methods cannot be used effectively in tiered seating lecture type classrooms.	FALSE	17%	64%	19%	22%	73%	5%
6 Flipped classes take more faculty preparation time than traditional lecture classes.	FALSE	18%	12%	39%	52%	39%	9%
7 The most common engagement method employed in engineering courses is the "problem-based learning" method.	TRUE	61%	11%	28%	84%	6%	10%
8 There are certain courses where engagement teaching methods are not appropriate and a traditional lecture-based course should be used exclusively.	FALSE	18%	49%	33%	15%	67%	18%
9 After this workshop, I do not expect to improve my effectiveness as a teacher of undergraduate engineering courses.		5%	76%	18%	4%	90%	5%
10 After this workshop, I expect to improve my effectiveness as a teacher of graduate engineering courses.		73%	1%	25%	82%	5%	13%

Surprisingly, the majority of participants answered all of the questions correctly in the pre-workshop quiz, indicating at least some exposure to these topics. Of less surprise is that the number of participants who answered correctly on the post-workshop quiz increased significantly. The less definitive results for questions 3 and 5 are believed to be a reflection on the quality of the questions rather than on participant understanding. A total of 38 respondents that answered "true" to question 6 added the caveat that this would only be true in the first year the module was taught. One interesting result is the response to question 8. While the number of participants answering correctly increased, the increase was lower than for other questions. However, even taking this into account, the results suggest that some instructors were not convinced that active learning methods were appropriate for every subject.

In response to the additional post-workshop quiz question, "Since completing this workshop, are you planning to increase the percentage of recitation time that is devoted to engagement teaching methods?", 79% of the participants answered "yes."

Additional questions were added to each quiz to obtain qualitative information. For example, the most common concerns with utilizing the material taught during the workshop were having adequate preparation time and student acceptance.

At the end of the workshop, participants were asked as a group exercise to recall as many of the active learning topics that were covered in some fashion in the workshop without referring to their notes. Most participant groups identified around 12 separate methods. Often the groups included other concepts that were covered in the workshop but were not "active teaching methods" per se such as, "don't let students upward delegate their problems to you," or "textbook based teaching" in their lists. The total number of methods/concepts identified by at least one group was 31, which pretty much included every concept and method that was presented.

Each individual participant was then asked to identify the top/most important three items on their lists for them personally. No attempt was made to define what "top" or "most important" meant. This was left to each individual. An overwhelming majority identified the flipped instructional method as their top item. The next most commonly selected (at least 1/3 of responses) were: working in groups, case studies, problem-based learning, and using pre-quizzes to ensure students do assigned readings prior to attending class.

In response to the question, "Were your initial concerns or questions about engagement teaching methods addressed in the workshop?", 74% responded "yes," 25% responded "mostly/some," and only 2% responded "no."

In conclusion

A workshop was developed to assist UK university engineering instructors in improving their modules through better module design and the adoption of active learning methods. The workshop is judged to have been a success since 79% of the responses to a post-quiz question stated that they planned to increase their use of active learning methods in their instruction and 99% of the responses indicated that all, most, or some of their initial concerns and questions about using these methods were addressed in the workshop. It was also very encouraging that the flipped instruction method was the top/most important item from the workshop for most of the participants.

Note

1 http://ethics.iit.edu/eelibrary/case-study-collection; Sciencecases.lib.buffalo.edu/cs/collection/; https://alexanderstreet.com/products/engineering-case-studies-online

References

Anderson L, Krathwohl D & Bloom B (2001) *A Taxonomy for Learning, Teaching, and Assessing: A Revision of Bloom's Taxonomy Of Educational Objectives.* Boston, MA: Allyn & Bacon

Aronson N & Arfstrom K (2013) *Flipped Learning in Higher Education* Url:www.flippedlearning.org/cms/lib07/VA01923112/Centricity/Domain/41/HigherEdWhitePaper%20FINAL.pdf

Bloom B, Engelhart M, Furst E, Hill W & Krathwohl D (1956) Taxonomy of educational objectives: The classification of educational goals, in *Handbook I: Cognitive Domain*, New York: David McKay Company

Bonwell C & Eison J (1991) Active learning: Creating excitement in the classroom, in *ASHEERIC Higher Education Report No. 1*, Washington, DC: George Washington University

The Cornell University Center for Teaching Innovation (2017) *Problem-Based Learning* Url:www.cte.cornell.edu/teaching-ideas/engaging-students/problem-based-learning.html

Felder R & Brent R (2009) The ten worst teaching mistakes, *Chemical Engineering Education*, Vol. 43, No. 1, pp. 15–16

Felder R, Woods D, Stice J & Rugarcia A (2000) The future of engineering education: II, teaching methods that work, *Chemical Engineering Education*, Vol. 34, No. 1, pp. 26–39

The Flipped Learning Network (2016) Url:http://flippedlearning.org/site/default.aspx?PageID=1

Freeman S, Eddy S, McDonough M, Smith M, Okoroafor N, Jordt H & Wednderoth M (2014) Active learning increases student performance in science, engineering, and mathematics, *Proceeding of the National Academy of Science*, Vol. 111, No. 23, pp. 8410–8415

Hake R (1998) Interactive-engagement vs. Traditional methods: A six-thousand-student survey of mechanics test data for introductory physics courses, *American Journal of Physics*, Vol. 66, No. 1, pp. 64–74

The Oxford Living Dictionaries (2017) *Case Study Definition 2* Url:https://en.oxforddictionaries.com/definition/case_study

Prince M (2004) Does active learning work? A review of the research, *Journal of Engineering Education*, Vol. 93, No. 3, pp. 223–231

Wiggins G & McTighe J (1998) *Understanding by Design*, Merrill Education/ASCD College Textbook Series, Alexandria, VA: ASCD

Summary of Part 3

Readiness for the workplace is an important aspect of the formation of future engineers. But although the importance of education and formation of engineers is recognized, there is no consistent and robust approach available to us for assessing the effectiveness of various pedagogical methodologies, in particular those aimed at developing important core competencies related to employability of the graduates. The iTeach project described in chapter 7 aimed to develop such a robust and objective framework. Even though the project evaluated its validity for a range of pedagogical methodologies used in the particular case of chemical engineering, in a range of geographical and educational contexts, its validity should easily cross-correlate across other engineering disciplines. The basis of the framework and the results of its testing are briefly reviewed in this chapter to encourage engineering educators to quantitatively evaluate the effectiveness of their pedagogical approaches.

This focused piece of practical work is followed in chapter 8 by a more philosophical exposition of what our future engineers should look like. The world that they will inherit and live in is fast moving and unpredictable; the way we teach engineers to be able to face the challenges they might encounter has to undergo a radical rethink. Enterprising skills, creative and critical ways of thinking, dispositions, and attitudes will have a much more critical role to play than the transmission of inert knowledge. Permission to fail and the exercise of imagination, 'playful tinkering' and embracing change will become part of the new repertoire of solving the problems of tomorrow. The engineers of the future will have to use their intuition and inspiration to *visualize* and *create* imagined worlds. Creativity and imagination will go hand in hand in building the world of tomorrow asking, 'What if?'

To do this we need to create learning contexts that generate a sense of curiosity, the imagination running wild, where there is excitement and pleasure in our students; we need to kindle their desire to be part of something bigger than themselves. The process will no doubt seem chaotic at times, but it is at the edge of chaos that creativity thrives; it is where imagination is at play that real learning takes place. We must endeavour to build a transformative, character building curriculum, where our future engineers are developed around the concept of learner transformation of being and becoming, facilitated through the process of coming to know and to understand.

However, in order to deliver these changes successfully, teachers also have to adapt to the new practices of delivering, assessing, and providing feedback. The process requires a cultural change, to both teachers and learners, towards a deeper understanding of the learning process itself rather than delivery and learning of a particular set of skills. There will be giving and receiving critique by both sides as both learn from each other in a culture of continuous reflection, an environment where freedom and imagination will be encouraged and failure and retrial are permitted. Knowledge should and will continuously be contested, so the ability for critical reasoning will be taught. Dispositions, tendencies to engage with the world around them, such as the *will to learn, a will to engage, a preparedness to listen, a preparedness to explore, to hold oneself out to new experiences,* and *a determination to keep going forward,* will have to be cultivated (Barnett, 2009). Qualities, the manifestations of dispositions, such as *courage, resilience, self-confidence, self-belief, self-motivation, carefulness, integrity, self-discipline, restraint, willingness to speak or to engage, respect for others, openness, commitment, enthusiasm, generosity, intellectual humility,* and *authenticity* will be instilled in our future engineers.

The concluding chapter 9 is a reflective piece on the need of a holistic approach to our engineering futures through a review of the innovative undergraduate degree program – a Bachelor of Arts in Liberal Studies in Engineering – a program that would infuse exemplary and substantive engineering content throughout a sequence of core courses rooted in the liberal arts. A program aiming to provide a smoother pathway into engineering, to better prepare engineering students for the "grand" challenges they might face in an uncertain future, and to provide liberal arts graduates with basic knowledge of engineering and technology.

A surprising number of institutions have been attempting to break the mould of the past (that is, lecture/recitation; students working as individuals in competition with their peers; canonical presentation of engineering sciences; single answer problems; cook-book laboratories; and technology focused design classes), through the use of project-based learning; design experiences that stress user interface; portfolios for assessing a student's progress; increased concern for teamwork and communication; and the, not unrelated, push to increase the diversity of students of engineering. Nevertheless, in general, it remains very difficult to convince one's faculty peers of the worth of educational innovation, especially of the sort we advocate here and, as a result, to make and sustain such changes.

Part 3

Linking education to employability

Chapter 7

Efficiency of teaching core knowledge and employability competencies in chemical engineering education

Jarka Glassey

This is an overview of the effectiveness and efficiency measures currently used in chemical engineering education in Europe. The findings of the iTeach European project consortium[1] are used as a basis for examining whether the chemical engineering education is seen as fit for purpose. A review of the learning outcomes of a chemical engineering higher education formation indicated a significant alignment of the requirements world-wide with some differences in the emphasis on fundamental science, related engineering disciplines, and information technology applications. Outcomes of the subsequent focus groups and semi-structured interviews with associated industrial network partners, as well as questionnaire surveys of wider labour market representatives, used to identify the skill gaps and requirements, indicated a high level of overall alignment amongst the stakeholder groups. State-of-the art procedures in assessing the effectiveness of teaching of core (chemical) engineering knowledge and of the development of professional skills and competencies required to increase the employability of the graduates was also reviewed. Together with the stakeholder consultation, this enabled a robust framework for supporting effective delivery of core knowledge and employability competencies to be formulated, as described in this chapter. The results of the pilot implementation of this framework are outlined and generic findings summarized.

Introduction

The continuous evolution of the chemical engineering (CE) profession and, with it, that of its education is widely recognized (e.g. Molzahn, 2004; Campbell & Belton, 2016). Sherlock stated (IchemE, 2016): "In the 21st century, the requirements of a growing and ageing population will have significant impact on society. With the global population expected to reach 8.5bn by 2030 and 11.2bn by the end of the century, demand on resources such as water, energy, food, and raw materials will be greater than anything we have experienced". The role of (chemical) engineers in helping to address grand societal challenges relating to secure supplies of energy, water, food and nutrition, and health and wellbeing has been clearly articulated and widely accepted. It is also clear that the effective formation of future generations of chemical engineers capable of continuously contributing to this agenda is critical. So for example, Shott et al. (2015) argue that it is important to include in the traditional chemical engineering curricula aspects of life sciences to enable graduates to contribute to the industrial biotechnology sector more effectively.

Another important aspect of the formation of the future engineers is the readiness for the workplace. On one hand this is continuously highlighted as an important aspect of the university-level education; on the other hand, it is recognized that certain skills and competencies are difficult to develop within such an environment and need to be acquired in real workplace settings (Cranmer, 2006). The importance of industrial internships in the formation of professional chemical engineers is argued by Glassey and Brown (2014). They also highlight, through the analysis of a recent survey of industrial placements/internship in chemical and process industries (concerning particularly longer term placements), that the economic fluctuations and business priorities may often affect the ability of the industrial partners to commit to such extensive involvement. More recently (and concurrently with the research reported here), Fletcher et al. (2017) discussed various aspects of employability skills from the students' and employers' points of view.

So, while the importance of education and formation of (chemical) engineers is recognized, a consistent and robust approach to assessing the effectiveness of various pedagogical methodologies, in particular those aimed at developing important core competencies related to employability of the graduates, is critical and long overdue. This is especially true given that "the competitiveness of the country and therefore our standard of living hinges on our ability to educate a large number of sufficiently innovative engineers" (Tryggvason & Apelian, 2012).

The iTeach project aimed to develop a robust and objective framework for assessing the efficiency of various pedagogical methodologies, in particular those facilitating the development of important core competencies related to employability. The project also evaluated its validity for a range of pedagogical methodologies used in chemical engineering in a range of geographical and educational contexts. The basis of the framework and the results of its testing are briefly reviewed in this chapter to encourage engineering educators to quantitatively evaluate the effectiveness of their pedagogical approaches.

Methodology

Exploration of the significance of learning outcomes

A review of the learning outcomes of a chemical engineering higher education formation was initially carried out. This was based on the requirements set out by the Bologna recommendations, the review carried out by the Working Party on Education of EFCE, and various professional accreditation requirements, including IchemE (2017), ABET (2017), Engineers Australia (2017), and ASIIN (2011). Separate questionnaires for academic, industrial, recent graduate, and student stakeholder groups were prepared on the basis of this review. Invitations to each of the stakeholder groups were sent out world-wide by all project partners and associated partners. The online questionnaires were completed over a period of three months.

Using the Statistical Package for the Social Sciences (SPSS), the quantitative data (i.e. all Likert-scale type questions) was analysed for descriptive information, including measures of central tendency (mean, standard deviation, minimum, maximum) and frequency counts. For single-choice questions, only frequency counts were conducted. In order to compare differences between abilities within the same "learning area," and between the results of different geographical locations for each ability, one-way analysis of variance (ANOVA) was used (Miller & Miller, 2005). Differences were identified by the estimation of confidence intervals for the means at 95% confidence, and by using Fisher's least significant difference (LSD) method. While some of the samples for specific geographic locations were relatively small (n < 14) and the data not distributed normally (confirmed using the Kolmogorov-Smirnov test), the validity of the methodology employed is still guaranteed through the central limit theorem (Miller & Miller, 2005). Group comparison was carried out after classifying the responses geographically using United Nations Geoscheme for Europe, created by the UN Statistics Division.[2] Thematic analysis (Braun & Clark, 2006) was employed on the open survey questions using the qualitative data analysis software package Nvivo 10. Respondents' comments were initially sorted into broad analytical categories corresponding to the survey questions. In a second analytical step, every statement in the broad categories was analysed for content and placed under an appropriate heading or thematic 'node' along with any other responses which were sufficiently similar (Young & Schartner, 2014).

Following the initial data analysis from the questionnaire responses, a template of questions was agreed upon by all partners to be used for the focus group semi-structured interviews at each partner country. Where possible, representatives of each of the three stakeholder groups were invited to attend the focus group discussions. These focus groups explored in more detail the differences in perceived importance of knowledge and skills required by the new generation of chemical engineering professionals (see following sections).

Framework development and testing

A range of indicators and measures of employability skills and teaching effectiveness collected as described above were analysed using decision-making methodology and multi-objective optimization to select the most appropriate methods to be included in the proposed assessment framework. Detailed discussions of the consortium partners took place during a one-day consortium workshop at the ECCE symposium in Nice 2015. This led to the development of a version of a framework to enable the evaluation of a single module/course and a specific pedagogical intervention. Consultations on the draft version of the framework were carried out with each national professional body/employer organization (associate partners), and the framework was modified as required.

The framework was piloted at each partner institution and both employability skills and core knowledge delivery were assessed against the proposed criteria in a module/course delivered within each partner institution. A range of methods of teaching were assessed. These included the use of recorded sessions for pre-lecture preparation, e-learning enabled delivery, and classical teaching methods, to ensure the robustness and broad validity of the framework.

In this stage of the project, each partner carried out preliminary pilot tests on different courses which helped realize some operational difficulties regarding pilot implementation of the assessment framework, for example that dramatic changes in the pedagogical methodologies are hard to implement within an academic environment with set quality procedures requiring significant lead times in most cases. Two additional examples are that the implementation of certain pedagogical approaches is easier in some courses and more complex to achieve in others, and that staffing changes within the period of testing may influence the results of the analyses. As a result, all partners decided that the assessment framework should be piloted for the same course, and chemical reaction engineering was elected due to its relevance to chemical engineering programmes, being core and common in all syllabi.

Results

Learning outcomes

Briefly, the consortium identified five major areas of learning outcomes based on the world-wide accreditation requirements for chemical engineering accreditation (Glassey et al., 2016, *https://research.ncl.ac.uk/iteacheu/*):

1) Underpinning Mathematics and Science (Mathematics, Chemistry, Physics, Biology, Information Technology (IT))
2) Core Chemical Engineering (Fundamentals, Mathematical Modelling & Quantitative Methods, Process & Product Technology, Systems, Safety, and Sustainability, Economics, & Ethics)
3) Engineering Practice and Design (Practical Skills, Data Interpretation & Analysis, Information Literacy, Industrial Standards & Quality Assurance, Systems Approach to Design, Technical Rigour in Design, Awareness of Safety, Health & Environment Issues, and Awareness of Business Drivers)
4) Advanced level – Master's programmes (Chemical Engineering Science Depth, Limitations of Current Engineering Practice, Awareness of

Emerging Technologies, Design in the Context of Uncertainty, Innovative Advanced Design, and Chemical Engineering Science Breadth)
5) Embedded Learning – General Transferable Skills (Problem Solving Skills, Communication Skills, Working Effectively with Others, Leadership Skills, Effective Use of IT, Project Planning & Time Management, and Continuous Professional Development)

The questionnaire responses from the stakeholders indicated a remarkable agreement in terms of the significance of each of these across Europe. For example, Figure 7.1 illustrates the perceived importance of the core chemical engineering learning outcomes (Figure 7.1a), engineering practice and design (Figure 7.1b), and advanced level (Figure 7.1c) by the academic community. Not surprisingly, high importance is assigned to all learning outcomes, with particular emphasis on the fundamentals and safety (core chemical engineering), data interpretation and analysis, and awareness of safety, health, and environmental issues (engineering practice and design) as well as chemical engineering science depth and innovative advanced design (advanced level). Other stakeholder groups broadly agreed with this level of significance, although there were a number of slight differences highlighted particularly in the focus group discussions.

The analysis of the focus group discussions revealed particular emphasis on areas of underpinning science and core chemical engineering that have been indicated as slightly less important in the questionnaires from some of the stakeholder groups. For example, the industrialists indicated a slightly lower importance for biology knowledge (see Figure 7.2), which was contradicted by the outcomes of the focus groups to some extent.

On the other hand, graduates in the UK and FYROM focus group discussions highlighted the importance of biology, which was perceived slightly less important by the industrial stakeholders responding to the questionnaire:

> I think biology's pretty important to me at the minute. It depends what industry you're gonna go in to, so at the minute I'm doing my research into biopharmaceuticals and biology's a big thing. It's hard to say which [underpinning science area] you think's most important cos it's subjective to what you're gonna do.
>
> (UK graduate)

> The industry in FYROM which is mostly developed is the food industry, and the foreign investments are focussed on food industry, and the importance of biology is big.
>
> (FYROM graduate)

This aligns with the arguments presented by Shott et al. (2015) and the increasing importance of the contribution of chemical engineers to the food and nutrition and health and wellbeing grand societal challenges.

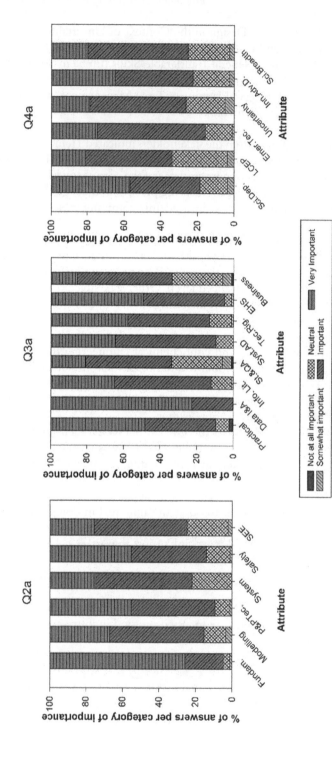

Figure 7.1 The perceived importance of Core ChE knowledge (a), Engineering Practice and Design (b), and Advance Level courses (c).

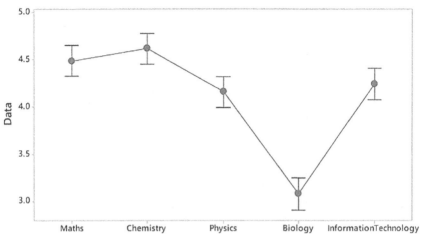

The pooled standard deviation was used to calculate the intervals.

Figure 7.2 The perceived importance of underlying science by the industrial respondents to the iTeach questionnaire on learning outcomes.

In terms of the perceived importance of the employability competencies by the academic community, Figure 7.3 clearly indicates a high level of importance assigned to all the categories (with slightly lower importance assigned to leadership). There was more variability in the relative importance of various employability competencies as perceived by the various stakeholder groups. For example, see Figure 7.4 for responses of the industrial stakeholder group, where greater importance is assigned to problem solving, communication, and teamwork, partly due to the fact that the latter skills could be effectively developed within industrial environment. The focus groups also indicated a much greater variability in this context.

An interesting feature to come out of the data is that many students and employers feel that there are important employability competencies which are not being addressed by current chemical engineering courses. These relate strongly to the notion of business management, i.e. entrepreneurship, Human Resource Management, cash flow, and managing uncertainty:

> Importance of business drivers, be able to work in groups, to be able to take some decisions in the context of uncertainty.
>
> (student, France)

> Project planning and time management should be strengthened. Business plan focus should be added to core competences.
>
> (employer, Portugal)

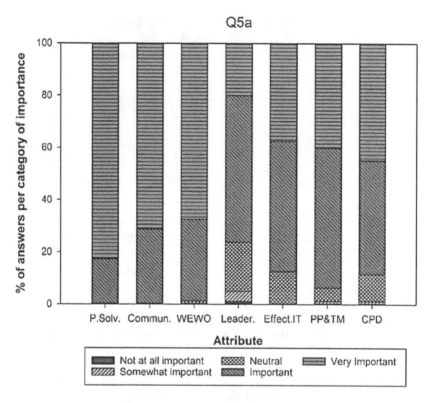

Figure 7.3 The perceived importance of employability competencies by the academic stakeholder group (col 1 = Problem Solving Skills, col 2 = Communication Skills, col 3 = Working Effectively with Others, col 4 = Leadership Skills, col 5 = Effective Use of IT, col 6 = Project Planning & Time Management, col 7 = Continuous Professional Development).

> In industry the focus is completely different . . . and I don't think we're adequately taught that in terms of a business focus.
>
> (graduate, UK)

One focus group participant also identified the importance of learning the English language in order to improve their career progression:

> Some graduates fail to get a good position because a good command of English is an absolute must in many of the largest companies which are multinational.
>
> (academic, Slovakia)

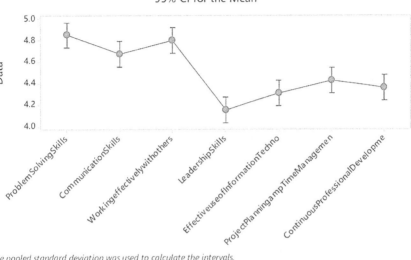

The pooled standard deviation was used to calculate the intervals.

Figure 7.4 The perceived importance of employability competencies by the industrial stakeholder group.

Some aspects of the analyses presented here are supported by arguments presented in Fletcher et al. (2017), although a number of features have been identified in this more extended European study that are being currently analysed in depth. Further detailed analysis, including geographical differences observed from the questionnaire responses, can be found on the iTeach website and the relevant publications.

Framework development and testing

Decision-making methodology and multi-objective optimization were used to identify the most appropriate methods for evaluating efficiency of pedagogical intervention. Further focus groups with stakeholder groups were carried out by each consortium member within their geographical areas to refine the initial framework. The final framework tool for individual module/course evaluation is implemented within Microsoft Excel as illustrated in Figure 7.5.

As a result, the assessment framework was piloted on an introductory level chemical reaction engineering course across all institutions, due to its relevance to chemical engineering programmes. In fact, the initial implementation results of the assessment framework showed agreement among partners in most metrics (Figure 7.6).

iTeach

Improving Teaching Effectiveness in Chemical Engineering Education

Version:	2016 1.0
Institution name:	*[Enter your institution name]*
User name:	*[Enter your name]*
E-mail:	*[Enter your e-mail]*
Course/Unit:	*[Enter the course/teaching unit designation]*
Pedagogical approach:	*[Select one]*
	[If selected "Other" please specify]

What is the Assessment Framework Tool?

A free and easy-to-use tool for institutions and organizations to assess, compare and communicate their efficiency regarding teaching a course. The tool provides quick and accurate answers to key questions such as:

- What influence does a certain pedagogical approach have on the learning process?
- How do employers assess the relevance of a certain course?
- What are the students' perception about what a pedagogy has on their learning process?
- Do graduates and students agree on the relevance of the formation and pedagogy of a certain course?
- Do academics and employers agree on the strategic nature of a course?

What does it do?

This tool allows the easy calculation of 6 metrics to assess the efficieny of teaching a given course. To this end, stakeholders must answer an online questionnaire available at the iTeach official website and the resulting data should be inserted into this iTeach tool to calculate Metrics 1-4 and 6; metric 5 is based solely on the students marks that are retrieved by the course/teaching unit professor, which should also be incorporated in this tool. The tool provides the tabular and graphical representation of the results in the last sheets.

Who developed the Assessment Framework Tool?

Figure 7.5 Example of the iTeach individual module/course evaluation framework: (this page) introductory page, (facing page) graphical output.

Improving Teaching Effectiveness in Chemical Engineering Education

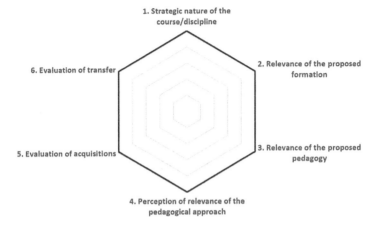

Figure 7.5 Continued

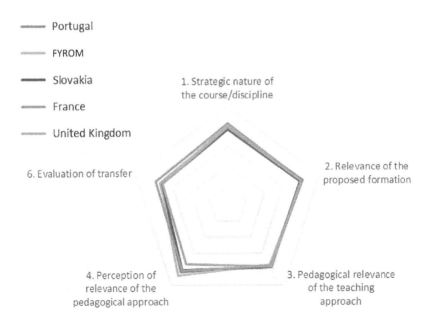

Figure 7.6 Results of the assessment framework applied to Chemical Reaction Engineering in iTeach partners, excluding metric 5 (contribution from TUD was not included due to absence of responses from employers).

The analysis of the results also indicated that the use of such a core module/course did not allow us to explore fully the discriminatory characteristics of the framework. In addition, some challenges in the interpretation of the metrics have been raised during the piloting stage and hence the framework was further refined into its current form.

Also, the response of the various stakeholders in completing the required questionnaires was rather disappointing (only a 13% response rate across all the invitations sent by all consortium partners (3660) – Figure 7.7). Furthermore, the use of different grading scales across HEIs revealed the necessity to develop a general formula for metric 5 (student acquisitions) that is independent of the adopted local grading scale (for details, see the iTeach website). The assessment framework was further improved with metric 5 and piloted in a subsequent project stage.

In order to address the above issues and to provide an opportunity for wider testing and multiplication of project results, a subsequent wider testing of the framework was carried out. During this stage of the project, the consortium undertook a wider testing of the updated framework for individual module/course and pedagogical approach evaluation, using also associate partners and volunteering institutions outside the consortium and, where possible, scientific and engineering disciplines other than chemical engineering (e.g. Electrical and Computers Engineering at FEUP or Industrial Engineering at IBU – see Table 7.1 for a full list of institutions and programmes that participated in this testing phase).

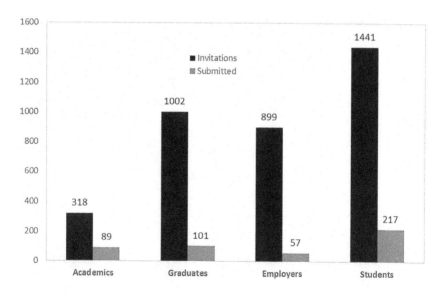

Figure 7.7 Stakeholders' response rate to the assessment framework questionnaires for piloting Chemical Reaction Engineering by all iTeach partners.

Table 7.1 List of courses, programmes, and institutions that applied the assessment framework tool across European institutions

	Institution	Course	Programme	Curricular year/semester
1	Newcastle University, UK	Reaction Engineering Stage 2	BEng/MEng Chemical Engineering	2 / 2
2	Newcastle University, UK	Reaction Engineering Stage 3	BEng/MEng Chemical Engineering	3 / 1
3	Newcastle University, UK	Reactor Systems Engineering CME3035	BEng/MEng Chemical Engineering	3 / 1
4	Manchester University, UK	Chemical Engineering Principles	Chemical Engineering	1 / 1
5	University Lorraine, France	Reaction Engineering	Chemical Engineering	1 (L3) / 1
6	University Lorraine, France	Reaction Engineering 2	Chemical Engineering	1 (L3) / 2
7	University Lorraine, France	Heat Exchangers Design	Chemical Engineering	1 (L3) / 2
8	University Lorraine, France	Fluid-Solid Unit Operations	Chemical Engineering	2 (M1) / 1
9	University Lorraine, France	Process and Reaction Engineering III	Chemical Engineering	2 (M1) / 1
10	University Lorraine, France	Safety and Sustainable Development	Chemical Engineering	2 (M1) / 1
11	IBU, FYROM	Reaction Engineering	Bachelor of Science in Chemical Engineering	3 / 1
12	IBU, FYROM	Design Project	Bachelor of Science in Chemical Engineering	4 / 2
13	IBU, FYROM	Engineering Economy	Bachelor of Science in Chemical Engineering	2 / 1
14	IBU, FYROM	Physics I	Bachelor of Science in Chemical Engineering	1 / 1

(Continued)

Table 7.1 (Continued)

	Institution	Course	Programme	Curricular year/semester
15	IBU, UKIM	Physical Chemistry	Bachelor of Science in Chemical Engineering	2 / 1
16	IBU, UKIM	Microbiology	Bachelor of science in Chemical Engineering	3 / 1
17	FEUP, Portugal	Reaction Engineering I	Integrated Master Chemical Engineering	3 / 1
18	FEUP, Portugal	Chemical Engineering Practice IV	Integrated Master Chemical Engineering	4 / 2
19	FEUP, Portugal	Reaction Engineering II	Integrated Master Chemical Engineering	3 / 2
20	FEUP, Portugal	Disperse Generation	Integrated Master Electrical & Computer Engineering	5 / 1
21	STU, Slovakia	Fundamentals of Reaction Engineering	Bachelor Chemical Engineering	3 / 1
22	STU, Slovakia	Laboratory of Separation Processes	Bachelor Chemical Engineering	2 / 2
23	STU, Slovakia	Advanced Heat Transfer	Master Chemical Engineering	1 / 1
24	STU, Slovakia	Fundamentals of Reaction Engineering	Bachelor Chemical Engineering	3 / 1
25	STU, Slovakia	Material Balances	Bachelor Chemical Engineering	1 / 1
26	STU, Slovakia	Technological Project	Master Chemical Engineering	2 / 1
27	TUDO, Germany	Reaction Engineering	Bachelor Chemical/Biochemical Engineering	3 / 1
28	STU, Slovakia	Design Project	Bachelor Chemical/Biochemical Engineering	4 / 1
29	STU, Slovakia	Conceptual Design	Master Chemical Engineering	1 / 2

Figure 7.8 shows examples of resulting radar plots for some of the courses, chosen as illustrative examples. The results of the assessment framework for all courses are available on the iTeach website. It is important to note that only the fully evaluated courses are listed in Table 7.1 and demonstrated in Figure 7.8. Whilst the scale of the radar plot suggests greater similarity between the two programmes and pedagogies, upon closer inspection it is possible to see higher ratings of the IBU course (Figure 7.8 bottom) compared to that at University Lorraine (UL, Figure 7.8 top). This is particularly evident in metric 1 (Strategic nature of the course/discipline), metric 2 (Relevance of the proposed formation), metric 4 (Perception of relevance of the pedagogical approach by the students) and metric 5 (evaluation of acquisition – based on the course makers relative to the performance of the cohort on the other courses in the same year, as well as the performance of previous cohorts of students). Similar deviations were observed for the other tested courses and the project team is currently analysing the results in more detail to identify any potential trends relating to geographical or discipline-specific features of the tested courses.

The above results confirm that it is possible to provide a robust quantitative evaluation of the specific pedagogical interventions in the delivery of core engineering knowledge and employability competencies, which account for subjective evaluations of all stakeholder groups (academic, student, and

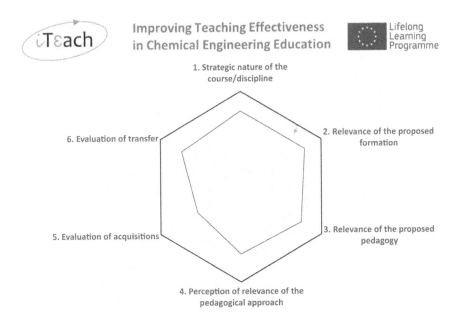

Figure 7.8 Examples of courses tested in the extended evaluation phase of the iTeach project: (this page) Industrial Process Conception (UL); (next page) Engineering Economy (IBU).

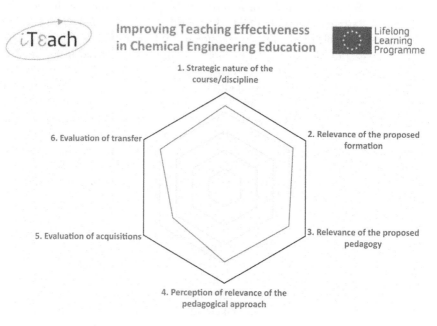

Figure 7.8 Continued

industrial) as well as quantitative statistical evaluation of performance on the tested courses.

Whilst arguably the success of the framework depends to an extent on the cooperation of the various stakeholder groups in providing their views, it is possible to use the framework with only partial contribution of stakeholders or missing information of the performance of students (e.g. see Figure 7.6). Whilst the benefits offered by the framework are more limited in such a case, it can still provide valuable insights into the efficiency a particular pedagogical intervention in engineering education.

Conclusions

This chapter presented the review of the chemical engineering learning outcomes and the framework for evaluating the efficiency of the delivery of core knowledge and employability skills, developed by iTeach. Detailed analysis of the requirements of various accreditation bodies indicated a reassuring consistency in learning outcomes assessed by these bodies. The resulting learning outcomes served as a basis for a survey of the significance and current methods of teaching the respective learning outcomes administered to academics across a wide range of European institutions offering chemical engineering courses.

The statistical analysis of the responses highlighted some differences in the perceived importance of underlying sciences (biology in particular), but showed a remarkable consistency across the core chemical engineering outcomes, engineering practice and design, advanced chemical engineering, and employability competencies. These conclusions align well with the trends in the published literature and recent surveys of industrialists and academics.

The framework for evaluating the effectiveness of delivering core engineering knowledge and employability competencies, developed on the basis of the research reported here, was tested widely both on chemical engineering and broader engineering and scientific courses across Europe. The results from this testing stage indicate that it is possible to use the framework to indicate the impact of various pedagogical interventions during engineering and science education and evaluate their perceived strengths and weaknesses. Further independent testing by the community will contribute to further evaluation and the validity of this approach.

Notes

1 https://research.ncl.ac.uk/iteacheu/
2 http://millenniumindicators.un.org/unsd/methods/m49/m49regin.htm

References

ABET Criteria for Accrediting Engineering Programs (2017–2018) Url:www.abet.org/accreditation/accreditation-criteria/criteria-for-accrediting-engineering-programs-2017-2018/

ASIIN (2011) Subject-specific criteria relating to the accreditation of Bachelor's and Master's degree programmes in mechanical engineering, process engineering and chemical engineering Germany

Braun V & Clark V (2006) Using thematic analysis in psychology, *Qualitative Research in Psychology*, Vol. 3, No. 2, pp. 77–101

Campbell G & Belton D (2016) Setting up new chemical engineering degree programmes: Exercises in design and retrofit within constraints, *Education for Chemical Engineers*, Vol. 17, pp. 1–13

Cranmer S (2006) Enhancing graduate employability: Best intentions and mixed outcomes, *Studies in Higher Education*, Vol. 31, pp. 169–184

EFCE Bologna recommendation Url:www.efce.info/Bologna_Recommendation

Engineers Australia (2017) Accreditation management system education programs at the level of professional engineer Url:www.engineersaustralia.org.au/about-us/accreditation-management-system-professional-engineers

Fletcher AJ, Sharif AWA & Haw MD (2017) Using the perceptions of chemical engineering students and graduates to develop employability skill, *Education for Chemical Engineers*, Vol. 18, pp. 11–25

Glassey J & Brown D (2014) *Enhancing Industry Exposure for Student Chemical Engineers*, Perth, Australia: Chemeca

Glassey J, Kockmann N, Meshko V, Porjazoska Kujundziski A, Polakovic M, Madeira M & Schaer E (2016) *Teaching Efficiency in Chemical Engineering*, August, Prague, Czech Republic: CHISA

IchemE (2016) *Chemical Engineering Matters*, 3rd Edition Url:http://view.digipage.net/00000074/00011131/00094513/

IchemE (2017) *Accreditation of chemical engineering programmes* Url: http://icheme.org/accreditation/university-accreditation/guidance.aspx

Miller JN & Miller JC (2005) *Statistics and Chemometrics for Analytical Chemistry*, 5th Edition, Harlow, Essex: Pearson Prentice Hall

Molzahn M (2004) Chemical engineering education in Europe: Trends and challenges, Trans IchemE, Part A, *Chemical Engineering Research and Design*, Vol. 82, No. A12, pp. 1525–1532

Shott I, Titchener-Hooker N & Seville J (2015) Pick a mix, *The Chemical Engineer*, Vol. 894, No. 895, pp. 35–36

Tryggvason G & Apelian D (2012) *Shaping Our World: Engineering Education for the 21st Century*, Hoboken, NJ: John Wiley & Sons Ltd

Young TJ & Schartner A (2014) The effects of cross-cultural communication education on international students' adjustment and adaptation, *Journal of Multilingual and Multicultural Development*, Vol. 35, No. 6, pp. 547–562

Chapter 8

Personal and professional skills: something they do teach you at university

Plato Kapranos

Introduction

It is largely recognized that our world is a world of constant flux, permeated by very rapid and relentless change; it is industrialized, globalized, and interconnected. It is also self-evident that engineers, throughout the history of development of human civilization, have played a major role in shaping our physical environment, and it is highly likely that they will continue to do so for years to come.

This expectation is not unfounded as evidenced by the fact that engineering graduates are in great demand, and it is highly probable that they will continue to be in demand for the foreseeable future because of the particular set of skills they possess; as Charles Handy succinctly puts it, we may experience a shortage of jobs, but there will never be a shortage of work to be done.

However, competition in the global job market is not a level playing field, as equally well qualified graduates offer their services at quite different competitive rates. Nevertheless, industry is also well aware that cheap labour is no longer as decisive a factor for competitiveness as it used to be. What appears to matter more are the dispositions, attitudes, and skills of employees, and therefore this important issue must be addressed in university curricula (Soeiro, 2009). Clearly a good degree from a reputable HE institution is something that will help the employability of our students; however, what is equally important now and in the future is an ability on the part of our students to persuade prospective employers that they are the right persons for whatever the potential employers need to get done.

Today's engineering graduates more often than not have to differentiate themselves from the competition by demonstrating their competences, i.e. knowledge, skills/know-how, attitudes, and personal attributes (Bacigalupo et al. (2016); Fink, 2009; Goldberg, 2006; Selinger, 2004; EU Guidebook, 2012). This trend appears to hold the developed countries of the EU, the USA, Canada, and Australia and to a lesser extent for developing countries where personal connections are still very important and play a major role in gaining employment.

The full impact of such trends in this competitive market place is not yet clear, but what is certain is that we will need more and more engineers with knowledge, skills, and enterprising and entrepreneurial mindsets to develop and produce the goods and services required by an expanding world economy. There is a clear need to train graduates that can think and act like professionals, with professionalism being much more than just acquiring specific skills and subject knowledge, but rather *a state of mind, a way of thinking and living.*

Knight and Yorke (2003) proposed a definition of employability in higher education as "A set of achievements – skills, understandings and personal attributes – that make individuals more likely to gain employment and be successful in their chosen occupations, which benefits themselves, the workforce, the community and the economy."

Clearly knowledge remains the main tool of the professional engineer, but additional skills are also needed to manipulate such knowledge into achieving specific goals. Of course, goals are influenced by attitudes, so it is important that our future professionals must be imbued by the 'right attitudes' during their years of training. Fostering the multitude of skills that professional engineers use in their daily tasks such as communication, networking, leadership, project management, time management, problem solving, arranging and facilitating meetings, dealing with conflict, dealing with Health and Safety issues, protecting Intellectual Property, and handling ethical issues, to name but a few, is fast becoming part and parcel of university training in UG and PG degree courses across the world.

The process of embedding such skills into the professional conscience of students is often facilitated by the use of problem-based learning (PBL) experiences (Kapranos, 2015, 2016; Terron-Lopez et al., 2016), where students have to deal and solve 'real problems' under realistic conditions and strict time deadlines. Such approaches allow students to quickly learn the value and use of good communication, networking, group task allocation, and time and project management, as they deliver their solutions to the scrutiny of academics, company managers, and their peers, through formal reports and presentations. Realistic exercises such as these have a positive effect on increasing motivation on the part of the students, and assist the development of professional attitudes towards the tasks se and the practical application, the practice, of the transferable skills we aspire to convey (Kapranos, 2014).

But whatever these 'skills' turn out to be, the underlining premise here is that students must have the ability to learn, i.e. they must 'learn how to learn,' learn the ability to *think critically*, and learn the ability to *be enterprising*; enterprising is used here in a wider context as the combination of behaviours, attributes, and competencies that enable the generation and application of ideas (QAA, 2018). Figure 8.1 shows the synergies between enterprise and employability.

If the skills we espouse to introduce and embed are indeed *enterprising skills*, then not only will they fulfil a more utilitarian purpose, but they also fulfil the *learning for the sake of learning* principle, that distinctly relates to the individual

Personal and professional skills

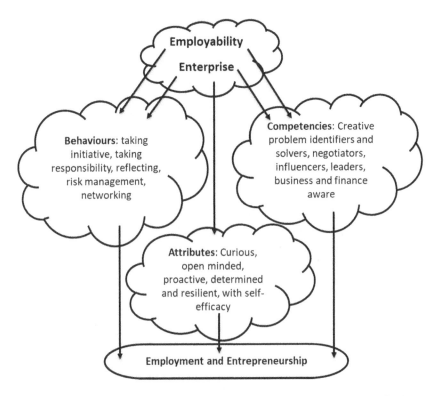

Figure 8.1 Synergies between enterprise and employability (QAA (2018), Enterprise and entrepreneurship guidance: Guidance for UK higher education providers, January 2018).

and their relationship with their environment and their relationship with others (Cullingford, 1990).

This is akin to the Socratic principles of self-knowledge combined with concern for others, leading us towards the wider development of a better and more just society – something that goes to the heart of civilization and more meaningful lives.

Current state of affairs

A recent CBI/Pearson Education and Skills Survey (2016) states that businesses look first and foremost for graduates with the right *attitudes* and *aptitudes*, those that will enable them to be effective in the workplace; nearly nine in ten employers (87%) rank these in their top considerations. In the same report, many businesses are satisfied with the basic skills and general graduate readiness for employment, with more than four in five firms reporting satisfaction or better with graduates' numeracy (91%) and literacy skills (86%), and nearly the same proportion satisfied or better with graduates' problem solving (79%) and communication skills (77%). These results appear to be at odds when contrasted with similar reports of only few years ago (Wendlandt & Rochlen, 2008; Andrews & Higson, 2008), indicating that the recent drive to narrow the employability 'skills gap' appears to have had some success.

The Joint Board of Moderators (2009), in their annual report, recommended that 'professionalism' can and should be embedded into engineering education in order not only make degree programmes more attractive to students but to ensure that graduates have the appropriate skills to work effectively in industry. The key aims they propose are appropriate *attitudes*, *skills*, and *knowledge*, including, amongst others, the ability to work with complex ill-defined problems, team working, and communication skills.

In a similar approach, the Vitae Researcher Development Framework (RDF) (2011) proposed the development of wider employment-related skills such as original, independent, and critical thinking, effective project management, personal effectiveness, communication skills, networking, and team working.

When selecting graduate recruits, it is very important for any business that the person will fit in with the culture of the business and the existing personnel. As a result, attitudes become equally important to aptitudes as both will enable new employees to blend and be effective in any workplace environment. Year on year, these are by far the most widely cited considerations among graduate recruiters. The reality for graduates is that simply gaining a degree will not be enough on its own to win entry to a successful career, and that developing the right skills and attitudes is critically important for a successful transition from education to the world of work (Lumley & Wilkinson, 2014). Currently there are more and more opportunities available to students to develop the necessary attitudes and aptitudes during their time in education. However, students are not always aware of their existence and must therefore be alerted of both their importance and made explicitly aware of how to get them and be encouraged to seize them.

The House of Commons Science and Technology Select Committee inquiry into Engineering Skills, on 18 June 2012 (Engineering UK, 2012), commented on global rapid changes in the world of work and the need to develop skills that are appropriate to the new contexts. Technical knowledge still remains essential and paramount, but there is a clear realization that cross-cutting skills, skills that enable graduates to become innovative developers and users of knowledge, are equally important for industry to remain competitive.

Industrial links and awareness of the challenges faced by engineering companies are viewed as key factors in adding value to any engineering educational provision. Embedding employability into core degree curricula has been a priority of stakeholders such as the government, universities, FE colleges, and employers for quite a while (Cole & Tibby, 2013). In the same document, a number of employability models have been considered, all having particular strengths, but one proposed by Dacre Pool and Sewell (2007) seems to capture the essence of employability with its various links. The difference between personal and professional development is subtle; on the one hand, *professional development* involves developing in a particular role, understanding what one does and improving it and with it. It involves enhancing the necessary skills to carry out a role as effectively as possible and is something that continues throughout a working life. Although it is foremost the acquisition of skills and knowledge for career advancement, it also includes an element of personal development. On the other hand, *personal development* is more about what skills are needed to achieve set objectives, both in a particular role and for life in general; it is about improving one's talents and potential, both in and out of the workplace.

Expectations of what a graduate engineer should look like have changed over the years, from the 'knowledgeable individual' towards 'someone who could display and utilize particular skills, competencies, and attitudes.' Barnett (2009) suggests that, "*knowledge* recedes from view and *'learning how to learn'* has become the new mantra (italics added by author)," even though this had been proposed a lot earlier in the Dearing Report (1997). Knowledge, as defined by the Oxford Online Dictionary (2018), is "facts, information, and skills acquired through experience or education; the theoretical or practical understanding of a subject."

Knowledge is directly linked to skills; skills are dependent on knowledge as well as certain abilities and personality traits. Skills are acts that require practice and as such skills are developed and enhanced through practice.

Dewey (1938) contends that knowledge is not something that exists externally and has to be appropriated by students; it is something that is created by the student who integrates and assimilates information, making it applicable through interaction and reflection.

Tacit knowledge, described as 'action oriented knowledge' or 'know-how,' (Sternberg et al., 1993) is goal oriented and perceived as personally useful, therefore it relates closely with personal values. Sternberg et al. (1995), formalized the distinction of two types of knowledge, *procedural knowledge* (knowing how) and *declarative knowledge* (knowing what), i.e. formal academic knowledge.

When we talk about combinations of Knowledge, Skills, Abilities, and Other personality characteristics (KSAOs), we do so in relation to *competencies*, defined by Kurtz and Bartram (2002), in terms of behaviour that delivers desired results or outcomes. So competencies are very much individual, as they are combinations of these characteristics and, as suggested by Campion et al. (2011), not dominated by any one of them.

Howard Gardner (1983, 2008, 1993) proposed his theory of multiple intelligences, two of which were *interpersonal* and *intrapersonal intelligence*, meaning the ability to understand others and the capacity to understand oneself, respectively. These were popularized by Goleman (1995) under the label *Emotional Intelligence* (EI), a key skill, if it is a skill and not a personality characteristic (Barrett,

2001), when dealing with people; more recent work on EI has proposed a mixed model where motives, social styles, and other traits not primarily concern or focus on emotional reasoning are added to relevant emotion-specific abilities (Myer et al., 2008).

Campbell et al. (1990) developed a hierarchical model of job performance based on eight components and three determinants as the basic building blocks.

> Should education be essentially the development of the individual, to enable him or her to lead a fulfilled life, or should education, supported by the State, be designed to help meet the requirements of society? Should education be seen as a manifestation of the development of the individual or a means of giving the individual the necessary knowledge and skills for employment?
> (Cullingford, 1990)

This has been an ongoing debate through the ages, but what sometimes gets overlooked in this debate is the more fundamental question of 'how do we learn?' Understanding how we learn forces us to think about the purpose of learning, what is to be learned, and how this can be communicated and achieved. Learning is an active process, and as part of this process learners are in perpetual involvement with their physical and social environment, i.e. with other people. Learning is a reflection both of character and ability; it is not the continuous accumulation of knowledge, as often perceived, but a state of perpetual change, adaptability, and the desire to question, examine, rethink, and reassess. Of course, some things might be learned unintentionally, but for most part, real learning depends on us *being willing* to learn something new; we must either be *willing* or *wanting* to learn. This infers recognition on our part of what is of interest to us and the exercise of choice on what we are willing to put an effort towards learning.

In today's competitive employment market environment this can be translated to 'what skills do I need to have in order to make myself more employable?' It therefore makes sense to acquire not only those skills that make one more employable, but the extra skills that will ensure when in employment one not only can keep their job but thrive in it.

In order to move towards integrating *enterprise* into our curricula involves change, and change does not come easily to most of us. "We are more comfortable teaching students what to think than we are teaching them how to think" (Greetham, 2010).

Educators prefer the tried and trusted, 'if it isn't broke don't fix it' approach in their teaching. Accepting new ideas appears to go through an evolutionary process described as *indignant rejection, reasoned objection, qualified opposition,* followed by *tentative acceptance*. What typically follows is *qualified endorsement, judicious modification, cautious adoption,* and *impassioned espousal* (Cullingford, 1990).

This reluctance to accept new ideas begins with lack of knowledge, being satisfied with not knowing (*subconscious incompetence*), followed by questioning the usefulness of knowing, 'what's in it for me?' (*conscious incompetence*), then by becoming uncomfortably aware of the new knowledge (*conscious competence*), and finally, through becoming confident enough and using the new knowledge (*subconscious competence*) (Cullingford, 1990).

What should the engineer of the future look like?

Barnett (2012) poses the question "if the future is unknown, what kind of learning is appropriate for it?" and typical responses by various researchers to that question have invariably been about skills: *generic skills, transferable skills, key competencies, core skills, underpinning skills, employment-related skills, professional skills, cross-cutting skills, soft skills, problem solving skills, self-assessment skills, critical skills*, etc. Bridgstock (2009); DeLa Harpe et al. (2000); Cole and Tibby (2013); Andrews and Higson (2008); Cryer (1998); Taylor (1998); Cajander et al. (2011); Wang et al. (2005); Zijlstra-Shaw et al. (2011); Bridges (2000); Woods et al. (2000); Bacigalupo et al. (2016); Hodge et al. (2007); Moore (2004).

Our world has been described by Bauman (2012) as a 'liquid world,' a world of universal transience where nothing is bound to last, let alone forever!

Of course this is not a new sentiment; over 2,500 years ago Heraclitus of Ephesus, quoted by Plato, pronounced "τὰ πάντα ῥεῖ καὶ οὐδὲν μένει" – "everything flows and nothing remains" – believing that change is ever-present and an integral part of the universe. What of course has changed in the intervening millennia is the rapidly increasing rate of change.

Bauman (2012) also provides us with a very eloquent and fitting metaphor regarding learning in the post-modern world, that of a "smart intelligent missile." He suggests that in order to hit a target in the past, ballistic missiles were very appropriate as the targets were clearly defined and mostly stationary. However, as Brown (2012) relates, the eras of stability are long gone and a new culture of learning, that must have imagination at its core, has to be the way forward.

Continuing with the missile metaphor, we need smart intelligent missiles that can constantly adapt, update and correct and even chose their targets as they go, in order to hit our moving, erratic, and unpredictable targets that most of the time are invisible to the gunners. So our future engineers need the ability to learn and learn fast, but also the ability to forget, change their minds, and revoke previous decisions. In a world of constant change, information rapidly goes 'out of date' and knowledge becomes a disposable commodity no longer in use to be thrown away, forgotten, or replaced.

Castillo (2002) and Sadler-Smith (2010) believe that most knowledge generated in our world of rapid change is inferred tacit knowledge because there is no time for it to be distilled, encoded and, communicated before the next shift happens. This greatly challenges the relevance of traditional pedagogies that have to do with explicit, rather than tacit, knowledge (Brown, 2012).

Brown also contends that there must be a shift from teaching explicit knowledge to learning tacit knowledge and that 'learning to be' is the kind of tacit knowledge that lies at the heart of communities of practice, such as engineering. So if knowledge (existing as a collectively attested set of understandings in the world) is receding from view according to Barnett (2009), should it be replaced by "knowing" (an individual's personal hold on the world)? That would mean learning has to be seen neither in terms of skills or knowledge but in terms of human qualities and dispositions (Barnett, 2012), moving from an *epistemological* educational change to an *ontological* one.

Dewey (1897) in *My Pedagogic Creed* also makes some very relevant comments to today's educational dilemma. He holds that the process of education starts unconsciously at birth – current research evidence supports that it starts even before birth in the womb – and continues throughout one's lifetime, shaping their personalities, characters, and ideas, through habit forming, feelings, and emotions. Education gives us the ability and the means to apply judgement when conditions demand it. Dewey sees the education process as integral part of life, evolving through repeated reconstructions of experiences. He does not see any difference between the process and the goal of education.

There is a lot of wisdom in Dewey's thoughts that echo our current predicament of how our engineers should be educated. It appears that a good place to start would be to train the individual learners to understand themselves, as their actions are based and are guided by their internal belief systems. Appropriate attitudes, behaviours, and feelings of confidence have to be cultivated in the learners in order to be able to face the challenges posed by their 'liquid' world. We have to give learners a clear sense of themselves and make their relationship with their world explicit; they must understand that it is only through investing in their selves and through continuous self-reflection that they will be able to formulate and take appropriate action to overcome future challenges and improve things. The best place to start with getting to know ourselves, is the Delphic pronouncement "Γνωθι Σ'Αυτον" – "Know thyself"; by questioning what our beliefs about learning are we are becoming aware of our own ignorance that in turn will provide the beginning of doubt, inevitably leading to wisdom; "Εν οιδα οτι ουδεν οιδα," i.e. the Socratic 'I know one thing, that I know nothing' (Kapranos, 2012).

Obviously, as we are moving from the conventional format of helping students to acquire knowledge and understanding to the new pedagogical approach concerned with ontological accomplishments such as *self-belief*, *self-motivation*, and *self-confidence*, we will require not only a student-based approach to teaching and learning but a rethink of the roles and relationships of teacher and learner, the curriculum, the assessment, the feedback, and the learning environment, i.e. the complete learning experience, taking a holistic view of the educational process in what Wood (2017) calls *holiploigy*.

He perceives the educational experience as an emergent process through complex interactions of curricula, teaching, learning, assessment, feedback, and educational philosophies resulting in the growth of both students and tutors. The term *holiploigy* is derived from the terms *holi*, meaning holistically on many different levels, and *ploigos*, meaning navigator in classical Greek; it describes the complexity of the overall process of teachers helping learners navigate through their learning experience whilst at the same time developing their own expertise. This approach sees education as a student-centred undertaking where the learners construct their own understanding and build their own skills, and where the main task of the teacher is to provide the necessary arrangements, the learning opportunities, for the process to take place. Such a learning process assumes that teaching should be about the human being and its place in the world. Biesta (2016) contests that view because he thinks that learners are no longer the subject of the educational process, but are rather co-creators of knowledge and makers of meaning. We are here discussing the education of engineers who by default are ones who have a major input in shaping our world, and there should be nothing stopping them to imagine the world they want to live in and help to create it; they can become masters of their future and not bystanders to it.

So it becomes incumbent upon us to instil in our engineering students the kind of *attitudes* and *values* that will assist them in their quest of shaping their future (Landy & Conte, 2013); *motivation* must be encouraged, developed, enhanced, rewarded, and strengthened (Hughes, 2012), as is a *sense of passion, desire, appreciation for beauty*, and above all *curiosity*, the fuel that powers the engine of human advancement (Higashino, 2010).

Motivation (Steward, 2008) has been described by Shellnut (1996) as the neglected heart of instructional technology. Keller (1979) refers to several elements of motivation, such as curiosity, expectancy, relevancy, and satisfaction and has accommodated them in his ARCS model (Keller, 1987).

We must also ensure that the concept of *metacognition*, the capacity to reflect upon one's own thinking (Brookfield, 1995) and thereby monitoring and managing it becomes second nature to them (Greeno et al., 1996).

Reflection; we all have an understanding of what it is, but according to Mezirow (1994), it can mean many things. It can be allowing our thoughts to wander over something, taking something under consideration, conceiving possibilities or alternatives, considering our assumptions as well as those of others, and of course reflecting on our own reflections (Mezirow, 1998).

Education for communicative competence involves cultivating the learner's ability to negotiate meanings and purposes instead of passively accepting the social realities defined by others. Of course, having to re-examine one's core ideas, belief systems, and abilities is not an easy process; in fact it is a highly emotionally charged experience, but if it is undertaken and successfully completed the results will be very beneficial in the long run (Bransford et al., 2005; Gopnik & Meltzoff, 1997).

Dewey (1897) believes that even if we think and act habitually, when based on values of good, truth, and beauty then the emotional part will take care of itself. Gardner (2008) in a similar vein believes that fundamentally education is about values. Unfortunately, we do not find it easy to talk about values.

Slavich and Zimbardo (2012), in their exposition on transformational teaching, talk about the fact that our efforts, be it conscious or unconscious, are about ensuring that students not only gain mastery of their course content but at the same time that they go through a transformation of their values, beliefs, skills, and attitudes relating to learning. The process is a dynamic interactive sharing of knowledge, as instructors view their courses as opportunities for life-changing experiences for their students that will result in their meaningful personal growth. Tutors no longer see themselves as someone that imparts information, but rather as someone that contributes in the way their students learn and live.

Along similar lines, Rosebrough and Leverett (2001) suggest that education should be about inspiring students and not just for providing information. The role of the educator is to prepare the students for life by providing them with the appropriate skills and also the right attitudes.

Gardner (2008) advocates that through our evolving curricula we are indeed exposing our students to, and having them think about, various ethical dilemmas. We do try and devise role-playing situations that reflect real life in order to school them in having meaningful employment and meaningful lives. We envision what kind of human beings we want them to be and what kind of world they would want to live in, and direct our efforts to shape their intelligence and characters towards such ends. Clearly then the challenge is laid out for us; the way we teach will influence the way our future professional engineers will behave, and in our fragile, chaotic, and complex world with its associated risks this is not a menial task.

Challenges and solutions in delivering the engineer of the future

The engineer for the 21st century, seems to fit the description of "the reasonable adventurer" (Heath, 1964), capable to "operate successfully in complex and ever-changing environments . . . built around six specific attributes: intellectuality; close friendships; independence in value judgments; a tolerance for ambiguity; a breadth of interest; and a sense of humour"(Jones, 2007; 2011).

In pedagogical terms our approach shifts more towards student-centred experiential learning, self-exploration, freedom, and continual reflection, not forgetting the element of enjoyment.

Alfred Whitehead, in the *Aims of Education and other Essays* (1929), states that

> There can be no mental development without interest. Interest is the *sine qua non* for attention and apprehension . . . without interest there will be no progress. Now the natural mode by which living organisms are excited

towards suitable self-development is, enjoyment . . . the development of character along a path of natural activity, in itself is pleasurable.

The success of learning will ultimately be put on more secure footing if there is constructive alignment between critical factors such as learning outcomes, learning activities (pedagogy), assessment, and feedback (Kapranos, 2014; Reeves, 2006; QAA, 2018; Jones, 2006; Ramsden, 1992).

To deliver these changes successfully, teachers have to adapt to the new practices of delivering, assessing, and providing feedback. The process will promote cultural changes, for both teachers and learners, towards a deeper understanding of the learning process itself rather than delivery and learning of a particular set of skills. There will be giving and receiving critique by both sides as both learn from each other; a culture of *continuous reflection* is to be fostered in an environment where freedom and imagination are encouraged and failure and retrial are permitted and not criticized; after all, isn't this is how we do learn and how science moves forward, from reflecting on "failure," as Firestein (2011) so eloquently discusses? Knowledge should and will continuously be contested, so the ability for critical reasoning will be taught. Dispositions, defined as tendencies to engage with the world around us, such as the *will to learn, a will to engage, a preparedness to listen, a preparedness to explore, to hold oneself out to new experiences,* and *a determination to keep going forward* will have to be cultivated (Barnett, 2009). Qualities, the manifestations of dispositions, such as courage, resilience, self-confidence, self-belief, self-motivation, carefulness, integrity, self-discipline, restraint, willingness to speak or to engage, respect for others, openness, commitment, enthusiasm, generosity, intellectual humility, and authenticity will be instilled in our learners. This is a character-building curriculum, developed around the concept of learner transformation of being and becoming, and this process is facilitated through the process of coming to know and to understand.

Barnett (2012), offers us a schema of the pedagogical options in an uncertain world, shown in Figure 8.2, that links challenges and opportunities. The quadrant that requires our attention is no. 4, the only one that offers a curriculum for educational transformation; unfortunately, that comes with high risk. The proposed curriculum is aimed at nothing less than the transformation of the human being through pedagogies that are characterized by uncertainty and will allow for human flourishing through exposure to dilemmas and uncertainties.

The pedagogical journey will be one of encountering strangeness, wrestling with it, and forming one's own responses to it. The openness in this quadrant means open relationships between teacher and student, relationships that involve vulnerability on both sides, and therefore are not without risks, but there are also opportunities with students getting to know each other as persons and getting to know, to a degree, their teachers. Being-for-uncertainty stands for certain kind of relationships with the world. It is characterized by certain kinds of dispositions discussed above that yield the dispositions desired by employers such as adaptability, flexibility, and self-reliance. When these dispositions

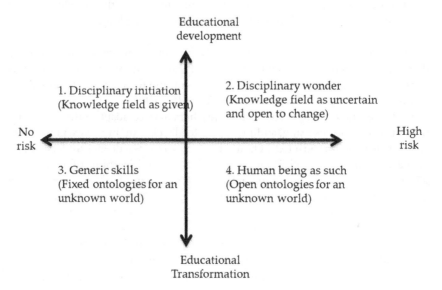

Figure 8.2 'Pedagogical options: Learning for an unknown future' by Ronald Barnett Higher Education Research & Development Vol 23:3 pp. 247–260 (2004).

are fostered, they offer the making of a *being* that may thrive in an uncertain changeable world. This process of self-formation, of individuals forming and transforming themselves, is the concept of *Bildung*, described by Christensen et al. (2006).

Diploma in personal and professional skills

In fitting with the above proposed themes of student-centred experiential learning, self-exploration, freedom to learn from failure in &low-risk environments, continuous reflection, and not forgetting the element of enjoyment, in the Department of Materials Science and Engineering at the University of Sheffield we developed a Diploma in Personal and Professional Skills for our student cohorts within the Doctoral Training Centre (CDT) for Advanced Metallics.

Students enrolling for the four year PhD training undertake a combination of parallel studies that form the Skills Diploma which aims to ensure that CDT graduates are equipped with the transferable skills as well as the technical knowledge and expertise they will need to succeed in their future careers. The course has been designed to cover the skills highlighted in the Research Councils UK (RCUK) Joint Skills Statement 2001 and the Researcher Development Framework.[1].

Learning outcomes of the PG diploma course

By the end of the course, students will be able to:

- Identify their personal strengths and weaknesses;
- Display the skills and behaviours needed to become a future research leader;
- Identify and describe their skills and competencies to future employers; and
- Provide robust evidence of their achievements beyond standard technical competence.

Personal Development Planning (PDP)

PDP is a continuous cycle of:

1. Self-assessment and evaluation
2. The identification of needs and goals
3. Planning a course of action to meet these needs and goals
4. Carrying out the action plan and recording the achievements
5. Reflecting on outcomes and evaluating progress, which should reveal new needs and goals.

Personal Development Planning is a process which involves keeping track of students' professional development as a researcher and reflecting on the skills that they acquire during the course of their research. In the course of their research they develop both specialist research skills and a broad range of 'transferable' skills (e.g. communication, leadership, team-building, time management). It is very important that students learn to be able to identify, evaluate, and record these skills that are very useful to them when they carry out their research, help them identify their Continuing Professional Development needs, and towards the end of their course how to apply for a job, prepare their CVs, and become skilled at interviews.

Being aware of gaps in their knowledge and skills and having a strategy for remedying them will help them to anticipate and avoid obstacles to the successful completion of their research. In particular, the thoughts and ideas generated by engagement with PDP helps them to have more structured and meaningful discussions with their supervisors. When putting together a CV or drafting answers to 'competency-based' questions on application forms, they will need to think about how to provide evidence that they have the skills that an employer is looking for. Most professional bodies now expect members to record systematically the steps that they are taking to keep their professional knowledge up-to-date, and many major employers expect the same of their employees. In the case of professional associations and regulatory bodies, keeping this kind of record may be a condition for continued membership/registration. Employers may use the record as a basis for making decisions about pay and promotion. Therefore, it is a good thing to get into the habit of evaluation, reflection, and planning before it becomes compulsory! The PDP is facilitated through an electronic version of a PDP log template with instructions for its completion; this must be kept updated and submitted to the CDT Manager every six months. The PDP process is supported by annual one-to-one meetings with a member of CDT staff, most likely the CDT Manager, and additional meetings may be arranged as necessary.

Course structure

- Transformative Technologies
- Personal Effectiveness Skills
- Introduction to Research Skills
- Doctoral Communication Skills
- Public Engagement Project
- Skills in Action (PhD)
- Business Operations
- Short Term Business Impact Study (EngD)
- SME Consultancy Project
- Innovation and Commercialization of Research
- Standards, Codes, and Specifications
- Career Skills
- Science & Engineering in the Media

Over the space of the four years, the graduates will undertake the above activities that are designed to deliver and embed the various skills. For example, under the Transformative Technologies module, students will learn how to introduce the idea and reality of emergent and potentially disruptive/transformative materials technologies, enable the identification, investigation, critical analysis, and exploration of market implications of such technologies, and through group work develop effective collaborative working attitudes. Under the Personal Effectiveness section, they are introduced to networking, working in teams, communication and presentation skills, time management, project management, creative thinking, getting motivated, assertiveness, and how to get the most from their supervision. Through the Introduction to Research Skills, students are prepared for their PhD research via workshops, conferences, and visits that provide them with knowledge of PhD milestones, the expectations of students and supervisors, and an appreciation of the broader industrial context of materials research, thus enabling them to make an informed choice of PhD topic. An introduction to working as a cohort and learning from each other's experience provides them with a forum to communicate their research findings to a scientific audience and receive feedback on their progress.

The Doctoral Communication Skills module exposes students to good practice in writing for an academic readership; develops skills in planning, drafting, editing, and proofreading; and explores the conventions used in academic writing in preparing work for publication or delivering presentations of scientific work to a general scientific audience.

Through the Public Engagement Project, training is provided in experience of public engagement activities. Students have the opportunity to design and carry out a project to disseminate research in materials science and engineering to a public audience. This helps students to gain confidence in communicating their subject, develop strong organizational and interpersonal skills, understand how to address the needs of individuals, learn to devise and develop projects, and teach methods appropriate to engage the audience they are working with, to inspire a non-specialist audience to engage with scientific concepts, and to create a replicable output that can be used in future public engagement activities.

With Skills in Action, an opportunity is provided for students to use their transferable skills, reflect on their progress, and identify areas for future development. The cohort is required to work together and in small groups to organize and deliver a series of journal club meetings and external speaker seminars. Attendance at journal club meetings and seminars broadens students' knowledge of their wider research field.

Through Business Operations, students learn to explore the operations function across a range of business types (services/products), to highlight the relevance and interdependence of key operations, whether internal or external to a given business, to understand the operational and strategic challenges facing operational managers in an ever-changing business environment, and to have an opportunity to develop a range of transferable skills in communication, information management, evaluation, and decision making. In addition, only the EngD students have the opportunity to experience working on a short-term project of relevance to their sponsoring organization, in contrast to their longer-term projects. The exact nature of the project is developed by the student in conjunction with their academic and industrial supervisors and the course director. This gives students a broader understanding of their sponsor's business beyond their project, provides them with direct experience of how the departments, systems, and processes within the company work together, and empowers them to devise, execute, and report a programme of work in response to a specific brief where timescales are short.

Through the SME Consultancy Project, students work in small groups on a two-week project tackling a real problem facing a local SME. Groups work with the business to understand the problem, plan and execute a strategy to solve it, and present their results and recommendations to the business (Kapranos, 2015, 2016).

The Innovation and Commercialisation of Research unit examines various aspects of the commercialization of research and is very much project-based; it allows students to develop commercialization ideas and business models which could be based on their own area of research and preparing them to focus beyond the laboratory. Students evaluate a business opportunity first-hand, developing a commercial business case based on the idea, and then preparing a business report and presentation. The unit is delivered as a series of lectures by speakers from the fields of enterprise and commercialization, along with study group tutorial sessions. There are also follow-on sessions and events to outline the opportunities available for research students who would like to take an idea to the next stage – perhaps as a start-up company or as a licencing opportunity.

The Standards, Codes, and Specifications is industrially led and aimed at exposing students to the use in practice of standards, codes, and specifications. This is undertaken through seminars, where real case studies are discussed from a range of sectors; examples include materials selection, process control, non-destructive evaluation, product release, and in-service inspection. Discussions cover topics such as the preparation and implementation of new specifications, the process of standardization, risks associated with the use of standards, and design constraints associated with the use of standards.

Finally, further consolidating their communication skills, students undertake an intensive three-day course delivered by experienced science journalists. Students work in groups to plan, prepare, deliver, and evaluate a radio programme and a broadcast news package. The course includes sessions on print journalism, and the role of and relationships between science and the media.

The Diploma in Personal and Professional Skills as part of the Doctoral training is a coherent program that aims to develop the complete person, the engineer with the right qualities and dispositions fit for the challenges of the 21st century.

In conclusion

The world that we live in and the one the future engineer will inherit is fast moving and unpredictable. How we teach engineers has to undergo a radical rethink. We have to move from the previous dogmas of the 'knowing student' and the 'skilled student' to the 'performative student' (Barnett, 2009): students capable to engage purposefully with their world.

Enterprising skills, creative and critical ways of thinking, dispositions, and attitudes will have a much more critical role to play than the transmission of inert knowledge. Permission to fail and the exercise of imagination, 'playful tinkering,' and embracing change (Brown, 2012) will become part of the new repertoire of solving the problems of tomorrow. The engineers of the future will have to use their intuition and inspiration to *visualize* and *create* imagined worlds. Creativity and imagination will go hand in hand in building the world of tomorrow, asking 'What if?'

To do this, we need to create learning contexts that generate a sense of curiosity, the imagination running wild, where there is excitement and pleasure in our students; we need to kindle their desire to be part of something bigger than themselves.

The process will no doubt seem chaotic at times, but it is at the edge of chaos that creativity thrives; it is where imagination is at play that real learning takes place.

Note

1 www.vitae.ac.uk/CMS/files/upload/Vitae-Researcher-Development-Framework.pdf

References

Andrews J & Higson H (2008) Graduate employability, 'soft skills' versus 'hard' business knowledge: A European study, *Higher Education in Europe*, Vol. 33, No. 4, pp. 411–422

Bacigalupo M, Kampylis P, Punie Y & Van den Brande G (2016) *EntreComp: The Entrepreneurship Competence Framework*, Luxembourg: Publication Office of the European Union; EUR 27939 EN; DOI: 10.2791/593884

Barrett GV (2001) *Emotional Intelligence: The Madison Avenue Approach to Professional Practice*, Paper presented at the 16th annual conference of the Society for Industrial and Organizational Psychology, San Diego, CA

Barnett R (2004) Pedagogical options: Learning for an unknown future, *Higher Education Research & Development*, Vol. 23, No. 3, pp. 247–260

Barnett R (2009) Knowing and becoming in higher education curriculum, *Studies in Higher Education*, Vol. 34, No. 4, pp. 65–77

Barnett R (2012) Learning for an unknown future, *Higher Education Research and Development*, Vol. 31, No. 1, pp. 429–440

Bauman Z (2012) *On Education-Conversations with Riccardo Mazzeo*, Cambridge: Polity Press

Biesta G (2016) The rediscovery of teaching: On robot vacuum cleaners, non-ecological education and the limits of the hermeneutical world view, *Educational Philosophy and Theory*, Vol. 48, No. 4, pp. 374–392

Bransford J, Vye N, Stevens R, Kuhl P, Schwartz D, Bell P, Meltzoff A, Barron B, Pea R, Reeves B, Roschelle J & Sabelli N (2005) Learning theories and education: Toward a decade of synergy, in *Handbook of Educational Psychology*, 2nd Edition (pp. 209–244), Mahwah, NJ: Erlbaum

Brookfield SD (1995) *Becoming a Critically Reflective Teacher*. San Francisco: Jossey-Bass Inc

Brown JS (2012) Learning in and for the 21st Century, in CJ Koh *Professional Lecture Series No. 4* (pp. 12–31), Singapore: National Institute of Education, November 21–22nd Url:www.johnseelybrown.com/CJKoh.pdf

Bridges D (2000) Back to the future: The higher education curriculum in the 21st century, *Cambridge Journal of Education*, Vol. 30, No. 1, pp. 37–55

Bridgstock R (2009) The graduate attributes we've overlooked: Enhancing graduate employability through career management skills, *Higher Education Research & Development*, Vol. 28, No. 1, pp. 31–44

Cajander A, Daniels M, McDermott R & von Konsky BR (2011) Assessing professional skills in engineering education, Proceedings of the 13th Australasian computing education conference (ACE 2011), 17–20 January 2011, Perth, Australia Sydney: Conferences in research and practice in information technology (CRPIT), Vol. 114, pp. 145–154 Url:http://crpit.com/Vol114.html

Campbell JP, McHenry JJ & Wise LL (1990) Modelling job performance in a population of jobs, *Personnel Psychology*, Vol. 43, pp. 313–333

Campion MA, Fink AA, Ruggeberg BJ, Carr L, Phillips GM & Odman RB (2011) Doing competencies well: Best practices in competency modelling, *Personnel Psychology*, Vol. 64, pp. 225–262

Castillo J (2002) A note on the concept of tacit knowledge, *Journal of Management Enquiry*, Vol. 11, No. 1, pp. 46–57

CBI/Pearson Education and Skills Survey (2016) Url:www.cbi.org.uk/cbi-prod/assets/File/pdf/cbi-education-and-skills-survey2016.pdf

Christensen J, Henriksen LB & Kolmos A (2006) *Engineering Science, Skills, and Bildung*, Aalborg, Denmark: Aalborg University Press

Cole D & Tibby M (2013) Defining and developing your approach to employability- A framework for higher education institutions, *The Higher Education Academy* Url:www.heacademy.ac.uk/system/files/resources/employability_framework.pdf

Cryer P (1998) Transferable skills, marketability and lifelong learning: The particular case of postgraduate research students, *Studies in Higher Education*, Vol. 23, No. 2, pp. 207–216

Cullingford C (1990) *The Nature of Learning, Children Teachers and the Curriculum*, London: Cassell Educational Ltd

Dacre Pool L & Sewell P (2007) The key to employability: Developing a practical model for graduate employability, *Education and Training*, Vol. 49, No. 4, pp. 277–289.

Dearing Report: National Committee of Enquiry into Higher Education (1997) *Higher Education on the Learning Society*, London: HMSO Url:www.educationengland.org.uk/documents/dearing1997/dearing1997.html

DeLa Harpe B, Radloff A & Wyber J (2000) Quality and generic (Professional) skills, *Quality in Higher Education*, Vol. 6, No. 3, pp. 231–243

Dewey J (1897) My pedagogic creed, *School Journal*, Vol. 54, pp. 77–80

Dewey J (1938) *Experience and Education*, 60th Anniversary Edition, Indianapolis, IN: Kappa Delta Pi

Engineering UK (2012) Url:http://epc.ac.uk/wp-content/uploads/2012/08/Engineering-Skills-Inquiry-EPC-FINAL.pdf

EU Guidebook Series (2012) How to support SME Policy from Structural Funds, in *Building Entrepreneurial Mindsets and Skills in the EU, Office for Official Publications of the EU*, Luxembourg: European Commission Directorate-General for Enterprise and Industry

Fink FK (2009) International perspectives of continuing engineering education, in Lappalainen, P (Ed.), *European Continuing Engineering Education – Conceptualizing the Lessons Learned* (pp. 45–51), Finland: Publishers SEFI and TKK Diploli

Firestein S (2011) *Failure: Why Science Is so Successful*, Oxford: Oxford University Press

Gardner H (1983) *Frames of Mind: The Theory of Multiple Intelligences*, New York: Basic Books

Gardner H (1993) *Multiple Intelligences: Theory and Practice*, New York: Basic Books

Gardner H (2008) Multiple lenses on the mind, in Huat CM & Kerry T (Eds.), *International Perspectives on Education* (pp. 7–27), New York: Continuum International Publishing

Goldberg DE (2006) *The Entrepreneurial Engineer – Personal, Interpersonal and Organizational Skills for Engineers in a World of Opportunity*, Hoboken, NJ: John Wiley & Sons Ltd

Goleman D (1995) *Emotional Intelligence*, New York: Bantam Books

Gopnik A & Meltzoff AN (1997) *Words, Thoughts and Theories*, Cambridge, MA: MIT Press

Greeno JG, Collins AM & Resnic LB (1996) Cognition & learning, in Berliner D & Calfree R (Eds.), *Handbook of Educational Psychology* (pp. 15–46), New York: Palgrave Macmillan

Greetham B (2010) *Thinking Skills for Professionals*, Basingstoke: Palgrave Macmillan

Heath R (1964) *The Reasonable Adventurer*, Pittsburgh: University of Pittsburgh Press

Higashino K (2010) *A Midsummer's Equation*, London: Little Brown Book Group

Hodge D, Pasquesi K & Hirsh M (2007) *From Convocation to Capstone: Developing the Student as Scholar*, Keynote address, Association of American Colleges and Universities Network for Academic Renewal Conference, April 19–21st, Long Beach, CA Url:www.miami.muohio.edu/president/reports_and_speeches/pdfs/From_Convocation_to_Capstone.pdf

Hughes C (2012) Passion for beauty: A model for learning, *Creative Education*, Vol. 3, No. 3, pp. 334–340

The Joint Board of Moderators (2009) Url:http://jbm.org.uk/uploads/JBM101_Annual Reportv3.pdf

Jones C (2006) Constructive alignment: A journey for new eyes, *Journal of Enterprising Culture*, Vol. 14, No. 4, pp. 291–306

Jones C (2007) Creating the reasonable adventurer: The co-evolution of student and learning environment, *Journal of Small Business and Enterprise Development*, Vol. 14, No. 2, pp. 228–240

Jones C (2011) *Teaching Entrepreneurship to Undergraduates*, Cheltenham, UK and Northampton, MA, USA: Edward Elgar Publishing

Keller JM (1979) Motivation and instructional design: A theoretical perspective, *Journal of Instructional Development*, Vol. 2, No. 4, pp. 26–34

Keller JM (1987) Development and use of the ARCS model of instructional design, *Journal of Instructional Development*, Vol. 10, No. 3, pp. 2–10

Kapranos P (2012) Diploma in personal and professional skills for centres of doctoral training-managing by instructional objectives, in Kapranos P & Brabazon D (Eds.), *Proceedings of 4th International Symposium for Engineering Education* (pp. 307–315), UK: The University of Sheffield, 18–20th July

Kapranos P (2014) Teaching transferable skills to doctoral level engineers-the challenge and the solutions, *Open Journal of Social Sciences*, Vol. 2, pp. 66–75 http://dx.doi.org/10.4236/jss.2014.25014

Kapranos P (2015) PBL for doctoral students in collaboration with SMEs: Thinking like a professional engineer, *Open Journal of Social Sciences*, Vol. 3, pp. 57–63 http://dx.doi.org/10.4236/jss.2015.36012

Kapranos P (2016) Use of industrial SME problem based learning to promote and embed professional and enterprising skills, in Bhamidimarri R & Liu A (Eds.), *Engineering and Enterprise – Inspiring Innovation* (pp. 83–92), Switzerland: Springer

Knight PT & Yorke M (2003) Employability and good learning in higher education, *Teaching in Higher Education*, Vol. 8, No. 1, pp. 3–16

Kurtz R & Bartram D (2002) Competency and individual performance: Modelling the world of work, in Robertson IT, Callinan M & Bartram D (Eds.), *Organizational Effectiveness: The Role of Psychology* (pp. 227–255), New York: John Wiley & Sons Ltd

Landy FJ & Conte JM (2013) *Work in the 21st Century: An Introduction to Industrial and Organizational Psychology*, 4th Edition (pp. 158–159), Hoboken, NJ: John Wiley & Sons Ltd

Lumley M & Wilkinson J (2014) *Developing Employability for Business*, Oxford, UK: Oxford University Press

Mezirow J (1994) Understanding transformation theory, *Adult Education Quarterly*, Vol. 44, No. 4, pp. 222–232

Mezirow J (1998) On critical reflection, *Adult Education Quarterly*, Vol. 48, No. 3, pp. 185–198

Moore T (2004) The critical thinking debate: How general are general thinking skills? *Higher Education Research & Development*, Vol. 23, No. 1, pp. 3–18

Myer JD, Roberts RD & Barsade SG (2008) Human abilities: Emotional intelligence, *Annual Review of Psychology*, Vol. 59, pp. 507–536

QAA (2018) *Enterprise and Entrepreneurship Guidance: Guidance for UK Higher Education Providers*, January Url:www.qaa.ac.uk/en/Publications/Documents/Enterprise-and-entrpreneurship-education-2018.pdf

Oxford Online Dictionary (2018) Url:https://en.oxforddictionaries.com/definition/knowledge Visited March 26th

Ramsden P (1992) *Learning to Teach in Higher Education*, New York: Routledge

Reeves TC (2006) How do you know they are learning? the importance of alignment in higher education, *International Journal of Learning Technology*, Vol. 2, No. 4, pp. 294–309

Rosebrough TR & Leverett RG (2011) *Transformational Teaching in the Information Age: Making Why and How We Teach Relevant to Students*, Alexandria, VA: ASCD

Sadler-Smith E (2010) *The Intuitive Mind, Profiting from the Power of your Sixth Sense*, Chichester, West Sussex: John Wiley & Sons Ltd

Selinger C (2004) *Stuff You Don't Learn in Engineering School – Skills for Success in the Real World*, Hoboken, NJ: IEEE Press and John Wiley & Sons Ltd

Shellnut BJ (1996) *John Keller – A Motivating Influence in the Field of Instructional Systems Design* Url:http://arcsmode.ipower.com/pdf/Biographical%20Information.pdf

Slavich GM & Zimbardo PG (2012) Transformational teaching: Theoretical underpinnings, basic principles, and core methods, *Educational Psychology Review*, Vol. 24, pp. 569–608

Soeiro A (2009) Third Mission of Universities and Engineering, in Lappalainen P (Ed.), *European Continuing Engineering Education – Conceptualizing the Lessons Learned* (pp. 53–60), Publishers SEFI and TKK Diploli

Sternberg RJ, Wagner RK & Okagaki L (1993) Practical intelligence: The nature and role of tacit knowledge in work and at school, in Reese H & Pucket J (Eds.), *Advances in Lifespan Development* (pp. 205–227), Hillsdale, NJ: Erlbaum

Sternberg RJ, Wagner RK, Williams WM & Horvath JA (1995) Testing common sense, *American Psychologist*, Vol. 50, pp. 912–927

Steward A (2008) *Getting the Buggers to Learn in FE*, London: Continuum International Publishing Group

Taylor A (1998) Employability skills: From corporate 'wish list' to government policy, *Journal of Curriculum Studies*, Vol. 30, No. 2, pp. 143–164

Terron-Lopez MJ et al. (2016) Implementation of a project-based engineering school: Increasing student motivation and relevant learning, *European Journal of Engineering Education*, Vol. 42, No. 6, pp. 618–631

Vitae Researcher Development Framework (2011) Url:www.vitae.ac.uk/vitae-publications/rdf-related/researcher-development-framework-rdf-vitae.pdf/view

Wang J, Fong YC & Alwis WAM (2005) *Developing Professionalism in Engineering Students Using Problem Based Learning*, Proceedings of the 2005 Regional Conference on Engineering Education, December 12–13, Johor, Malaysia, Session 02–001, pp. 1–9

Wendlandt NM & Rochlen AB (2008) Addressing the college-to-work transition –implications for university career councelors, *Journal of Career Development*, Vol. 35, No. 2, pp. 151–165

Whitehead AN (1929) New York: Palgrave Macmillan

Wood P (2017) Holiploigy-navigating the complexity of teaching in higher education, *Journal of Learning Development in Higher Education*, No. 11, pp. 1–9

Woods DR, Felder RM, Rugarcia A & Stice JE (2000) The future of engineering education – developing critical skills, *Chemical Engineering Education*, Vol. 34, No. 2, pp. 108–117

Zijlstra-Shaw S, Robinson PG & Roberts T (2011) Assessing professionalism within dental education: The need for a definition, *European Journal of Dental Education*, Vol. 15, pp. 1–9

Chapter 9

Breaking boundaries with liberal studies in engineering

Louis Bucciarelli and David Drew

Introduction

In January of 2015, a diverse group of teachers of history, literature, philosophy, anthropology, economics, and other domains in the humanities, arts, and social sciences came together with teachers of engineering at a workshop in Washington D.C. to explore possibilities for establishing an innovative undergraduate degree program – a *Bachelor of Arts in Liberal Studies in Engineering* (Bucciarelli et al., 2015).

The program would infuse exemplary and substantive engineering content throughout a sequence of core courses rooted in the liberal arts. It aims to provide a smoother pathway into engineering, to better prepare engineering students for the "grand" challenges they might face in an uncertain future, and to provide liberal arts graduates with basic knowledge of engineering and technology.

The National Science Foundation provided support for our workshop and, subsequently, we have received an NSF grant to explore the feasibility of establishing a program of this nature at a variety of colleges and universities. As part of this effort over the past two years, we have developed, and posted online, four modules that illustrate the integration of engineering content into courses in the liberal arts.

Engineering practice changed, engineering education challenged

Our motivation is rooted in the observation that the world of engineering practice has changed over the past few decades prompted, in large part, by an epidemic of innovation in information processing and computer technologies. The world of engineering education has experienced a corresponding disruption with challenges to traditional ways of preparing students for practice as evidenced by:

- A dramatic increase in the fraction of students choosing to major in Computer Science (Computing Research Association, 2017)
- At the same time, an increase in the number of students seeking to study across traditional disciplines, e.g., biology and engineering, management and engineering

- A broader definition of the design process that includes attention to the social context of design and often includes the arts
- Emergence of an ideology that stresses entrepreneurial prowess as a legitimate objective of undergraduate engineering education
- Increased student interest and participation in co-curricular activities, e.g., intercollegiate competitive design and build projects (Schuster et al., 2006); service learning; foreign study
- Faculty (and ABET) statements of the need to prepare students for work that requires sensitivity to the social/political context, negotiation with "stakeholders" who have different and often conflicting interests in, and awareness of, how culture can inform the design of products and systems (ABET, 2016–17)
- Faculty recognition of the impossibility of preparing graduates for all that they might be called upon to do in the future; emphasis on teaching students how to learn and life-long learning (Dutta et al., 2012)
- Attempts to open up engineering education to a more diverse population, e.g., women and under-represented minorities (Malcom-Pique & Malcom, 2013)
- An associated heightening of interest in, and legitimizing of research on, how to teach and reflection on what is it that is essential for engineering students to learn (Engineering Education Departments and Programs)

These are symptoms of how the engineering education as a system – students, faculty, and administration – is disturbed by, and attempting to accommodate, dramatic changes in engineering practice. They are a disjointed lot, seemingly unrelated and hard to attribute to any single cause, though in the future a historian might look back and construct a coherent story. (It's not enough to gloss the whole as a consequence of the "computer revolution." More needs to be said about the interests and practices of students and professionals.)

At a more fundamental level, significant, fully thought out, successful accommodation to the changes we see today in engineering practice is severely hampered by three entrenched, no-need-to-speak-of, beliefs:

- Preparation for the engineering profession requires but four years of undergraduate study; students commit prior to enrolling at university
- An essential component of that preparation must include success in a series of prerequisite courses in mathematics and science whose content has not changed for half a century, although "delivery" methods have changed
- The core requirements of a major must consist of courses, including engineering design, that are rooted in an ideology that sees the world of engineering practice as problems to be solved by the classical instrumental theories and methods taught in the engineering sciences. All else is of minor importance

If faculty hold to these tenets, then the current undergraduate engineering major, so full of requirements, presents few opportunities for change that would better prepare students for contemporary engineering practice: an openness to different perspectives; sensitivity to cultural values; ability to work with others, or negotiate; reflect on one's work; communicate clearly, or listen attentively; be eager to learn; and be open to moving on (National Academy of Engineering, 2004).

The prevailing ideology that stresses instrumental thinking infects student attitudes as well. Most all, save those who choose to double major or actively engage a minor in the liberal arts, follow along and see their humanities requirement as "soft," something to get through with as little distraction from the really important courses of their major (Shivani, 2017).

Yet there are promising signs that change is possible. At a surprising number of institutions there have been attempts to break the mould of the past (that is, lecture/recitation; students working as individuals in competition with their peers; canonical presentation of engineering sciences; single answer problems; cook-book laboratories; technology focused design classes). Think of project-based learning; design experiences that stress user interface; portfolios for assessing a student's progress; increased concern for teamwork and communication; and the, not unrelated, push to increase the diversity of students of engineering. And it's not that there is lack of recognition by funding agencies, by philanthropies, as well as by NSF, of the need for change. But, in general, it remains very difficult to convince one's faculty peers of the worth of educational innovation, especially of the sort we advocate here and, as a result, to make and sustain such a change.

Two design challenges

We propose the establishment of a new kind of undergraduate experience that would integrate engineering studies in with courses in the humanities, arts, and social sciences. Immediately, two challenges arise:

Rigid Structures: James Duderstadt (2009) has said that we are trying "to educated 21st Century engineers with a 20th Century curriculum in 19th Century institutions." As professors with decades of university experience and as observers of academia, especially the professorate, we recognize that universities are very s-l-o-w to change. Furthermore, innovations in higher education often are rejected as perceived threats to quality. We have realized that in proposing a closer integration of engineering education with the arts and humanities, including collaboration in teaching of faculty from both domains, we are trying to introduce some fluidity into a rigid structure, going against the grain. So while we have proposed a *Bachelor of Arts degree in Liberal Studies in Engineering*, we recognize that institutional change may need to occur; this would best be done in small steps. Moreover, we have underscored consistently that we are raising the bar for engineers, not creating "engineering lite."

A Narrow Demographic: To this day, most engineering students are white males. But most university programs have become more diverse demographically, along a number of dimensions, especially with regards to gender and ethnicity. A series of studies and task force reports, for example (Froyd, 2008) has suggested that the most effective way to diversify engineering enrolments is to broaden the coursework, address the social/political contexts of engineering practice, and explicate the implications of technology for society, especially in the early years of undergraduate study (Hill et al., 2010; Thaler, 2011).

Some have suggested that the under-representation of women in engineering, especially in computer science, is because they find the work too challenging. We offer a contrary interpretation: perhaps they don't find the content interesting and relevant enough. Consider a study by Wang et al. (2013), which studied 18-year-old college students, and then revisited the same students when they were 33. In one analysis, they compared the SAT scores of the students with whether or not they had chosen a STEM career 15 years later. They found that 49% of those with high quant scores and modest verbal scores were working in STEM. But only 34% of those with high quant scores and high verbal scores were working in STEM. Most of the missing 15% were women.

Two design requirements

Our advancing the idea of a new kind of undergraduate degree and calling it a *Bachelor of Arts in Liberal Studies in Engineering* is, in the main, a strawman, a socio-technical imaginary (Jasanoff & Kim, 2015), meant to move faculty of engineering and of the liberal arts to think seriously about the possibility that preparation for work as an engineer, for the vocation, requires now a firm basis in the liberal arts and that all graduates should be sensitive to and prepared to reflect upon, not just "impacts," but the complex social/political contexts of engineering practice at all levels – within the firm, the community, nation, the world.

The core idea goes as follows:

> [T]ake exemplary, substantive content of the 'traditional' undergraduate engineering program – the engineering sciences, the laboratory tests, the design projects – and subject this to study from the perspectives of the humanities, arts, and social sciences as well as engineering. The method is to build on the content and form of instruction in today's engineering program but dramatically transform both content and form to achieve the goals of a liberal arts program – 'critical thinking' is the key phrase in this regard – while attending to the fundamentals of the traditional engineering course of study. To do this, 'fundamentals' must necessarily be redefined.
>
> (Bucciarelli and Drew, 2015)

We also put forward, as a second "design requirement," that

> [T]he program's structure, course requirements, and conduct should engender a sense of community among students and among faculty. Students should see the program as their intellectual home.
> (Bucciarelli and Drew, 2015)

The aim is to encourage students to identify as a group, a community, and see themselves as standing apart from their peers who have chosen to major in traditional fields. Those seeking this new form of undergraduate education will be strengthened in their resolve and professional identity formation by participation in a cohort experience. Supplemental instruction programs built around co-operative study groups have dramatically increased success rates in undergraduate STEM fields at institutions as diverse as Harvard, Cal Poly Pomona, and Texas Southern University (see, for example, Bonsangue & Drew, 1995).

Rooted in the liberal arts

> Ruefully – and with some embarrassment at my younger self's condescending attitude toward the humanities – I now wish that I had strived for a proper liberal arts education. That I'd learned how to think critically about the world we live in and how to engage with it. That I'd absorbed lessons about how to identify and interrogate privilege, power structures, structural inequality, and injustice. That I'd had opportunities to debate my peers and develop informed opinions on philosophy and morality. And even more than all of that, I wish I'd even realized that these were worthwhile thoughts to fill my mind with – that all of my engineering work would be contextualized by such subjects
> Chou, 2017

We see a program in *Bachelor of Arts in Liberal Studies in Engineering* as an antidote, a way to engage students in engineering, even entrepreneurship, while rooting learning in specially designed courses in the humanities, arts, and social sciences that stress reflective thought and practice, show the importance of cultural values, listening, reading, and open discussion with peers. Think of the program not as "engineering lite," but as "liberal arts enriched." Think of the program as pre-professional.

The challenge is in how to integrate "exemplary engineering content" in with the teaching/learning of literature, philosophy, history, anthropology, sociology, government, economics ... in a way that contributes to enriching the host course and engenders an understanding and critique of the engineering in context?

Perhaps the best way to illustrate a way forward is to show how three colleges have met the challenge.

At Wellesley College, Amy Bazaert, an instructor responsible for the college's engineering course offerings, and Catia Confortini, Associate Professor of Peace and Justice Studies, collaboratively teach *Intersections of Technology, Social Justice, and Conflict*. The course is jointly listed – ENGR 305/PEAC 305. For students in the Peace and Justice Interdepartmental Major within the School of Liberal Arts, the course is a required, "capstone" course. For these eight (of 14) students, the assigned engineering exercises set the experience apart from their other P&J requirements. The engineering students see it as different from what they are accustomed to doing in Brazaert's other courses; Confortini's assignments press students to think hard about the context of technology.

Three technologies (socio-technical systems) were studied: human-powered water pumps, drones, and cook stoves. The *Liberal Studies in Engineering* online module, *Techno-Anthro Two Pumps*, served as a resource for the water pump segment. Student exercises were evenly split; half were defined by Professor Confortini and asked students to write a paragraph (75–100 words) posing a question prompted by the readings. Half were assigned by Professor Bazaert. These "Tech assignments" were in the form of engineering analysis of the technology, consisting of background reading, mathematical estimation exercises grounded in the fundamental equations of the associated technology, exploration of the design requirements, and processes associated with the technology.

Another example is at Purdue Polytechnic, where Todd Kelley, Professor of Design Thinking at Polytechnic, collaborates with Sherylyn Briller, Professor of Anthropology in the College of Liberal Arts, in teaching a design and project-based course *TECH 22000, Designing Technology for People*. Although the course is housed in Polytechnic, of the 45 students enrolled in the course roughly half of the students are majors in anthropology, with the other half being majors in engineering technology. Both Professors Briller and Kelley are active and teaching in every meeting of the course. The course is structured around a major group project whose purpose is to use ethnographic methods to explore user experiences and develop a new design solution (Briller et al., 2017).

At Smith College, one of the few liberal arts colleges offering an accredited engineering undergraduate major, Professors Susannah Howe, director of the Engineering Design Clinic, Suzanne Gottschang, from Anthropology, and Domminique Thiebaut, from Computer Science, collaborate in "coaching" a team of students in an engineering capstone design course. The course brought students majoring in Anthropology together with students of engineering. The small team was charged with designing a digital version of a screening questionnaire for paediatric toxic stress. In this, they worked closely with the Baystate High Street Health Center. For the students majoring in Anthropology, there exist few opportunities at the undergraduate level to work on a project in the "real world."

These examples illustrate what we see as essential features of a Liberal Studies in Engineering teaching/learning experience.

- The mixing of engineering in with the liberal arts requires the collaboration of faculty from both domains – in planning as well as in teaching. "Turn teaching" will not suffice. That is primary.
- Students too are mixed. Some are intent on studying engineering; others are majors in the liberal arts. In a full Liberal Studies program, we see classes of students with different interests; some may go on to pursue an engineering degree, others may follow different paths (Bucciarelli and Drew, 2015)
- All three courses are specifically required to complete a major – at least for some of the students. They are not simply elective
- All three examples engage students actively. At Wellesley, classroom discussion is the norm, and discussion is prompted by questions students themselves pose (and write out before class). At Purdue Polytechnic and at Smith College, students do projects, in teams

It is notable that, in all three examples, the liberal arts faculty was a Professor of Anthropology. One can see how Anthropology is a good fit with engineering design, with its concern for the vagaries of human use or misuse of a product or system.

Four modules illustrate "infusion"

The *Techno-Anthro Two Pumps*, used as a resource at Wellesley College, engages faculty from the liberal arts (Anthropology) and engineering (Fluid Mechanics) in the analysis of the fate of two, human-powered pumps in sub-Saharan Africa. The reader should not get the idea that Anthropology is the only liberal arts field that can be integrated with engineering in the classroom. The module is but one of four posted online.[1]

Another, *Science and the Courts*, builds upon a recent decision of the US Supreme Court in which a citizen of the State of New Mexico was arrested and charged with driving while intoxicated (DWI) on the basis of evidence obtained from the analysis, via gas chromatography, of a blood sample. The individual, a Mr. Bullcoming, petitioned the Supreme Court, claiming that the way the evidence was presented in a New Mexico court violated the confrontation clause of the Sixth Amendment of the Constitution. The US Supreme Court agreed.

The objective of the module is to move students to reflect on the source of authority in science, the integrity of data obtained via sophisticated instruments, and the qualifications of the individual running the machinery; in addition, they would be asked to consider what is required in making the results of laboratory tests understood and useful in contexts other than that of the laboratory itself – in this case the context of the courts.

Along with study of briefs submitted to the court, the decision itself, and the Sixth Amendment of the US Constitution, *Science and the Courts* would have students doing an experiment using Thin Layer Chromatography (TLC), a cruder method than gas chromatography, but one that, working on the same fundamental principal, provides a way to identify compounds and determine their purity.

Doing the lab exercise, students should gain a sense of how things can go wrong; how doing a laboratory procedure requires fine tuning ingredients to obtain "good data" – all this should be journaled in a lab notebook. Students will learn that to do an experiment, one must know a good bit about the outcome before one starts. The question of "bias" due to an experimentalist's foresight can be introduced at this point. A more general question regarding human error – as contrasted with other sources of error – might also be put on the table.

Contrasting the machinery required to do Thin Layer Chromatography with that deployed in Gas Chromatography can lead to a discussion of how the experimentalist's (and theorist's) knowledge and know-how is captured and resides in the machine itself. Where, then, lies the authority in science (and engineering)? Is it in the "wonderful machine" itself – so a "surrogate's" presentation of the evidence in court is allowed? Or does the authority rely upon the standing of the scientist(s) whose theoretical and craft work framed and inspired the design and production of the machine? What about the lab technician, the licenced operator of the instrument? What does he or she contribute to this picture? What if the actual person, technician, who ran the test, is required, as the US Supreme Court ruled, to present the evidence in court? What must he or she "know" about the workings of the machinery if we are to accept the data as evidence? One author of this piece is licenced to drive an automobile, but would not claim that he could explain the cause of every knock, whine, stall, or reverberation whenever such might occur. The other drove a large truck (about the size of a semi) while a graduate student, but, if engine trouble developed, he was instructed to step aside, as that "was a different union."

A third module, *Galileo and the Resistance of Beams*, is meant for use in a course in the History of Science and/or in an engineering course in Statics and Strength of Materials. Students read the original source (in translation) of Galileo's analysis of conditions for fracture of a cantilever beam subject to a large weight at its free end.

Galileo's model and fundamental result are wrong (according to today's treatment) but his scaling laws were, and are, correct. Students are asked to consider how an engineering theory can be both wrong and right.

An excerpt from a letter of Descartes, what we would call a book review of Galileo's *Dialogue Concerning Two New Sciences*, prompts reflection on the differences in thought and practice of scientists and engineers today. To relieve students' anxiety, the module explains how today's engineers analyse a cantilever beam. Students, in an engineering problem set, are asked to compare Galileo's result with the result found in today's textbook.

The fourth module, *Engineering Narrative, Gender, and a Computer Science Exercise*, is meant for use in a course in Gender and Science and/or a course in Computer Science.

The module's objective is to lead students to reflect on engineering instruction, how it both constrains and enables, limiting one's thinking about the real-world context of an assigned exercise (if there pretends to be one) while providing the student with knowledge of the powerful instrumental ideas and methods used in engineering problem solving. In particular, our interest is in studying the way exercises are stated and addressed in engineering coursework. Part of this is what the engineering student is schooled not to see, to ignore, for this is an indication of values as much as any explicit statement of what is good, what is right, what is just.

To give the reader a sense of the power of the instrumental ideas and methods that take priority in engineering education, we solve a computer science exercise that might be assigned in an introductory CS course. That same exercise provides material and focus for the study of values implicit in an engineering narrative.

For most all of the exercises a student encounters in an engineering science course, their narrative is carefully constructed to lead the student on without revealing too much about how to solve the problem. Most are sparsely written, providing only that information essential to framing a solution. Including excessive information that may lead the student astray is considered bad form. But infrequently, one encounters an exercise whose narrative is more interesting in its own right. The Computer Science exercise we treat is of this nature.

Whatever the form of a narrative clothing the instrumental ingredients of a problem, the student's job is to see through the problem's presentation and draw out the mathematical structure that will enable a solution. This underlying structure is fixed relative to the freedom authors have in constructing a narrative. The end of a chapter in an engineering textbook will include a good number of problems, each a different story, but the logic that applies for doing the exercise is one and the same if one digs deep enough. The power of the scope of applicability of the engineering sciences is displayed in this way.

Narrative, when prevailing unquestioned and apparently needing no articulation (everyone is in on it), can blind ourselves to the possibility that things can be different, that different stories are possible, that presumptions can be called into question. There is a now famous little story about fish that makes the point (Wallace, 2005):

> There are these two young fish swimming along, and they happen to meet an older fish swimming the other way, who nods at them and says, 'Morning, boys, how's the water?' And the two young fish swim on for a bit, and then eventually one of them looks over at the other and goes, 'What the hell is water?'

This module is intended to move students to shift their thinking off its 'default setting'; to become sensitive to the water they swim in – without drowning. Creativity requires this kind of awareness, this kind of openness to a bigger world – the water we all swim in – and that things may be different.

Possible venues, strategies for implementation

A module does not a curriculum make. What then is the *Bachelor of Arts in Liberal Studies in Engineering* curriculum? What are the program's requirements? Where would it be housed? Who are the faculty?

We have been negligent. We have said very little about a curriculum, a set of requirements. We do this because we don't want to foreclose the possibility of innovation in curricula that would fit local constraints (and opportunities). Or – another way of saying this – we believe that the core idea of infusion of engineering in with the liberal arts can be accomplished at a wide range of institutions of higher education. Community colleges, liberal arts colleges, as well as research universities are all possible venues. Development of a program at a liberal arts college would require the participation of engineering faculty recruited from a neighbouring institution or hired directly by the liberal arts college.

Development of a full program would best be done in stages. The end goal is to put in place a sequence of courses, rooted in the humanities, arts, and social sciences, with engineering infused that is open to all students. Some might be seeking to enrol in a program that keeps open the possibility that they might pursue a degree in engineering; others might be recognizing the pervasive influence of technology in changing the ways we work and play and seeking an engineering-enriched program in the liberal arts that might better prepare them for pursuing a professional degree in management, public policy, or even education, law, or medicine.

Because of this dual nature, the "pathway" might be housed in a school of humanities or in a school of engineering. We see the former as the better choice to ensure that the transformation in the students' ways of seeing the world that we propose is achieved.

The required core sequence of liberal arts courses infused would allow ample time aside from this core for students interested in engineering to elect courses that would prepare them for admission to a master's level program in engineering, in computer science, in technology and policy, in management, or the like. For those students whose interests lie elsewhere, they could choose their electives concentrated in a field in the humanities, the arts, or the social sciences in preparation for say medical school or law school.

The core sequence itself would be designed, and courses chosen, to satisfy the university's or college's general education requirements. Both of these possibilities would require extensive negotiation among faculty concerned. The aim is not educational innovation by "adding on" but by transformation of what exists.

Whatever the final form, collaboration among faculty of the liberal arts and of engineering will be required – at least until the program is established and its main goals met as measured by the sense of community evident in program participants (faculty and students) and by its record of attracting students and graduating individuals who value, in retrospect, their choice of a program rooted in the liberal arts as a foundation for their life, and life's work.

Reflections

In the wake of the January 15 workshop, attendees were invited by Gary Downey, editor of the journal *Engineering Studies*, to submit commentary on our proposal to establish a BA in *Liberal Studies in Engineering*. These, together with our lead article *Liberal Studies in Engineering – a Design Plan*, were published together as volume 7, numbers 2 and 3 of the journal (Engineering Studies, 2015).

Several commentators, as did we, found fault with the presumption that preparation for the engineering profession requires but four years of undergraduate study. Karl Pister, Chancellor Emeritus, Univ California (Judson King & Pister, 2015), Professor Emeritus of Chemical and Biomolecular Engineering wrote:

> Recognize up front that the essential confining problem is the fact that engineering in the USA places the professional degree in engineering at the bachelor's level. The present lack of breadth in engineering education is a manifestation of the constraints that come from squeezing everything into a nominally four-year degree. All other major professions place the professional degree at the graduate level and thereby build upon a broad, less-specified undergraduate education.

Likewise, Susan Silbey (2015), Professor of Sociology and Anthropology at MIT, viewed the constraints of the four-year undergraduate degree as the "elephant in the room." She points to features of the four-year degree that move critics to advocate reform.

> [In its embrace of instrumental reasoning], the degree becomes a magnet for those who want education to be an instrumental activity with a clear means-ends relationship – it should pay for itself through immediate lucrative occupation.
>
> The four-year degree encourages tightly packed curricula with limited opportunities for random exploration and inquiry....
>
> Because it is a four-year degree lacking general educational cultivation, engineering is conventionally relegated to lower ranks in prestige hierarchies than law or medicine.

Sharon Jones (2015), then Dean of Engineering & Professor at the University of Portland, writes that an AB pre-professional degree leads her to imagine

> an outcome that allows students to progress through their curriculum, while maintaining their motivation and confidence, and gaining a full range of competencies needed to both frame and solve engineering problems. . . . Imagine their satisfaction when told that a pre-professional AB Engineering degree can be used to either help their success in just about every other career path, but if they decide they like engineering enough, they can practice professionally after completing a one- or two-year graduate degree program intentionally designed for them.

But this "revolution that is needed in engineering education"

> can only happen if there is seamless entry from the AB Engineering degree to professional graduate programs in traditional engineering disciplines.

Throughout the workshop, frequent note was made of the overwhelming emphasis in engineering education on instrumental methods and problem solving skills. How, if Liberal Studies in Engineering aims to move students (and faculty) to pay serious attention to cultural context and to critically reflect on questions of equity, of sustainability, of robustness, security, privacy, bias – to take seriously the competing interests of so-called "stakeholders" – how to manage the tension between the drive to solve the (engineering) problem and the recognition that context matters and sometimes can seem to overwhelm? Peter Kroes, Professor of Philosophy at Delft, the Netherlands, argued that

> any program in Liberal Studies in Engineering (LSE) should first and foremost be based on *intrinsic goals*, which can go hand in hand with *instrumental goals*. In particular, LSE has to critically reflect on the increasing dominance of precisely instrumental thinking in and outside engineering, a kind of thinking that appears to lock us up into an Iron Cage.
>
> (Kroes, 2015).

He goes on to discuss the nature of pedagogical collaboration at Delft University of Technology, which takes the form of co-teaching.

> Co-teaching means that the development of the content and the teaching of these courses is done by staff members from the engineering and philosophy departments. Since engineers and philosophers are jointly responsible for these courses, they have to enter into a dialogue about teaching goals and about how they can be achieved

So, as we concluded in the previous section, collaboration between faculty of engineering and faculty of the liberal arts will be essential in both planning and teaching. We hold that intense collaboration of this kind can go a long way in changing the culture of engineering education. Gary Downey (2015), in a concluding essay to this special issue, says as much:

Perhaps the mutual learning that might result from systematically juxtaposing engineering and the liberal arts could indeed achieve transdisciplinary moves that transport instructors and learners alike beyond existing forms of knowledge and expertise, producing new images and practices of engineering formation that just might travel.

Note

1 For access to the modules, "register" at https://edge.edx.org/courses/MIT/0.123x/Sandbox/about

References

ABET (2016–17) *Criteria for Accrediting Engineering Programs* Url:www.abet.org/accreditation/accreditation-criteria/criteria-for-accrediting-engineering-programs-2016-2017/

Bonsangue M & Drew D (1995) Increasing minority students' success in calculus, *New Directions for Teaching and Learning*, Vol. 1995, No. 61, pp. 23–33

Briller S, Kelley T & Wirtz E (2017) Designing for People, *Anthropology News* Url:www.academia.edu/28605431/Designing_for_People

Bucciarelli L & Drew D (2015) Liberal studies in engineering – a design plan, *Engineering Studies*, Vol. 7, No. 2–3, pp. 103–122, DOI: 10.1080/19378629.2015.1077253

Bucciarelli L, Drew D, Tobia S (2015) *Liberal Studies in Engineering – Workshop Report; Support Was Provided by the NAE*, the Teagle Foundation, by the Dean of Humanities, Arts, and Social Sciences at MIT and by the Dean of the School of Education at Claremont Graduate University

Chou T (2017) *Title of the Piece by from Which the Quote Was Taken, Is Instructive: Leading Silicon Valley Engineer Explains Why Every Tech Worker Needs a Humanities Education* Url:https://qz.com/1016900/tracy-chou-leading-silicon-valley-engineer-explains-why-every-tech-worker-needs-a-humanities-education/

Computing Research Association (2017) *Generation CS: Computer Science Undergraduate Enrollments Surge Since 2006* Url:http://cra.org/data/Generation-CS/

Downey GL (2015) Opening up engineering formation, *Engineering Studies*, Vol. 7, No. 2–3, pp. 217–220, DOI: 10.1080/19378629.2015.1121612

Duderstadt J (2009) *Engineering for a changing world: A roadmap to the future of engineering practice, research, and education*, in Grasso D & Burkin M (Eds.), *Holistic Engineering Education: Beyond Technology*, New York: Springer

Dutta D, Patil L & Porter JB Jr. (2012) Sustaining American competitiveness in the 21st century, in *Lifelong Learning Imperative in Engineering*, NAE, University of Illinois. Url:www.nap.edu/read/13503/chapter/1

Engineering Education Departments and Programs (Graduate) Url:http://engineeringeducationlist.pbworks.com/w/page/27610307/Engineering Education Departments and Programs (Graduate)

Engineering Studies (2015) Vol. 7, No. 2, p. 3 Url:www.tandfonline.com/toc/test20/7/2-3?nav=tocList

Froyd J (2008) *White Paper on Promising Practices in Undergraduate STEM Education*, Texas A&M University, commissioned paper for NAS Board on Science Education STEM Education Workshop, June 30th

Hill C, Corbett C & St. Rose A (2010) *Why So Few? Women in Science, Technology, Engineering, and Mathematics*, Washington: AAUW

Jasanoff S & Kim SH (2015) *Dreamscapes of Modernity-Sociotechnical Imaginaries and the Fabrication of Power*, Chicago: University of Chicago Press

Jones S (2015) The need for intentional graduate pathways for students in liberal studies and engineering pre-professional programs, *Engineering Studies*, Vol. 7, No. 2–3, 214–216, DOI: 10.1080/19378629.2015.1062485

Judson King C & Pister KS (2015) How best to broaden engineering education? *Engineering Studies*, Vol. 7, No. 2–3, pp. 150–152, DOI: 10.1080/19378629.2015.1062489

Kroes P (2015) Critical thinking and liberal studies in engineering, *Engineering Studies*, Vol. 7, No. 2–3, pp. 126–128, DOI: 10.1080/19378629.2015.1062491

Malcom-Pique LE & Malcom SM (2013) Engineering diversity: Fixing the educational system to promote equity, *NAE: The Bridge*, Vol. 43, No. 1, 15 March Url:www.nae.edu/19582/Bridge/69735/69743.aspx

National Academy of Engineering (2004) *The Engineer of 2020: Visions of Engineering in the New Century*. Washington, DC: The National Academies Press, pp. 40–41, DOI: 10.17226/10999

Schuster P, Davol A & Mello J (2006) *Student Competitions The Benefits And Challenges* Paper presented at 2006 Annual Conference & Exposition, Chicago, IL. Url:https://peer.asee.org/1055

Shivani P (2017) *STEM Study Suggests UCSB Humanities are "Soft and Useless"*, Url:https://theblacksheeponline.com/uc-santa-barbara/ucsb-study-suggests-humanities-are-soft-and-useless

Silbey S (2015) The elephant in the room: Constraints and consequences of a four-year undergraduate engineering degree, *Engineering Studies*, DOI: 10.1080/19378629.2015.1062488

Thaler A (2011) *Interdisciplinarities-Students' Perceptions of Interdisciplinary Engineering Education in Europe*, Gender and Interdisciplinary Education for Engineers (GIEE) Conference, Paris, pp. 209–221

Wallace D (2005) who according to *The Guardian*, was 'the most brilliant writer of his generation' began his commencement address to graduates of Kenyon College in May, 2005 with this story Url:www.theguardian.com/books/2008/sep/20/fiction

Wang MT, Eccles JS & Kenny S (2013) Not lack of ability but more choice: Individual and gender: Differences in choice of careers in science, technology, *Engineering, and Mathematics Psychological Science*, Vol. 24, No. 5, pp. 770–775

Summary of Part 4

This final part moves through chapter 10, beyond the cognitive domain (relating to straightforward acquisition of knowledge) into the affective domain (identifying, understanding and addressing how people learn), conative domain (associated with behaviour and mental processes related to goal directed action, volition, striving), and psychomotor domain (relating to learning and physical movement, coordination and motor skills) in order to explore education through the two I's, the twin lenses of *implementation* and *innovation*, in order to help educators to determine more effectively what they are attempting to achieve, and to provide insights into more meaningful approaches to mapping learner progression.

It considers what happens beyond the threshold of human consciousness and challenges the way we educate and, in particular, the way that we assess our students. It proposes that we may inadvertently be contributing to reported declines in creativity and innovation competencies if we continue to consider learning in terms of content delivery, as opposed to learner generated interest and development. If, as suggested by the previous chapters, we are to prepare our students for a world of change, where nothing remains the same for long, knowledge that we 'tell' may be quickly superseded. However, the ability to harvest knowledge in a timely way, that is suited to their context, and can be robustly communicated and defended, will enable students to be independent thinkers, not dependents who rely primarily on recall.

The two I's provide a simple and pragmatic way to engage educators and to lead them towards more insightful ways of working, ones that help to strike a meaningful balance between implementing what is known and innovating to meet future demands.

The next chapter, 11, picks up and expands on the theme of the need for a holistic and interdisciplinary approach to enterprise education and makes the case for enfolding enterprise education into the lives of every university graduate by unfolding enterprise education from the formal curriculum. The primary claim is that enterprise resides within the lives of each individual student and not in the curriculum of learning institutions, and that the challenge for learning institutions is to work with what each student naturally brings to the table.

The chapter reviews the contemporary literature of transformational learning, competency-based learning and enterprise learning and offers a new model of enterprise learning is that is student-based, not institution-based, and concludes by discussing the key changes required for all participants and highlights the need to elevate such planning above other discipline-based norms and planning procedures.

Finally, we are all aware that moments of insight have played a key role in the evolution of technology over the decades, so the final chapter, 12, explores the role played by off-task breaks in triggering the unconscious processing of ideas. By breaking up the working day with low effort routine tasks and breaks, individuals can significantly enhance their creativity. Taking time away from the job becomes the key link in the creativity process. The chapter concludes with a look at managing creativity and innovation through the careful management of off-task breaks during the innovation process.

Part 4

The affective side of education

Chapter 10

Through the lenses of the two I's: implement or innovate?

Andy Penaluna

Purpose

The purpose of this chapter is to present outlines that assist the classification of learning and assessment practices, so that they are pertinent to developing innovators. It discusses the hurdles that educators may face and offers ways to navigate and manage learning that adds clarity of purpose.

Design/methodology/approach

The chapter is based on a staged narrative literature survey including new policies and guidance materials that have been supported by academic inquiry, plus the author's own research.

Findings

Globally, education has been charged with developing effective teaching and learning innovators who can help to produce much needed high-quality learning systems. This assumes that teaching and learning theories and practices can help to determine appropriate learning outcomes to match this need, and at scale. This cannot be achieved using metrics that accurately pre-determine what a learner will achieve, simply because innovation by its very nature should surprise us.

Practical implications

Several practical recommendations are posited in a step by step discourse, however central to the debate is the distinction that needs to be made between goal-focused assessment strategies that can predict outcomes and measure against them, and strategies where the goal emerges as learning progresses, or responds to weakly defined problems that enable flexibility of thought.

Social implications

Innovations in education are often regarded with some suspicion, and concerns arise over changes and what losses may result. The assumption in this chapter is that the goal of raising the quality and scale of learning for innovation in education will positively affect education itself and respond to calls for change.

Originality/value

The originality of the paper is in its systemic approach to a long-standing question: do we want learners to copy experts, or do we wish them to challenge norms and provide new innovations to consider and test? Or do we need both? In exposing the hurdles and through the provision of aligned arguments, this chapter provides stimulus for thought and further enquiry.

Introduction and context

In order to meet the demands of international calls to address perceived skills gaps (Cedefop, 2017; World Economic Forum, 2016), bodies such as the European Commission (2013) are calling for more education and training that supports entrepreneurial learning, growth, and growth mindsets (Dweck, 2007). There is also an assumption that appropriate education can alleviate poverty (Sivakumar & Sarvalingam, 2010). In response, educators are being challenged to enhance their learners' abilities to be creative and innovative, to be able to respond positively to change, and to meet the challenges that the new world of work will bring.

An emerging body of policy and expert guidance literature is emerging that attempts to support this shift (Bacigalupo et al., 2016; QAA, 2018), however practical and empirically proven approaches are rare, with some studies in schooling in the USA suggesting that there is a creativity crisis in education (Kim, 2011), and that there has been a 20% decline in creativity in 20 years.

Viewing education through the twin lenses of implementation and innovation may help educators to determine more effectively what they are attempting to achieve, and may also provide insights into more meaningful approaches to mapping learner progression.

Discussion – where are we now?

Unlike clearly defined goal-focused education that proliferates science and business and management studies and similar educational offerings, we need to think beyond the limitation of testing learners through writing 'about' creativity and innovation, and support strategies that develop the competencies themselves. Assessment models that are reliant primarily on examination strategies can only test students' knowledge, and not their capacity to become innovators themselves.

At the centre of this argument is the premise that creative thinking is dependent on the development of divergent thinking strategies – ways of assisting enlightenment through the production of as many alternative solutions as possible (Gardener, 1982; Gomez, 2007), and not one correct solution that can be told and critiqued/reviewed. This requires 'visioning skills' where learners are required to create "multiple and intangible mental constructions" (Guba & Lincoln, 1994, 110). We must remain cognizant that few of these outcomes can be described as accurate or correct, because as yet they do not exist.

As creativity is the thought and mental construct that precedes innovation, however, its development and progression mapping is emerging as a critical requirement, not least because the development of artificial intelligence and robotic behaviour can easily be replicated when a standard approach, that based on norms as opposed to criteria, is the focal point of reference. Moreover, in a world of consistent change, comparisons with past work may well yield fewer insights into issues of causality that we might wish (Covey, 2000).

Most educational environments predict student outcomes so that they can be assessed with some ease. In its simplest of forms, multiple-choice questionnaires enable tick box responses and automated assessment. Most examinations are evaluated against norms and expectations, with model answers and suggested cannons of thought given to examiners to enable them to gauge how 'correct' the learner's response is.

In some circumstances this is appropriate, because we wish to live in an engineered world where an excellent understanding of robust processes and materials negates risk, for example, understanding material strengths and mathematically developed algorithms that test structures help us to ensure that they will not collapse. When proposing new structures however, should the architect constantly refer to norms and standards, or should they extend their thinking into potential opportunities for different materials, different combinations, or simply different environments into which to place their structures? Robots have already been developed that can match bricklayer skills, and outperform them by up to three times in terms of productivity (SAM, 2017). If we know exactly what to do, robots can be trained to copy it.

To develop this discussion, carefully contrived step-by-step stages in curriculum planning predict and schedule learning sessions for each successive topic, and generally tell the students what they are expected to achieve. In this case the curriculum is effectively content, and content has to be delivered within carefully pre-designed packages that can be evaluated by peers and experts. New course development and evaluation therefore usually occurs some time ahead of the course delivery, and this compounds the predictability aspects of the process because some time has passed and change may have occurred.

Discussion – where could we go next?

To help us to start to consider the alternatives, what are the essential premises that we need to consider? For example, we know that creative solutions surprise, bring new ideas to the table, and are often based on seeing things in different ways. Creative people 'pivot' their ideas (Crilly, 2018); they change and adapt according to the latest circumstances and environments. Moreover, these environments are subject to constant change – often at some considerable pace.

The ability to pivot, though tightly coupled with design, is under researched in the entrepreneurship literature (Shane & Ulrich, 2004), though with the introduction of various 'design thinking' approaches, it is gaining prominence. Once a solution has been found to a problem it can be difficult to disassociate with any new idea or thought. Kuhn (1962) introduced this by stating that the development of accepted facts and theories negated the opportunity to seek out anomalies, which in turn limits the opportunities for new paradigms to develop. For new research to develop, he asserts, an episodic approach that recognizes changes in patterns is required.

This 'flow' of idea generation is explored and discussed in depth by Csikszentmihalyi (1996), and it requires emotional engagement through disengagement with norms and expectations. The newness of the idea that may evolve is the motivation, not its correct nature. This flow of discovery is enjoyable, and various goals emerge; they are not predicted at outset. Synthesis as opposed to analysis is another key construct, as linking disparate knowledge and taking the views of others into account enables the linking and connecting of previously missed insights.

According to scholars such as Linsey et al. (2010) and Jansson and Smith (1991), the ability to change direction or pivot one's thinking is a prerequisite to creative success in uncertain environments, and it is a measurable barrier that can be predicted and accounted for. When exploration is limited by preconceived ideas and norms, it is necessary to develop tactics and approaches that force divergent and alternative thought (Penaluna et al., 2014). According to Sarri et al. (2010), creativity and innovation learning is an imperative, and is well understood by entrepreneurs once the premise is explained.

However, Simonton (1999) estimated it takes around ten years to learn the skills needed to achieve the kinds of abilities required, and research into brain functionality informs us that there is a physical dimension to this learning. The 'plasticity' of the brain and its growth is dependent on the learning experience, and much of the experience of learning to be creative takes place under the radar of conscious thought (Dijksterhuis & Meurs 2006).

Thinking deeper and deeper or thinking wider and wider?

There is another dimension to consider. As education develops the learner's abilities, their knowledge becomes more silo-based. We choose topics for school exams, choose subjects to study at university, and by the time we reach a PhD a contribution to knowledge may be well argued and methodologically sound, but extremely small and focused. This is acknowledged to be problematic when it comes to learning as an innovator where breadth not depth of thinking is required (Serdyukov, 2017). Schumpeter (1934) tells us that new mental connections and new associations of thought sit behind innovation and its development. Termed 'aha moments' within cognitive neuroscience research (Kounios & Jung-Beeman, 2009), these are thoughts that come to mind when relaxed. They typically manifest themselves as new ideas that suddenly occur in the mind, often solving problems in a momentary flash of inspiration. This requires breadth as well as depth of thinking, and recognizing subconscious thinking that is brought to consciousness through reflective practice is one way of achieving this. The type of insight that is needed to be innovative requires the ability to see things in different ways, and the preparatory brain state influences the type of thinking needed; it is "characterized by remote associations amongst problem elements" (Kounios et al., 2006, 889).

However as Dane (2010) explains, cognitive enrichment through deeper knowledge and understanding of the norm has a tendency to develop fixedness, which has to be traded off within task environments that circumnavigate previously fixed 'knowns.' In short, the more you know about a topic, the less you see alternatives that enable flexible thought and holistically derived alternatives, and unless a challenge is posited, you are unlikely to change your view.

Thus the notion of challenge to fixedness is introduced, and this could potentially be the primary role of the innovation educator, as we will discuss now.

The role of the educator, guide-on-the-side, meddler-in-the middle, or simply sage-on-the-stage?

Driven by her desire to develop what is becoming known as second-generation creativity, McWilliam (2009) asks about the role of the educator in terms of the challenges that they present to learners. The sage-on-the-stage is your delivery of knowledge teacher; they know all the answers and the learner, in their eyes, will always be dependent upon their wisdom. In contrast, the guide-on-the-side suggests a passive mode, where the teacher only interjects if required to do so. Thus, she introduces the meddler-in-the-middle, the teacher who teaches through interventionist questioning and continually challenges. They encourage rigorous thinking and ensure relevance remains a central construct, so that the learners know and understand the context(s) within which they are being challenged. This requires the setting of 'Wicked Problems' (Head & Alford, 2015), where no exact solution is known, and there is potential for a number of alternative proposals.

Command and control is not the ethos of these educators, nor is their intervention passive or laissez faire. They are active and energetic, demonstrate thoughtfulness themselves, and are frequently prepared to be proven wrong by their learners. They see this as progress as they learn too. This aligns with what we understand about the nature of wishing to be understood through empathy, and has much to do with 'mirror neurones' in our brain; the mechanism by which we ensure that we copy others in order to fit in, which is not dissimilar to being tribal in nature (Ferrari & Rizzolatti, 2014).

The term 'role model' sits well here, as it considers two theoretical aspects: the way that people identify with other people that they connect with within social roles, and the matching of psychological and cognitive skills that lead to imitation that is evidenced through patterns of behaviour. The potential of role models to have an impact can be extended to whether or not an educator has the ability to practice what they preach, in order to have an indirect impact on the learner. This in turn places emphasis on the educator (Lindquist et al., 2012), who within experiments in visioning and memory, supports the research from educators Blakemore and Frith (2005) who assert that the brain mirrors what it sees. Hence according to this argument, a proactive and engaging educator will be more effective than a passive educator who either simply delivers content, or passively sits by when learning is taking place. They are the meddler-in-the-middle.

Tell, conspire, or support: the contrasting roles of pedagogy, andragogy, and heutagogy

As we have discussed, many educational establishments consider learning in terms of content delivery, as opposed to learner-generated interest and development. A curriculum is planned some time in advance, and success measures reflect clear alignment with the planned lessons and procedures. In this kind of learning environment, content is key and nothing should be missed out if at all possible, as it may conflict with later planned sessions. The learner is primarily a passive recipient of the expert's knowledge, which is told to them.

However, predetermining what the learning outcomes will be and filling all the perceived gaps on behalf of the learner presents us with a problem; it instils a reliance on the system as it does not empower the student to develop their own learning independently. This setting of tasks that develop the learner is the responsibility of the educational institution, which will align the pedagogy with pragmatic considerations such as timetables and staff expertise. Neither must we forget that as a term, pedagogy describes the art and science of teaching children, and is based on the Greek meanings for 'child' and 'leader of' (Knowles et al., 2015), so the question arises, as we are dealing with adult learners: should this suffice?

Andragogy was introduced by Knowles (1968) as a means to take into account the perspectives of adult learners, who have different motivations and bring their experiences and knowledge to learning environments. It takes into account that maturity brings a different orientation to learning and that motivation to learn is typically aligned to issues of relevance and personal goals. In practice this means the educator and learner will harvest and share knowledge in what might be considered to be a team effort. The educator is the team leader and the learner a team player. Together new knowledge emerges through this partnership of minds, and through joint experiences and shared understandings.

Importantly, in these types of approaches there is a degree of self-determination on the part of the learner. Self Determination Theory (Ryan & Deci, 2000) suggests that increased motivation is the result of self-negotiated learning journeys. The central pillars of the theory require some level of pre-existing competence, a degree of autonomy, and relatedness to the topic or subject being studied. Competence derives from positive experiences on meeting challenges, and autonomy links these successes to opportunities, especially when choices have been offered to the learner (Rigby et al., 1992).

In empirical works, Ratelle et al. (2007) studied formal Self-Directed Learning in teenagers, evidencing that learners who were given more autonomy became more dedicated to learning. Similar studies looking into the role of parents as leaders of learning came to similar conclusions, suggesting that their aspirations for growth, enhanced networking and relationships, and engagement in societal problem solving were significantly strengthened (Williams et al., 2000).

Creating choices for learners can be developed through challenges such as wicked problems (Rittel & Webber, 1973), where no known solution exists, and nothing is ever 'correct.' However, multiple solutions can be found discussed and selected from a range of ideas. Solutions are based on context and timing, and what is right today may not be right tomorrow. Complex problems can vary in their wickedness (Alford & Head, 2017), and the most successful may be difficult to explain, as they bring new ideas and new insights that need to be carefully explained to make sense. Often the success can be seen in the iterative responses and not the final outcome (Head, 2010). In these scenarios, learning can be co-created and learner and educator co-conspire to find solutions to problems that neither may have pre-conceived.

Jones et al. (2014) draw these strands together and suggest a next step, that of the third approach, in a set entitled Academogy (Jones & Penaluna, 2018). Heutagogy (Kenyon & Hase, 2010) looks at nature's way of learning, and whilst this does not exclude the educator, it repositions them as mentor and supporter, to someone who is already a self-directed learner. Heutagogy signifies mature adult learning, which leads to self-efficacy and almost total independence. The learner is helped to both learn and unlearn (Smith, 2015); they become creative in situations where knowledge is incomplete and environments may be unfamiliar. In short, they continuously learn to learn, can discard previous learning when it is no longer helpful and develop personal insights into what needs to be learned next. The teacher's role is that of supporter and mentor, whose experience helps to guide the process forward, but not decide its ultimate goals or approaches.

Mind matters

Given the role played by the unconscious in creative thought, one clearly cannot manage the direction of insights and thought patterns that emerge. However, one can shape the overall creative process, through the careful management of interruptions and breaks. Therefore, walking away from the job is no longer seen as unproductive, but a key element in the creative process. This involves educating educators and managers.

(Breslin, 2016)

Unconscious thought is often disregarded in educational contexts, as it is difficult to rationalize, predict, or evidence. However, according to cognitive neurologists (Jung Beeman, 2005; Kounios et al., 2006) this is where creative thoughts develop, and only come into consciousness once in a relaxed state of mind where psychomotor activities enable the brain to bring their new ideas to conscious thought (Kounios et al., 2006). Breslin (2016) talks of 'off-task activities' that relates to this mind state. It aligns with Csikszentmihalyi's (1996) discussions on the flow of creative thoughts and, above all else, highlights that tension and stress result in less creative outputs. In practical terms, an examination context would most likely inhibit new idea generation.

Reflection is often cited as a means of drawing out such thinking, but relies on a comprehensive understanding of memory types and the neural linkages that can be made. Whereas those familiar with analytical approaches to learning expect learning to evolve predominantly from analysis, insightful thinkers either come up with an idea spontaneously or wait until later for it to emerge. Experiments by Salvi et al. (2016) support this, and perhaps surprisingly offer a new perspective, one that suggests that quick insightful (gut) answers are often more correct than those that have been laboured over analytically. The question remains, however: how do educators encourage reflection that draws out unconscious thought?

First of all, we have considered recognized types of memory and how they interact (see Figure 10.1).

We work with memory in many ways, but sensory memory where we become aware of context change is fleeting, as is working memory. Much of education aims to develop long-term memory, though research suggests that surprisingly little is actually recalled unless used in context and emotionally charged in some way. Known as 'sticky learning' (Inglis et al., 2014), this is what most educationalists seek to encourage – memory that lasts. Promoted neurologically through the differing types of explicit memory, memories are the type that we can recall and recollect with relative ease, traditionally the territory of examinations and tests.

Synthesis, however, is where creative thought originates, and bringing together memories can provide successful routes to questioning the mind itself. By systematically encouraging thought through questions, educators can assist the drawing out of previous unconscious thoughts such as implicit and procedural memory. Here, part of our discussion reminds us of our meddler-in-the-middle teacher, who has learned to develop curious thinkers through their questioning technique.

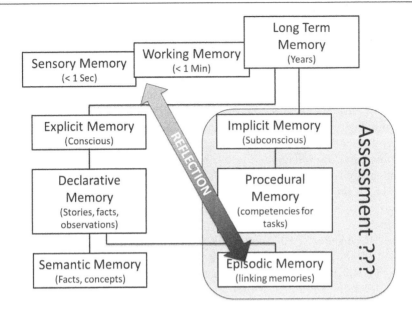

Figure 10.1 Memory types and their relationship to evaluative reflection.
Source: author's own work

Based on the premise that curiosity prepares the brain for learning and that topics that intrigue us are more likely to be remembered (Gruber et al., 2014), the dopamine circuit in our brains encourages us to learn when intrigued. This has been evidenced in experiments such as Romeo et al. (2018), whose work on conversational exposure explores two-way dialogues and their impact on learning when compared to single way dialogues – as experienced in lectures.

This debate can be summarized when we consider our synapses, the minute junctions between our brains that, when linked, transmit signals across the brain. These consolidate memory when they receive rewards that make us feel good (Domenico & Ryan, 2017). They can operate in two ways. The first is known as synaptic efficiency, which is when through regular use mental connections are reinforced. Repetition is the key and as any UK citizen knows when attempting to cross a road in Europe, it can lead to blind 'non thinking' procedural memories, as we cannot help but look the wrong way.

Conversely, Synaptic Plasticity relates to flexibility of thought, newness, and novelty development and relies on empathy and holistic, not detailed and focused perspectives. Plasticity is what enables us to adapt and develop our brain for changing circumstances, and is widely understood to relate to creativity (El-Gaby et al., 2015; Penaluna et al., 2011).

From complexity to pragmatism, introducing the two I's model

The idea of the two I's approach originated during a European Commission debate on education and training, where 'neutral introductory speakers' were charged with stimulating debate and, through their questioning of delegates, push new ideas to the fore (European Education and Youth Forum, 2014). The complexity of the debates discussed here formed much of the discussion, and the aim emerged to attempt a simple construct that could guide teachers and educators towards understanding when they were either supporting or killing creativity through their teaching. Later research would suggest this to be timely, as the challenges of learning to be creative not only had an impact on learners, as evidenced by Kim (2011), but also reflected the confidence of teachers.

The OECD uses "7+3" framework for innovative learning environments (OECD, 2017) reported through their Teaching and Learning International Survey (TALIS) that only 25% of teachers thought that their innovation is valued, let alone rewarded. Moreover, they also reported that leadership in the area takes creativity and often courage to implement (OECD, 2014). The European Commission's MEP Michaela Šojdrova (2017) picks up the commentary and noted that according to the 'Switch On Europe' report, three out of four European teachers do not feel encouraged to bring innovation into the classroom.

Thus the notions of pivoting one's thinking to change direction, encouraging breadth and not just depth of thinking, came to the fore. The teachers' roles in raising curiosity through sequentially questioning learners' responses in an engaged way, as opposed to simply telling or talking about a topic, had to be rationalized and revisited, so as to be useful to those who were either managing education, or for those charged with delivering it in a more confident manner.

Initial testing took place at a joint EU and OECD workshop consisting of 27 country representatives in Potsdam in 2015, and was subsequently published by the OECD as part of policy-making and practitioner guidance (Penaluna & Penaluna, 2015).

Through the alternative lenses of the two I's, educators are asked if within a given project or task, they want students to implement what is known, or innovate to find new solutions. They are directed to consider if they wish to evaluate through a normative process or a criterion referenced approach and how that might impact the learning, so as to ensure that it is constructively aligned, to ensure that the assessment matches the learning task requirements (Biggs, 2003).

To illustrate this pragmatic approach, examples of potential learning outcomes in the two I's model are provided in Table 10.1.

By throwing the focus on assessment strategies, the educator has to carefully consider the type and nature of learning activity that will promote the required outcome. Thus a virtuous circle is established.

Table 10.1 Two I's model

Implementation: Doing things that are determined by others and matching against their expectations. Can the student come up with a good idea that fits the problem?	Innovation: Producing multiple and varied solutions that respond to change and often surprise. Can the student come up with multiple ideas that respond to changing circumstances and see the problems that led to the problem?
Does the student's solution match the expectation of the test or examiner?	Does the solution surprise through new insights and alternative answers?
Can the solution be easily compared and contrasted to previous work and understandings?	Does the solution offer new insights and potentially challenge accepted understandings? Make links that were not made before?
Can the student write and follow a detailed business plan?	Can the student respond positively to short term and ever-changing venture environments? (Any business plan is temporary.)

Summary and conclusions

We have considered what happens beyond the threshold of human consciousness, it has challenged the way we educate and, in particular, the way that we assess our students. If we continue to consider learning in terms of content delivery, as opposed to learner-generated interest and development, it proposes that we may be contributing to reported declines in creativity and innovation competencies.

If we are to prepare our students for a world of change, where nothing remains the same for long, knowledge that we 'tell' may be quickly superseded. However, the ability to harvest knowledge in a timely way, that is suited to their context, and can be robustly communicated and defended, will enable students to be independent thinkers, not dependents who rely primarily on recall.

The two I's provide a simple and pragmatic way to engage educators and to lead them towards more insightful ways of working, ones that help to strike a meaningful balance between implementing what is known and innovating to meet future demands.

Ultimately, the aim has been to make the assumed and invisible visible, so that thoughtful educators can decide on appropriate strategies that match their own students' learning needs.

References

Alford J & Head B (2017) Wicked and less wicked problems: A typology and a contingency framework, *Policy and Society*, Vol. 36, No. 3, pp. 397–413

Bacigalupo M, Kampylis P, Punie Y & Van den Brande G (2016) *EntreComp: The Entrepreneurship Competence Framework*. Seville: European Joint Research Centre

Biggs J (2003) *Aligning Teaching for Constructing Learning*, Paper prepared for the UK Higher Education Academy, Url:www.heacademy.ac.uk/system/files/resources/id477_aligning_teaching_for_constructing_learning.pdf
Blakemore SJ and Frith U (2005) *The Learning Brain: Lessons for Education*, Malden, Oxford and Victoria, Australia: Blackwell Publishing
Breslin D (2016) Enhancing and Managing Group Creativity Through Off – Task Breaks, in Kapranos P (Ed.), *Proceedings of the 6th International Symposium for Engineering Education* (pp. 77–84), July 14–15th
Cedefop (2017) *Skill mismatch: The European experience, European Skills and Jobs Survey Presentation*, International Labour Office, Geneva May 11–12th Url:www.ilo.org/wcmsp5/groups/public/ – ed_emp/ – ifp_skills/documents/presentation/wcms_554337.pdf
Covey SR (2000) *The Brave New Workplace: Strategies to Excel in a World of Change*, Presentation during the Sixth Annual Worldwide Lessons in Leadership Series, 15 November. Niagara College, Niagara Falls, Canada.
Crilly N (2018) 'Fixation' and 'the Pivot': Balancing persistence with flexibility in design and entrepreneurship, *International Journal of Design Creativity and Innovation*, Vol. 6, No. 1–2, pp. 52–65
Csikszentmihalyi M (1996) *Creativity: Flow and the Psychology of Discovery and Invention*, New York: Harper Perennial.
Dane E (2010) Reconsidering the trade-off between expertise and flexibility: A cognitive entrenchment perspective, *Academy of Management Review*, Vol. 35, pp. 579–603
Dijksterhuis A and Meurs T (2006) Where creativity resides: The generative power of unconscious thought, *Consciousness and Cognition*, Vol. 15, No. 1, pp. 135–146
Domenico SI & Ryan RM (2017) The emerging neuroscience of intrinsic motivation: A new frontier in self-determination research, *Frontiers in Human Neuroscience*, Vol. 11, Article 145
Dweck C (2007) *Mindset: The New Psychology of Success*, New York: Ballantine Books
El-Gaby M, Shipton OA & Paulsen O (2015) Synaptic plasticity and memory: New insights from hippocampal left – right asymmetries, *The Neuroscientist*, Vol. 12, No. 5, pp. 490–502
European Commission (2013) *Entrepreneurship Action Plan: Reigniting the Entrepreneurial Spirit in Europe*, Brussels: European Commission; Luxembourg: Publications Office of the European Union
European Education and Youth Forum (2014) Future priorities of the ET 2020 Strategic Framework for European Cooperation in *Education and Training and Synergies with Youth Policy*, Brussels: European Commission Education and Training; Luxembourg: Publications Office of the European Union
Ferrari PF & Rizzolatti G (2014) Mirror neuron research: The past and the future, *Philosophical Transactions of the Royal Society B: Biological Sciences*, Vol. 369, No. 1644
Gardner, H. (1982). *Art, Mind and Brain. A Cognitive Approach to Creativity*, New York: Basic Books
Gomez JG, What Do We Know About Creativity? *The Journal of Effective Teaching*, Vol. 7, No. 1, pp. 31–43
Gruber JM, Gelman BD & Ranganath C (2014) States of curiosity modulate hippocampus-dependent learning via the dopaminergic circuit, *Neuron*, Vol. 84, No. 2, pp. 486–496
Guba, E. G., & Lincoln, Y. S. (1994). Competing paradigms in qualitative research. in Denzin NK & Lincoln YS (Eds.), *Handbook of Qualitative Research*, 2, 163–194, London: Sage
Head BW & Alford J (2015) Wicked problems: Implications for public policy and management, *Administration and Society*, Vol. 47

Inglis H, Dawson KL & Nishioka RY (2014) *Sticky Learning: How Neuroscience Supports Tteaching That's Remembered*, Minneapolis: Fortress Press

Jansson DG & Smith SM (1991) Design fixation, *Design Studies*, Vol. 12, No. 1, pp. 3–11

Jones C, Mataly H, Penaluna K & Penaluna A (2014) Claiming the future of enterprise education, *Education + Training*, Vol. 56, No. 8/9, pp. 764–775

Jones C, Penaluna A & Penaluna K (2018) *Entrepreneurship Education: Classification, Reasoning, Outcomes, Ways and Networks*, Proceedings of the 2018 ACERE Conference, held in Brisbane, Australia 6 to 9 February

Jung-Beeman M (2005) Bilateral brain processes for comprehending natural language, *Trends in Cognitive Science*, Vol. 9, No. 11, pp. 512–518

Kenyon, C & Hase, S. (2010) Andragogy and heutagogy in postgraduate work, in T Kerry (Ed.), *Meeting the Challenges of Change in Postgraduate Higher Education*, London: Continuum Press

Kim KH (2011) The creativity crisis: The decrease in creative thinking score on the torrance tests for creative thinking, *Creativity Research Journal*, Vol. 23, No. 4, pp. 285–295

Kounios J, Frymiare JL, Bowden EM, Fleck I, Subramaniam K, Parish YB & Jung-Beeman M (2006) The prepared mind: Neural activity prior to problem presentation predicts subsequent solution by sudden insight, *Psychological Science*, Vol. 17, No. 10, pp. 882–890

Kounios J & Jung-Beeman M (2009) The Aha! moment: The cognitive neuroscience of insight, *Current Directions in Psychological Science*, Vol 18, No. 4, pp. 210–216

Knowles MS (1968) Andragogy not pedagogy, *Adult Leadership*, Vol. 16, No. 10, pp. 350–352

Knowles MS, Holton III EF & Swanson RA (2015) *The Adult Learner: The Definitive Classic in Adult Education and Human Resource Development*, 8th Edition. New York: Routledge

Kuhn TS (1962) *The Structure of Scientific Revolutions*, Chicago, IL: University of Chicago Press

Lindquist KA, Wager TD, Kober H, Bliss-Moreau E, & Barrett LF (2012) The brain basis of emotion: a meta-analytic review. *Behavioral Brain Sciences*, Vol. 35, No. 3, pp. 121–143

Linsey JS, Tseng I, Fu K, Cagan J, Wood KL & Schunn C (2010) A study of design fixation, its mitigation and perception in engineering design faculty, *Journal of Mechanical Design*, Vol. 132, p. 041003

McWilliam EL (2009) Teaching for creativity: From sage to guide to meddler, *Asia Pacific Journal of Education*, Vol. 29, No. 3. pp. 281–293

OECD (2014) *Innovative Learning Environments: The Importance of Innovating Learning* Url:www.oecd.org/education/ceri/ILE_Brochure.pdf

OECD (2017) The OECD "7+3" framework for innovative learning environments, in *The OECD Handbook for Innovative Learning Environments*, Paris: OECD Publishing

Penaluna A, Coates J & Penaluna K (2011) Creativity-based assessment and neural understandings: A discussion and case study analysis, *Education + Training, Emerald Publishing*, Vol. 52, No. 8/9, pp. 660–678

Penaluna A & Penaluna K (2015) *Entrepreneurial Education in Practice, Part, 2 – Building Motivations and Competencies*, Entrepreneurship 360 Thematic Paper, Paris: Organisation for Economic Co-operation and Development (OECD) and the European Commission (DG Education and Culture).

Penaluna K, Penaluna A, Jones C & Matlay H (2014) When did you last predict a good idea? Exploring the case of assessing creativity through learning outcomes, *Industry and Higher Education*, Vol. 28, No. 6, pp. 1–12

QAA (2018c) *Enterprise and Entrepreneurship Education: Guidance for UK Higher Education Providers*. Gloucester: The Quality Assurance Agency for Higher Education

Ratelle C, Guay F, Vallerand R, Larose S & Senécal C (2007) Autonomous, controlled, and amotivated types of academic motivation: A person-oriented analysis, *Journal of Educational Psychology*, Vol. 99, pp. 734–746

Rigby CS, Deci E, Patrick BC & Ryan R (1992) Beyond the intrinsic-extrinsic dichotomy: Self determination in motivation and learning, *Motivation and Emotion*, Vol. 16, pp. 165–185

Rittel HWJ & Webber MM (1973) Dilemmas in a general theory of planning, *Policy Sciences*, Vol. 4, No. 2, pp. 155–169

Romeo RR, Leonard JA, Robinson ST, West MR, Mackey AP, Rowe ML & Gabrieli, JDE (2018) Beyond the "30 million word gap": Children's conversational exposure is associated with language related brain function, *Psychological Science*, Vol. 29, No. 5, pp. 700–710

Ryan R & Deci EL (2000) Self-determination theory and the facilitation of intrinsic motivation, social development, and well-being, *American Psychologist*, Vol. 55, pp. 68–78

SAM (2017) *Semi Automated Mason: This Bricklaying Robot Can Build Walls Faster Than Humans*, Url:www.youtube.com/watch?v=2-VR4IcDhX0

Salvi C, Bricolo E, Kounios J, Bowden E & Jung Beeman M (2016) Insight solutions are correct more often than analytic solutions, *Thinking and Reasoning*, Vol, 22, No. 4, pp. 443–460

Sarri K, Bakouros I & Petridou E (2010) Entrepreneur training for creativity and innovation, *Journal of European Industrial Training*, Vol. 34, No. 3, pp. 270–288

Schumpeter JA (1934) The theory of economic development: An inquiry into profits capital credit, interest and the business cycle, *Harvard Economic Studies*, Vol. 46

Serdyukov P (2017) Innovation in education: What works, what doesn't, and what to do about it? *Journal of Research into Innovative Teaching and Learning*, Vol. 10, No. 1, pp. 4–33 https://doi.org/10.1108/JRIT-10-2016-0007

Shane SA & Ulrich KT (2004) 50th anniversary article: Technological innovation, product development, and entrepreneurship in management science, *Management Science*, Vol. 50, pp. 133–144

Simonton, D. K. (1999), *Origins of Genius, Darwinian Perspectives on Creativity*, New York: Oxford University Press

Sivakumar M & Sarvalingam A (2010) *Human Deprivation Index: A Measure of Multidimensional Poverty*, Munich Personal RePEc Archive. Url:https://mpra.ub.uni-muenchen.de/22337/1/MPRA_paper_22337.pdf

Smith C (2015) The art of unlearning, *Harvard Educational Review* (Fall), Vol. 85, No. 3, pp. 413–414

Šojdrova M (2017) *Entrepreneurship Education: Unused Potential so Far*, Url:www.euractiv.com/section/economy-jobs/opinion/entrepreneurship-education-unused-potential-so-far

Williams GC, Hedberg VA, Cox EM & Deci EL (2000) Extrinsic life goals and health risk behaviors in adolescents, *Journal of Applied Social Psychology*, Vol. 30, pp. 1756–1771

World Economic Forum (2016) *The Future of Jobs: Employment, Skills and Workforce Strategy for the Fourth Industrial Revolution*, Global Challenge Insight Report. Url:http://www3.weforum.org/docs/WEF_Future_of_Jobs.pdf

Chapter 11

Enterprise education

Outside classrooms, inside students' hearts

Colin Jones

Introduction

The world of work for university graduates has never been more challenging; gone are the long nurturing careers that offered a ladder of gradual opportunity. Now, students must present themselves to a world of work already sufficiently developed so that their potential value-creating abilities can be seen from day one on the job. This suggests that the role of educating professionals, such as engineering, medical, or law graduates, needs to change in order to prepare students for this increasingly complex world. This chapter contemplates the nature of such change, positing a holistic approach that combines existing approaches to engineering and enterprise education. The aim being, to outline a dynamic foundation for graduate learning that supports preparing graduates for the challenges of tomorrow's unknown.

Engineering education is often described as being highly experiential in nature (Gadola & Chindamo, 2017) and specifically based upon developing a capacity for decision-making (Killen, 2015). Although cast from different elements, enterprise education is also based on experiential learning, focused on student development and geared towards exploration of the unknown (QAA, 2018). Both domains of education share an interest in developing the minds, hearts, and hands of students' (Shulman, 2005), vis-à-vis their capacity to operate successfully in complex and ever-changing environments. Both forms of education have for many years also been mindful of developing students to understand and exploit technological innovation (Steiner, 1998). Therefore, an opportunity exists presently to contemplate a greater integration of enterprise education into engineering education, as is occurring in other domains of education.

At this point in time, it is important to be clear what enterprise education equates to in the context of this chapter. Following the lead of QAA (2018, p. 7), enterprise education is defined as

> the generation and application of ideas, which are set within practical situations during a project or undertaking. This is a generic concept that can be

applied across all areas of education and professional life. It combines creativity, originality, initiative, idea generation, design thinking, adaptability and reflexivity with problem identification, problem solving, innovation, expression, communication and practical action.

Alternatively, entrepreneurship education is defined as "the application of enterprise behaviours, attributes and competencies into the creation of cultural, social or economic value. This can, but does not exclusively, lead to venture creation." So, the focus is not on directly supporting engineering graduates to commercialize their ideas, but rather upon initially aiding their development as graduates capable of operating successfully in complex and ever-changing environments. The remainder of the chapter is structured as follows. First, the notion of enterprising engineering graduates is contemplated. Following this, the notion of contemporary enterprise is considered. Then, the possibility of a signature pedagogy for enterprise education is discussed. This is followed by consideration of the opportunities to integrate aspects of enterprise education within engineering education, and the tools that could be used to facilitate such a process. The chapter concludes by drawing attention to the importance of scholarship of teaching and learning as a guiding shadow throughout this process.

Enterprising engineering graduates

It is quite reasonable to expect that engineering graduates would be quite enterprising. While this may be true in some programmes, the recent research of Male et al. (2010) suggests that, in addition to competency deficiencies related to practical engineering, there are also deficiencies related to business competencies, self-management, communication skills, problem solving, and teamwork – the direct focus of enterprise education. The recent work of Lucas et al. (2014) provides excellent insight into the developing scholarship of teaching and learning in the domain of engineering education. In drawing upon the idea of a signature pedagogy (Shulman, 2005) for engineering, they highlight the value of developing certain habits of mind. While admirable, it could be argued that this focus falls short of what would be required to develop truly enterprising engineering graduates, as we will discuss below.

The idea of an engineer's habits of mind (Lucas et al., 2014) is based on a logical desire that engineering graduates should be able to think and act like engineers. Attention is directed to attributes like curiosity, open-mindedness, resilience, resourcefulness, collaboration, reflection, and ethical consideration in the hope that they will underpin the learning required to make things that work, using problem solving, visualizing, systems thinking, and other adaptive processes. Implicitly, a clear focus on the developmental pathway of each student is advocated in this approach. However, what is missing is an explicit call for deep reflection through which to support such transformative learning

(Mezirow, 1978). However, the enterprise education literature increasingly addresses both issues, with personal development via deep reflection very much the status quo.

The work of Jones (2007; 2011) highlights calls for a type of graduate, a reasonable adventurer, capable of creating opportunities for satisfaction in all aspects of their life. Resurrecting the original ideas of Heath (1964), the reasonable adventurer is built around six specific attributes: 1) *intellectectuality*; 2) *close friendships*; 3) *independence in value judgements*; 4) *a tolerance of ambiguity*; 5) *a breadth of interest*; and 6) *a sense of humour*. These six attributes map easily onto notions of a desirable type of engineering graduate as well. In both approaches, assumptions are made that the students' repertoires of habits, while relatively stable, are plastic enough to be altered through engagement with frequent learning experiences, followed by personal reflection. Thus, we are concerned with the students' habits of mind that can be modified through interaction with all other elements of the learning environment. Here, the process of reflection, often overlooked, or taken for granted, is pivotal to the development of the student. We can demonstrate this by considering the idea of a signature pedagogy for enterprise education.

Contemplating enterprise education

Shulman (2005) notes that pedagogy is not merely teaching methods, the curriculum, or the individual process of design and/or assessment; it is the unique combinations of their usage in ways that are distinctive to a particular domain of education. In the context of enterprise education, there is a solid agreement (Gibb, 2002; Jones, 2011; Pittaway & Edwards, 2012; Neck & Corbett, 2018; QAA, 2018) that students of enterprise and entrepreneurship should learn *about*, *for*, and *through* enterprise/entrepreneurship. Not surprisingly, the domain has developed a wide variety of experiential education processes (Cooper et al., 2004) to support student learning. These three underlying approaches provide a silhouette of a signature pedagogy that is transformative in nature and also viewed as an

> activist pedagogy combining the elements of constructivist and critical pedagogy that empowers students to examine critically their beliefs, values, and knowledge with the goal of developing a reflective knowledge base, an appreciation for multiple perspectives, and a sense of critical consciousness and agency.
>
> (Ukpokodu, 2009)

Shulman (2005) warns against the development of a signature pedagogy that is compromised, insisting that a balance across its fundamental dimensions of practice (i.e. habits of heart, mind, and hands) must be achieved. Here is an identifiable contribution that enterprise education can make to engineering education. Adding additional focus onto the habits of heart of the engineering student supports the transformative development of the habits of hearts and hands. We cannot assume that learning will occur through an objective process; we must enable the subjective to also participate, equally. This will most likely represent a challenge to the average student, for it entails greater discomfort than the mere confusion of being temporarily lost between lessons. The work of Daryl Sharp provides many useful insights here.

> The development of personality from germ-state to full consciousness is a curse as well as a gift. That's because its first fruit is the segregation of the individual from the undifferentiated herd. That means isolation, and there is no more comforting word for it.
>
> (Sharp, 1995, p. 48)

The process of reflection required to support the development of desirable attributes in our graduates demands more of both educators and students than either is typically will to give. This is what makes enterprise education potentially so useful, and so difficult to domesticate. The challenge remains to provide a consistent focus on the underlying generative mechanisms (Bennett & George, 2003) and the conditions (Tsoukas, 1989) through which a student's habits of heart, mind, and hands can be developed for enterprising behaviour, whilst at the same time respecting the individual student learner. This requires that learning not be only measured against assumed standards, but also each student's comprehension of their own learning journey.

Introducing enterprise education into engineering education therefore provides students with additional opportunities to transcend concepts and ideas through personal experience (Hart, 2001). Doing so also requires that the educator steps back from doing things for their students. As Lindeman (1926, p. 48) noted, the "teacher who does things for others which they might have accomplished for themselves thereby weakens the capacity and worth of citizens, workers and students." An increasing feature of enterprise education is to "beg individuals to give us their difference, not their sameness. Nothing exciting can happen in a world of uniformities and homogeneities" (ibid, p. 53). This perhaps creates a contrast to engineering education, nevertheless, "we need, then, to be educated for self-expression because individuality is the most precious gift we have to bring to the world – and further, because the personal self can never be adequately represented by proxy. Personality becomes dynamic in terms of intelligent self-expression" (ibid, p. 57). For enterprise education, transformative learning is more than changing one's meaning perspective, it is the development of personality through altering one's habits of heart, mind, and hands in the pursuit of freedom from those factors that inhibit or frustrate; its natural outcome is an increased capacity for self-negotiated action. "We live in freedom when we are conscious of a degree of self-direction proportionate to our capacities" (ibid, p. 79). Given the recent trend towards hiring graduates with a strong interest in, and capacity to utilize, their underlying personalities, it can be argued that this intense focus on the individual in enterprise education has something to offer engineering education.

Signature pedagogy for enterprise education

A signature pedagogy for enterprise education should be developed with those factors that unite the learning context of its students. For example, students of enterprise (and engineering) are quite likely to hold many naïve assumptions regarding the processes of creating new value and/or their enterprising abilities. They are also both likely to face relatively unknown futures, in the sense of Barnett's (2004) liquid knowledge. Where they most likely differ from engineering students is that enterprise students typically face a delayed career progression, with the average age of successful entrepreneurs significantly beyond the average graduation age. There is a need for overconfidence and narcissism (Navis & Ozbek, 2016) to have been beaten down by life experiences and a greater appreciation of reality to develop. They may also differ somewhat in their immediate needs, vis-à-vis their engineering education. Whereas enterprise students can be seen to contemplate varied destinations, and thus present different requirements of education, engineering students may be expected to require more homogeneous *general* needs (Tyler, 1949).

A consequence of these similarities and differences is that one can see the possibilities for integrating enterprise education into engineering education, whilst also seeing challenges. Enterprise education increasingly employs heutagogical-learning processes (Hase & Kenyon, 2000) to support self-determined learning (Jones et al., 2014). Through this process, the actual aspirations and interests of the individual student potentially form a starting point in the student's learning. The ultimate aim is to develop self-directed students (Lindeman, 1926) who will develop a capacity for self-negotiated action. A process of transformative learning (Mezirow, 1978) separates the passive student from becoming the self-directed student. Transformative learning provides the means to develop students' capacity to feel, think, and act into habits of heart, mind, and hands, vis-à-vis a specific vocational context.

While there is likely to be a willingness to develop enterprising engineering students, doing so through using an authentic signature pedagogy for enterprise education will mean trade-offs in the signature pedagogy for engineering. In line with the desire for engineering graduates to present with excellent interpersonal skills, an additional focus on deep reflection needs to accompany any integration of enterprise education. Given the natural focus on experiential forms of education, this shouldn't be too challenging. However, there is reflection in the form of afterthought or recorded observation, and then there is the uncomfortable process of really getting to know oneself; it is the later that is required. The next issue relates to the timing of the education itself.

Viewed in the context of a coordinated process, education is often, relatively domesticated. Yet, this is exactly the opposite of what is required to support enterprise education. We need to allow education to occur anytime, anyplace, and at any pace (Bramante & Colby, 2012) to ensure it is authentic and effective. While this is entirely possible for enterprise education, perhaps this represents a challenge for engineering education, the experience of which is often controlled and not located in the ordinary lives of its students.

Integrating enterprise and engineering education

A way around this is not to seek integration by means of equality, but rather to use enterprise education practices to support and reinforce contemporary engineering education outcomes. The seminal ideas of Tyler (1949) continue to shine a light on the importance of the *source* of educational objectives. We can ask what behavioural changes are sought by the students, in addition to the generic context-specific needs of engineering students, that can be known in advance to support the needs of a diverse cohort. The work of Tyler was expanded upon by Biggs (1999) and his consideration of constructive alignment. Constructive alignment was conceived by Biggs (1999) as a template through which educators could achieve alignment across learning outcomes, learning activities and related assessment methods. Its application to the domain of entrepreneurship education was initially considered by Jones (2006; 2009), with the idea now well accepted by enterprise educators. This original consideration initially raised concerns about the nature of peer-assessment methods used within the process of constructive alignment. In more contemporary settings, the assumption that educators can specify precisely what learning outcomes are appropriate for enterprise education are now conflicted by the emergence of heutagogical learning in our domain (see Jones et al., 2014). Heutagogical learning, or self-determined learning, elevates the social situation and aspirations of each individual student. Like the ideas of Barnett (2004), educating for the unknown starts with addressing the ontological assumptions of the student. So, the passion of each individual student is considered as an organizing factor vis-à-vis how learning outcomes are determined, rather than merely a useful factor in increasing student engagement in pre-determined learning activities. In Figure 11.1, a simple way to visualize this situation is proposed.

By combining the pedagogical influence and direction of the educator with the student's immediate needs, we can account for both sides of the constructive alignment coin. Now the general, overarching needs identified by the educator and the immediate needs of each individual student provide the inputs for authentic context-based learning. For example, consider the engineering educator that sees the general needs of his or her students as developing a capacity for decision making around technology. Now let's consider the immediate needs of a given student, let's say, to develop an online app to support a community project. An opportunity exists for an alignment of needs, with the

Figure 11.1 Combining pedagogical and heutagogical inputs.

student's needs naturally being subsumed within the overarching needs of the educator. Therefore, consistency between the student's desired learning outcomes (LO) and the educator's general assessment methods (AM) is possible via a specific type of negotiation between educator and individual student. This negotiation must focus on two specific processes: responsibility agreement and resource agreement.

Responsibility agreement relates to the understanding achieved between the learner, educator, and any other related stakeholders concerned with who needs to do what for the learning process to occur alongside the student's exploration of their passion. Likewise, resource agreement relates to the student (potentially with assistance) identifying the type of resource profile required to support the learning activities (LA) to occur alongside the student's exploration of their passion. Taken together, these ideas of immediate and general needs and a reformulation of the idea of constructive alignment provide the impetus for viewing enterprise education as a process of perspective transformation; a potentially important ingredient in the development of engineering graduates for the 21st century. Importantly, this approach does not contravene the original basis upon which constructive alignment was developed (Biggs, 2017).

Tools of integration

Having established the opportunities to integrate enterprise education into engineering education, and having identified constructive alignment as a sound pedagogical process to guide such integration, now a specific tool of integration is offered for consideration. Activity theory can be used to consider how engineering education can identify opportunities for improvement that are directly aligned to student development. Activity theory (Engeström, 1987; 2001) illustrates the multiple factors that work together to support engineering education as an education activity. Developed from the early Russian/Soviet psychology of the 1920s and 1930s, and the seminal thinking of Vygotsky (1978), the key idea is that in order to achieve outcomes (such as knowledge and/or capabilities) we must use human activities and tools to do so. The activities occur in particular contexts, such as in institutions and/or, more broadly, in communities. Communities in turn are associated with rules that influence the nature of how activities occur.

Activity theory has previously been applied to education, with the recent work of Barnes (2012) as an excellent example. Barnes describes the six key components of activity theory, as highlighted in Figure 11.2, in the following manner. First, we are concerned with the subjects; in our context, these are the students, educators, support staff, and those who observe and/or influence the subjects' behaviour. Second, in terms of tasks and outcomes, we can view this simplistically in terms of generic learning outcomes (Kennewell, 2010), but more realistically, we need to factor in the ideas related to the personal development of our students, where we can envisage enterprise education making a contribution to engineering education. Logically, this will provide greater opportunities to align specific enterprise education initiatives with specific desirable outcomes that can be better measured. Third, we need to consider the tools being used within the activity. Broadly speaking we have a curriculum,

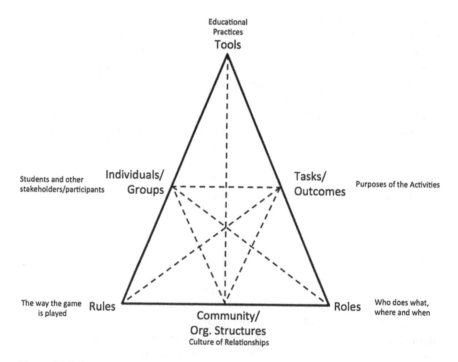

Figure 11.2 Activity system model
Source: adapted; from Engeström Y (1999))

and various processes and strategies that we use to foster and encourage learning. These can include internal tools, largely controlled by the educator, tools introduced from the local community, such as problem contexts and external contributors, and also tools introduced by students that are related to their own project-specific focus.

Fourth, we have communities and organizational structures. This is a complex area where boundaries between likely networks of activities systems are formed. Clearly, we can have very localized communities, national communities, and increasingly, international communities. For example, in the context of engineering education, we can anticipate specific levels of students' individual focus, given the freedom typically afforded to students to pursue individual projects related to their own aspirations in enterprise education. As a consequence, we need to be mindful to not only view our communities from micro, meso, and macro perspectives (Barnes, 2012), but also within each of those three levels. Fifth, the notion of the roles or the division of labour is complicated in the context of enterprise education. While there remain many pedagogically driven enterprise education programmes, many are increasingly identifying with notions of heutagogy and andragogy (Jones et al., 2014; Jones, 2016). As a result, the roles performed within the activity of enterprise education are many and varied. Again, as noted by Barnes (2012), this introduces important questions about not merely the roles performed, but also the transfer of power related to these roles. Sixth, the final component of the model is the rules employed vis-à-vis the activities performed.

Engeström (2001) outlines five key principles that control the use of activity theory. First, the primary unit of analysis is the activity setting itself. Second, the importance of multi-voicedness, or enrolling multiple perspectives, interests, and traditions associated with the activity setting are used to surface contradictions through which transformation and innovative change is possible. Third, the idea of historicity is used to ensure the processes of change within the system over time are comprehended as much as possible. Fourth, the search for contradictions within the activity system identifies the tensions through which system transformations are logically possible. Fifth, the principle of expansive learning dictates that only through embracing the identified contradictions can we truly and honestly contemplate the nature of change required to improve the activity system. After all, viewed from the perspective of activity theory, it is the system that is prioritized over the six individual components. In summary, activity theory provides a means for enterprise education to be viewed as a component within the broader activity system of engineering education, where improvements, large or small, are always possible.

Activity theory provides a structured way to seek out contradictions that may decrease the efficiency of engineering education. It also provides a means of integrating enterprise education into engineering education in ways that ensure the consistency of both approaches. One way to imagine this would be to imagine an activity system for both approaches, and then seek to integrate across rules, tools, roles, and outcomes. Doing so would enable strategic aims to guide a process of contradiction identification, where solutions are designed to address previously identified aims.

Conclusions

The view has been expressed that enterprise education can add value to engineering education. The idea of a signature pedagogy for enterprise education represents a vehicle for the scholarship of teaching and learning in the same way it does in engineering education. There may be potential issues associated with the development of teaching practice using the process of academagogy (McAuliffe & Winter, 2013), or scholarly leading in the context of engineering education. However, such issues are at the heart of the scholarship of teaching and learning given that our collective focus is upon enriching, rather than restricting, the quality of education. The signature pedagogy outlined for enterprise education (as contrasted against engineering education) draws upon many seminal ideas (Lindeman, 1926; Tyler, 1949; Mezirow, 1978). Thus, a scholarly foundation from the past continues to inform our possible actions in the future (Boshier & Huang, 2008). Aligning signature pedagogies is argued to be good scholarship of teaching and learning. It is about basing quality teaching and learning upon three fundamental dimensions, developing within our students the habits of heart, mind, and hands appropriate for enterprising behaviour, in the context of engineering education. Achieving such integration is aimed at initiating our students into the best values and behaviours through which to participate more fully in their potential futures, a fundamental aim of scholarly teaching (Glassick et al., 1997).

References

Barnes J (2012) *Changing Perceptions of ICT at KS3: A Critical Investigation using Activity Theory*, Unpublished dissertation, University of Wales, Trinity Saint David.

Barnett R (2004) Learning for an unknown future, *Higher Educations Research & Development*, Vol. 23, No. 3, pp. 247–267

Bennett AL & George A (2003) *Case Studies and Theory Development in the Social Sciences*, Cambridge, MA: MIT Press

Biggs J (1999) *Teaching for Quality Learning at University*, Philadelphia: Open University Press

Biggs J (2017) Personal communications

Boshier R & Huang Y (2008) In the house of scholarship of teaching and learning (SoTL), teaching lives upstairs and learning in the basement, *Teaching in Higher Education*, Vol. 13, No. 6, pp. 645–656

Bramante F & Colby R (2012) *Off the Clock: Moving Education from Time to Competency*, London: Sage Publications

Cooper S, Bottomley C & Gordon J (2004) Stepping out of the classroom and up the ladder of learning: An experiential learning approach to entrepreneurship education, *Industry and Higher Education*, Vol. 18, No. 1, pp. 11–22

Engeström Y (1987) *Learning by Expanding: An Activity-Theoretical Approach to Developmental Research*, Helsinki: Orienta-Konsultit Oy

Engeström Y (1999) Innovative learning in work teams: Analysing cycles of knowledge creation in practice, in Engeström Y, Miettinen R & Punamäki R (Eds.), *Perspectives on Activity Theory*, Cambridge: Cambridge University Press

Engeström Y (2001) Expansive Learning at Work: Toward an activity theoretical reconceptualization, *Journal of Education & Work*, Vol. 14, No. 1, pp. 133–156

Gadola M & Chindamo D (2017) Experiential learning in engineering education: The role of student design competitions and a case study, *International Journal of Mechanical Engineering Education*, Vol. 42, pp. 281–287

Gibb AA (2002) Creating Conducive Environments for Learning and Entrepreneurship; living with, dealing with, creating and enjoying uncertainty and complexity, *Industry and Higher Education*, Vol. 16, No. 3.

Glassick C, Huber M & Maeroff G (1997) *Scholarship Assessed: Evaluation of the Professoriate*, San Francisco: Jossey-Bass Publisher

Hart T (2001) *From Information to Transformation*, New York: Peter Lang

Hase S & Kenyon C (2000) *From Andragogy to Heutagogy*, Melbourne: Ultibase

Jones C (2006) Constructive alignment: A journey for new eyes, *Journal of Enterprising Culture*, Vol. 14, No. 4, pp. 291–306

Heath R (1964) *The Reasonable Adventurer*, University of Pittsburgh Press, PA

Jones C (2007) Creating the reasonable adventurer: The co-evolution of student and learning environment, *Journal of Small Business and Enterprise Development*, Vol. 14, No. 2, pp. 228–240

Jones C (2009) Enterprise education: Learning through personal experience, *Industry & Higher Education*, Vol. 23, No. 3, pp. 175–182

Jones C (2011) *Teaching Entrepreneurship to Undergraduates*, Cheltenham, UK and Northampton, MA, USA: Edward Elgar Publishing

Jones C (2016) Enterprise education: Towards the development of the heutagogical learner, *The All Ireland Journal of Teaching and Learning in Higher Education*, Vol. 8, No. 1, pp. 2541–2457

Jones C, Matlay H, Penaluna K & Penaluna A (2014) Claiming the future of enterprise education, *Education + Training*, Vol. 56, No. 8/9, pp. 764–775

Kennewell S (2010) Analysing the impact of information technology on activity and learning, in McDougall A, Murnane J, Jones A & Reynolds N (Eds.), *Researching IT in Education: Theory, Practice and Future Directions*. Abingdon: Routledge

Killen C (2015) Three dimensions of learning: Experiential activity for engineering innovation education and research, *European Journal of Engineering Education*, Vol. 40, No. 5, pp. 476–498

Lindemann E (1926) *The Meaning of Adult Education*, New York: New Republic

Lucas B, Claxton G & Hanson J (2014) *Thinking Like an Engineer*, London: The Royal Academy of Engineering Url:www.raeng.org.uk/publications/reports/thinking-like-anengineer-implications-full-report

Male S, Bush M & Chapman E (2010) Perceptions of competency deficiencies in engineering graduates, *Australasian Journal of Engineering Education*, Vol. 16, No. 1, pp. 55–68

McAuliffe M & Winter A (2013) Distance education and the application of academagogy: A case study, *International Journal of Innovation, Creativity and Change*, Vol. 1, No. 2, pp. 1–15

Mezirow J (1978) Perspective transformation, *Adult Education*, Vol. 28, No. 2, pp. 100–110

Navis C & Ozbek O (2016) The right people in the wrong places: The paradox of entrepreneurial entry and successful opportunity realization, *Academy of Management Review*, Vol. 41, No. 1, pp. 109–129

Neck H & Corbett A (2018) The scholarship of teaching and learning entrepreneurship, *Entrepreneurship Education and Pedagogy*, Vol. 1, No. 1, pp. 8–41

Pittaway L & Edwards C (2012) Assessment: Examining practice in entrepreneurship education, *Education + Training*, Vol. 54, No. 8/9, pp. 778–800

QAA (2018) *Enterprise and Entrepreneurship: Guidance for UK Higher Education Providers* Url:www.qaa.ac.uk/en/Publications/Documents/Enterprise-and-entrpreneurship-education-2018.pdf

Sharp D (1995) *Who am I Really?* Toronto: Inner City Books

Shulman L (2005) Signature pedagogies in the professions, *Daedalus*, Vol. 134, No. 3, pp. 52–59

Steiner C (1998) Educating for innovation management: The engineering educators' dilemma, *IEEE Transactions on Education*, Vol. 41, No. 1, pp. 1–7

Tsoukas H (1989) The validity of idiographic research explanations, *Academy of Management Review*, Vol. 14, No. 4, pp. 551–561

Tyler R (1949) *Basic Principles of Curriculum and Instruction*, Chicago, IL: The University of Chicago Press

Ukpokodu O (2009) The practice of transformative pedagogy, *Journal on Excellence in College Teaching*, Vol. 20, No. 2, pp. 43–67

Vygotsky L (1978) *Mind and Society: The Development of Higher Psychological Processes*. Cambridge, MA: Harvard University Press

Chapter 12

Enhancing and managing group creativity through off-task breaks

Dermot Breslin

Moments of insight have played a key role in the evolution of technology over the decades. But how can these ephemeral and enigmatic 'eureka' events be managed? This chapter explores the role played by off-task breaks in triggering the unconscious processing of ideas. By breaking up the working day with low effort routine tasks and breaks, individuals can significantly enhance their creativity. So, taking time away from the job becomes the key link in the creativity process. This research therefore points to the careful management of off-task breaks during the innovation process.

Introduction

In this chapter, I explore the impact of off-task breaks on the creative process in individuals and groups. Research in cognitive psychology has identified a positive link between off-task breaks and creativity (Simon, 1996; Smith, 1995). It is seen that taking time away from a problem can boost creativity, once the individual returns to the task. Some suggest that during such incubation breaks, unconscious problem-solving processes allow creative ideas to emerge (Bowers et al., 1990; Smith, 1995) through processes of association (Dijksterhuis & Nordgren, 2006; Zhong et al., 2008). Incubation thus refers to the temporary shift away from an unsolved problem to allow a solution to emerge (Wallas, 1926). Given this link between off-task breaks and creativity, some have explored further key characteristics of the incubation period. For instance, when one engages in low cognitive effort tasks during the incubation period, creativity is enhanced (Baird et al., 2012). Breaks should thus be viewed as an essential part in the creative process, as one cannot consciously think one's way towards a more creative outcome. Whilst past research has focused on the role played by incubation breaks in individual creativity, less focus has been paid to its role in the group creative process. Enhancing group creativity through off-task breaks is an important future endeavour for both educators and managers. The importance of breaks has important implications for our understanding of the UK productivity gap. Working more, it seems, is not the solution to increased productivity; this is an important lesson for UK PLC, i.e. UK considered as a Public Limited Company, as it strives to close the gap with its European neighbours.

Individual creativity and off-task breaks

The unconscious and off-task breaks

Both a passive and an active interpretation have been put forward to explain this positive effect of off-task breaks. Adopting a passive approach, the mental set-shifting or forgetting-fixation argues that putting ideas aside can reduce associations with incorrect solutions and allows new ones to emerge (Smith & Blankship, 1989), as the individual takes a fresh look at the problem. This passive view of incubation results in associations with incorrect solutions being reduced. So not thinking about a problem may result in wrong heuristics, and approaches becoming less accessible and/or being forgotten, and as a result providing the impetus for a fresh look (Dijksterhuis, 2004). Other, more active interpretations of incubation have emerged with the unconscious having an active role in idea processing (Koestler, 1964). Zhong et al. (2008) suggest that unconscious thought (task-related thought processes that occur while conscious attention is directed elsewhere) facilitates the discovery of remote associations, as opposed to the passive role of relaxation suggested by the forgetting-fixation or mental set-shifting hypothesis, noted previously. In other words, the individual continues to think about the problem in the absence of any conscious attention (Dijksterhuis, 2004), as our unconscious mind continues to work on ideas below the level of consciousness (Wallas, 1926). Dijksterhuis (2004) proposes that with unconscious thought, disorganized sets of information become reorganized into clearer and more integrated representations of information in memory. Through a process of continued associative activity, information is clustered, resulting in a more organized representation (Dijksterhuis, 2004). Therefore, Dijksterhuis and his colleagues argue that unconscious thought excels at integrating and associating information and is capable of carrying out associative searches across a broad range of background knowledge (Dijksterhuis & Nordgren, 2006). Extending this view, Zhong et al. (2008) put forward a two-step process, in which unconscious thought associates and creates the novel idea, which is then transferred to consciousness. But how can this process be managed, and crucially, how can we trigger such moments of unconscious thought?

Mind wandering and off-task breaks

Recently a group of psychologists have explored in more depth the cognitive processes underpinning off-task breaks. Specifically, they have found that when one engages in low cognitive demand tasks during an incubation period, the mind wanders (Baird et al., 2012). These episodes of mind wandering enhance creativity more than if one does nothing during the break, or if one is engaged in a more cognitively demanding task (Baird et al., 2012; Sio & Ormerod, 2009; Webster et al., 2006). Baird et al. (2012) thus posit that mind wandering might enhance the process of unconscious association. On the one hand, engaging in an off-task activity allows the mind to wander, triggering unconscious associations and insight. On the other, this incubation task cannot be too cognitively demanding, as this in turns limits the working memory resources left for unconscious thinking (Smallwood & Schooler, 2006). Therefore, with simple or automatic tasks, mind wandering occurs as attention shifts from the primary task to one's memories (Smallwood & Schooler, 2006), with information processing being decoupled in a sense from the task in hand (Smallwood et al., 2003). The more repetitive and automatic the off-task activity, the less executive control is needed in performing it (Smallwood & Schooler, 2006). So the more routine and automatic the incubation task, then the lower the cognitive effort needed to complete it, and thus the frequency of mind wandering should increase (Antrobus, 1966; Giambra, 1995; Smallwood et al., 2003; Smallwood et al., 2004). In summary, when an individual engages in familiar and routine tasks during off-task breaks, the greater the likelihood mind wandering will occur, and with this the associated benefits of increased creativity through unconscious through processes.

Group creativity and off-task breaks

Group creativity and social-cognitive factors

Whilst past research has identified a positive link between off-task breaks and the creative process in individuals (Simon, 1996; Smith, 1995), less attention has been paid to the effect of breaks on group creativity. Do off-task breaks in which group members reflect individually on the group task improve group performance post-incubation? Do off-task breaks, in which individuals socialize together, have a positive or negative effect on the creative process in groups? Whilst the effect of breaks on individual creativity largely relates to cognitive processes, the group creative process is shaped by an interplay between cognitive, social, and motivational factors (Paulus & Brown, 2007). First, the group setting allows individuals to share ideas, and to contribute towards the ideas of others. Compared to individuals working on their own, contributions from others can trigger a process of association, as individual ideas become exhausted. This process of association leads to unique combinations being generated (Dugosh et al., 2000; Paulus, 2000), and can also result in the retrieval of less common ideas (Dugosh & Paulus, 2005). Second, heightened levels of social interaction facilitate exchanges between individuals, and a back-and-forth conversation flow (Harvey, 2013; Van Oortmerssen et al., 2015). This can lead to an interaction flow (Van Oortmerssen et al., 2015) as one individual builds on the ideas of others, in a snowballing of concepts; the greater the interaction and production of ideas, the greater the opportunity for the cross fertilization of ideas noted before. Third, as individuals become more involved in the group process, through intensified social interactions, they are increasingly motivated to share and listen to the contributions of others (Paulus & Brown, 2007). These three interconnected factors thus act to facilitate the group creative process. Social forces facilitate the production of larger pools of ideas, which in turn provide the cognitive stimulation for each member to generate new ideas (Dugosh et al., 2000). Generated ideas in turn need to be noticed and attended to as members integrate them into their own knowledge systems. The more motivated members become, then the more open they are to communication, and to attending to the contributions of others (Paulus & Brown, 2007). Conversely, without motivation to attend to ideas, cognitive processes are limited, detrimentally affecting group outcomes. In this way, social forces influence the motivation of individuals to engage (Paulus & Brown, 2007). Off-task breaks can be seen to affect this interplay of social and cognitive forces in a number of ways, impacting the fluency of the creative process, and the quality of ideas generated and selected.

Individual versus group breaks

First breaks influence the social processes within the group, and with this, the production of ideas through interactions. Off-task breaks in which individuals reflect separately on the group task can interfere with these socialization processes, impairing the development of group cohesion and familiarity. For example, in a study of negotiation processes, Harinck and Dreu (2008) found that when individuals took individual breaks after a group session, they spontaneously reflected on competitive aspects of the group task. After the break, these competitive thoughts impaired collective efforts towards joint outcomes. In this same study, when groups took no break, or breaks in which they were cognitively distracted, joint outcomes post-break were improved (Harinck & Dreu, 2008). Harinck and Dreu (2008) concluded that taking individual off-task breaks is unhelpful for the group task. Competitive thoughts during these breaks act to increase self-interest, resulting in less integrative behaviours after the break (Harinck & Dreu, 2008). Following this line of argument, individual breaks are seen to interfere with the process of socialization occurring in groups (Breslin, 2018a). This constrains the interaction of group members post-break, and with thus constrains the creative fluency, or total number of ideas generated, in the group (Paulus, 2000).

Second, breaks interfere with the cognitive processes underpinning group creativity. It has been argued that breaks, in which group members individually reflect on the task following the group activity, can allow the individual to integrate ideas from the group session with their own generated ideas, resulting in new ideas and combinations of ideas post-incubation (Dugosh et al.,

2000; Paulus & Yang, 2000). Off-task breaks thus allow time for individuals to process ideas from the group. Paulus et al. (1996), however, found no difference in performance between cases in which individual breaks followed group creative tasks, and cases where group breaks followed individual creative exercises. This would suggest that the cognitive benefits derived from individual breaks following the group creative process are questionable. When one considers the group process, there is an interplay between the socialization processes noted above and key cognitive processes underpinning group creativity (Paulus & Brown, 2007). In this manner, intensifying the degree of social interaction and participation can be seen to also increase the quality of those ideas generated. As individual off-task breaks impair the process of socialization within the group, the generation of ideas through interaction is constrained, and with this the opportunity for members to attend to and build on the contributions of others. Following this argument, Breslin (2018a) argued that the quality of ideas is decreased post-break, in groups where individuals are alone during the break, relative to the no break case. Therefore, this research suggests that off-task breaks in which individuals engage in separate individual activities have a detrimental impact on group creativity (Breslin, 2018a). The key therefore in group tasks is to take breaks together.

Group processes and naturally occurring breaks

The activities of groups develop over time in pace with other time-based cycles including personal, organizational, and institutional cycles. For example, in an education environment, group tasks follow assignment deadlines, tutorial timetables, and tutor engagement sessions. In an industrial setting, group processes follow product development cycles, project management stages, annual budgeting cycles, etc. The synchronization of group processes with other external temporal patterns is known as entrainment. These cycles of activity vary from daily routines to broader monthly and annual calendars. On the one hand, temporal entrainment can trap or lock a group into a routine, making it difficult to schedule the off-task breaks needed to trigger creativity. On the other hand, entrainment naturally identifies pauses or interruptions in time cycles that groups can use to "stop and think" about their work progress (Okhuysen, 2001), and to maximize opportunities for change (Zellmer-Bruhn et al., 2004). The more a group works together, and the more familiar they are with each other, then the greater the probability that they will use interruptions (Okhuysen, 2001). Indeed, Breslin (2014) found that as groups develop over time, they generate more ideas and spend more time in divergent thought when completing group creativity exercises. Familiarity can lead to interruptions in three ways (Okhuysen, 2001). First, social norms within the group may encourage interruptions aimed at diffusing tensions or building bonds. Second, as the group gets to know each other, there is less chance for negative reaction if someone interrupts work, for example by joking or clowning around. Third, familiar groups can express disagreements without the risk of escalation. In summary, group processes naturally follow cycles of entrainment with other temporal rhythms occurring at the level of the individual, organization, or wider institution. These cycles lead to distinct pauses or interruptions, which create opportunities for off-task breaks and creativity. Furthermore, the more familiarity develops within the group, then the greater the probability such pauses will naturally occur.

The time of the day effect

Individual creativity and time-of-day

Finally, when considering the effect of breaks, attention must be paid to the time-of-day effect. Past research has shown that an individual's behavioural and cognitive function changes over the course of the day. This circadian rhythm is linked to physiological changes in body temperature and hormone production over the course of the day. The circadian rhythms of individuals differ between morning and evening types, which are termed chronotypes. Morning types wake up early, are more active in the morning and go to bed earlier in the evening. Evening types are less active in the morning, staying awake later in the night. The distribution of morning and evening types varies with age. For instance, children tend to shift from morning to evening types as they reach adolescence (Kim et al., 2002; Roenneberg et al., 2004). This prominence of evening types continues into young and college age adults, reversing back to morning types in older generations (Adan & Almirall, 1990; Giampietro & Cavallera, 2007; Intons-Peterson et al., 1998; May & Hasher, 1998). Scholars have explored time of day effects on cognitive functions associated with the creative process. May and Hasher (1998) focused on the notion of inhibitory processes, which control the flow of information from thought and perception (e.g., Hasher et al., 1999), and thus act to suppress the processing of distracting or task unrelated information. Inhibition has a number of effects on information processing (Hasher et al., 1999; May & Hasher, 1998), including restricting attention to only relevant, task-oriented stimuli, suppressing information that was but is no longer relevant to the task, and restraining the production of strong responses. These three inhibitory functions may be impaired at off-peak relative to peak times (May, 1999). Wieth and Zacks (2011) showed that reduced attentional control at a non-optimal time of day can positively affect performance on insight problems. Specifically, they argue that when evening types perform better at insight problems in the morning, which is their non-optimal time of day (Wieth & Zacks, 2011). They therefore point to a relationship between cognitive performance and an individual's circadian arousal. Others similarly showed that individuals were less able to ignore additional distracting information during their non-optimal time of day compared to their optimal time of day (Breslin, 2018b; May, 1999; May et al., 2005). In summary, the effectiveness of off-task breaks on individual creativity would seem to depend on the time at which such pauses were scheduled.

Group creativity and time-of-day

When considering socialization processes in groups, previous research has found a link between variations over time and individual circadian rhythms. Morning types for instance, who have an energy peak during the working day, are seen to be more conscientious (Jackson & Gerard, 1996), reflecting a dutiful/conformist personality style (Diaz-Morales, 2007). DeYoung et al. (2007) found a link between morning types and stability, as represented by neuroticism (reversed), agreeableness, and conscientiousness. Randler (2009) further links morning types and proactivity. Morning types are also seen to prefer social values (conservation, self-transcendence) over individual values (Vollmer & Randler, 2012) and tend towards cultural collectivism and having a low tolerance of ambiguity (Fabbri et al., 2007), conforming more to social laws and norms. When one considers processes of socialization, morning types would thus seem to be key players in collective activities, working towards group goals and serving as critical actors in team building exercises. Morning types are early risers, and so begin the working day in synch with their individual biological clocks. This alignment between individual and social rhythms might extend to a wider alignment between individual and social behaviours and values (Vollmer & Randler, 2012) over the course of the working day. Therefore, an apparent tendency towards conformance and conscientiousness within this group may be reflective of a synchronization between individual and collective diurnal rhythms. While morning types are associated with social traits such as conformance, conscientiousness, and agreeableness, some suggest that evening types exhibit behaviours which reflect more problems in coping with social demands than morning types (Mecacci & Rocchetti, 1998). Vollmer and Randler (2012) found that evening type adolescents had a greater preference for individual values (openness to change, self-enhancement) rather than social values. Vollmer and Randler (2012) further argue that because evening types struggle to comply with early social schedules, they often decide against pro-social behaviours of getting up early. As a result, they are less likely to conform to wider social constraints. This misalignment between social and biological times can result in a 'social jetlag' (Wittmann et al., 2006), which can lead to less proactivity than morning types (Randler, 2009), and even to anxiety, as evening types are expected to perform tasks during their non-optimal time of day (Diaz-Morales & Sanchez-Lopez, 2008). Interestingly, evening types have also been associated with different cognitive styles, having a higher ability to think creatively (Fabbri et al., 2007; Giampietro & Cavallera, 2007), being more intuitive, and more likely to have an unconventional/dissenting personality style (Diaz-Morales, 2007). Evening types are thus seen to be intuitive, impulsive, and creative, inclined towards cultural individualism and with a high tolerance of ambiguity (Fabbri et al., 2007). While the pro-social behaviours of morning types may reflect the synchronization between their individual biological clocks and social rhythms, the more individualistic behaviours of evening types likewise reflects a mismatch between the two.

In addition to chronotype, key processes of socialization may depend on levels of motivation, energy, and alertness that alter over the course of the day depending on the individual's body clock or circadian rhythm. For example, Hasler et al. (2008) found that behaviours associated with positive affect (socializing, laughing, and singing) varied according to circadian rhythms. In this latter study, it was seen that individuals peaked in terms of behaviours such as laughing and socialization between eight and ten hours after they woke. Clearly if these peaks occur during the working day (as in the case of morning types) then such individuals may exhibit higher levels of pro-social behaviours. Evidence from this research would thus suggest that when an individual's body clock is out of synch with the timing of the task in hand, then the individual concerned may behave in a more individualistic manner. These less pro-social behaviours might negatively impact upon the group creative process in a number of ways. First, conversations within the group can become dominated by one person effectively blocking comments from other members (Nijstad et al., 2002; Rietzschel at el., 2006). Second, free riding may occur, where some individuals sit back and contribute less, or engage in social loafing as they don't feel accountable as individuals (Karau & Williams, 1993). Finally, during non-optimal times of day the individual may feel more apprehensive about negative evaluations by others, and as a result feel inhibited to express ideas due to social anxiety (Camacho & Paulus, 1995; Rietzschel at el., 2006).

On the other hand, heightened levels of social interaction experienced during an individual's daily peak can enhance the creative process by facilitating exchanges between individuals. In this manner, individuals build on the contributions of others, leading to back-and-forth conversations (Harvey, 2013; Van Oortmerssen et al., 2015) as one idea triggers further associations in a snowballing of responses. With increased levels of interaction among team members, group members stimulate further ideas between themselves, leading to a process of cross-fertilization (Nijstad & De Dreu, 2002; Paulus et al., 2000). The more individuals are exposed to the ideas of others, then the more this process of cognitive stimulation occurs (Paulus & Yang, 2000). As a result, one would expect the number of ideas generated to increase as socialization within the group intensifies during daily peaks. Breslin (2018b) found that student groups reached a creative peak around the lunchtime period, despite individual differences in chronotype. During this lunchtime peak, groups were twice as productive creatively as first thing in the morning, or during the afternoon post-lunch period (Breslin, 2018b).

Managing off-task breaks

In light of this review of recent literature, educators and managers should look towards enhancing and managing the creative process in individuals and groups through off-task breaks. Breaks should be seen not as an impediment to productivity, but an essential element in the creative process. First, educators and managers need to be more aware of the opportunities created by breaks (Zellmer-Bruhn et al., 2004). Staudenmayer et al. (2002) for instance found that engineers and managers did not recognize the potential for change in interruptions. Second, managers need to set expectations for change, adaptation, and creativity within groups during breaks (Staudenmayer et al., 2002; Zellmer-Bruhn et al., 2004). Third, and reflecting on the research noted previously, guidance can be given on how to structure daily group activities, in terms of the nature, duration, frequency, and timing of off-task breaks. In this way, groups can learn to manage the process and maximize benefits for the ongoing needs of the organization.

The nature of the off-task break

When considering individual creativity, the type of off-task break completed has an important influence on incidences of mind wandering, with past experimental work looking at the impact on creativity of different incubation tasks from high cognitive demand (e.g. counting backwards, visual memory tests) to low cognitive demand (e.g. reading) (Sio & Ormerod, 2009). As noted above, when task demands are high, idle cognitive processes – and with this mind-wandering events – are reduced. On the other hand, when routine and habitual tasks are completed in a repetitive and automatic manner, mind-wandering processes are triggered. Therefore, it is important to identify tasks which are repeated routinely within the daily rhythms of the group, such as eating, reading, or going for a walk. Research has shown how renowned creative individuals develop and stick to rigid daily routines, in which their periods of work are interspersed with off-task breaks when they go for a walk, socialize with friends, etc. (Currey, 2013). Engaging in these low effort activities enhances opportunities for mind wandering, and with this insight. When considering the group creative process, collaborative group breaks are seen to increase the quality of the creative process, relative to individual breaks, no breaks, or more competitive group breaks (Breslin, 2018a). Breslin (2018a) thus calls for groups to engage in participative activities during breaks, in which each member is encouraged to get involved. In other words, more of a Swedish Fika coffee break and a race in the park!

The duration and frequency of off-task breaks

The length of the off-task break can also have an effect on mind wandering, and with this creativity (Sio & Ormerod, 2009). Sio and Ormerod (2009) argue that with a long preparation period in which an impasse has been reached, incubation effects can have a positive effect on creative problems. In these cases, a strategic shift in restructuring the problem is achieved during incubation. However, there is no standard on what is considered a long or short incubation period. For instance, Smith and Blankenship (1989) consider 15 minutes a long incubation period. The length of the incubation might also be considered relative to the preparation time worked on the problem before incubation. There has been little prior research which has explored the effects of frequency of off-tasks breaks and creativity. For instance, is it beneficial to develop repeated periods of problem-solving-incubation-selection on the same problem over time, or are fewer extended problem-solving-incubation-selection sequences better? Future research might also investigate these three areas by tracking individuals over a period of time. In this way, a more fine-grained assessment of the immediate impact of task type, incubation period, and incubation frequency on the group creative process can be obtained. Self-reports of behaviour can include diary (beeper) methods in which the individual records the frequency, sequence, and duration of behaviours during the day. These logs might be further supported by observations, or through shadowing activities.

Individual or group off-task breaks

As noted above, when groups take breaks it is important that they take these breaks together (Breslin, 2018a). By splitting up and taking breaks individually, important socialization processes are interrupted which impair social, cognitive, and motivational factors underpinning group creativity (Paulus & Brown, 2007). The key issue with group breaks is to engage all members together in the off-task activity (Breslin, 2018a). In this manner, both the fluency of the creative process and quality of ideas generated is facilitated and even enhanced by additional group forming activities during the break.

The timing of off-task breaks

In light of recent research which points to a link between creativity and an individual's non-optimal time-of-day (May, 1999; May & Hasher, 1998; Wieth & Zacks, 2011), the benefits of off-task breaks might be maximized when taken during these times. With this insight, individuals can thus identify when occurrences of mind wandering are more likely to occur. In conclusion, it is argued here that off-task breaks are likely to be more effective when they coincide with the individual's non-optimal time-of-day. As the individual is more likely to be distracted during these periods, then opportunities for mind wandering are increased. When considering groups, the lunchtime period is seen to be the most productive (Breslin, 2018b). Therefore, scheduling activities between 11:00 a.m. and 2:00 p.m. doubles creative productivity relative to the early morning or late afternoon. In addition, the mix of chronotypes across members introduces an important element of diversity which in itself may further enhance the creative process (Volk et al., 2017). Future research might explore the notion of group chronotype diversity. Volk et al. (2017) suggest that when teams understand chronotype diversity, they can enhance performance by altering the timing and pacing of their work to match the different energy peaks of group members. Equally, team performance can be impaired if chronotype differences among members are not recognized and understood within the group (Volk et al., 2017). As noted before, future research might be designed to create and investigate groups with different levels of chronotype diversity.

In summary, individuals and groups should seek to organize their day to get the most out of off-task breaks. The exact timing, duration, frequency, and nature of these breaks may change depending on the complexity of the problem being worked on. As noted above, the more complex the problem, then the more frequent and longer breaks should become. In addition, it is noted that groups in which individuals are familiar with each other are more effective self-organizers, including when organizing breaks (Okhuysen, 2001). Indeed, Okhuysen (2001) found that when pauses are imposed by management, the adaptiveness of the group decreases. Therefore, while educators and managers understand the importance of breaks, and set the agenda for these incubation periods (Staudenmayer et al., 2002; Zellmer-Bruhn et al., 2004), micro-level organization needs to be managed by the group itself.

Conclusions

Given the role played by the unconscious in creative thought, one clearly cannot manage the direction of thought patterns that emerge. However, one can manage the overall creative process through the careful management of these unconscious moments. Therefore, walking away from the job is no longer seen as unproductive, but a key element in the creative process. This will involve educating educators and managers, and changing the mindset of time-keeping administrators on the importance of breaks. Breaks should no longer be viewed as instances in which employees 'slack off,' but as an essential and critical part of the creative process in groups.

References

Adan A & Almirall H (1990) Adaptation and standardization of a Spanish version of the morningness-eveningness questionnaire: Individual differences, *Personality and Individual Differences*, Vol. 11, No. 11, pp. 1123–1130

Antrobus JS, Singer JL & Greenberg S (1966) Studies in the stream of consciousness: Experimental enhancement and suppression of spontaneous cognitive processes, *Perceptual and Motor Skills*, Vol. 23, No. 2, pp. 399–417

Baird B, Smallwood J, Mrazek MD, Kam JW, Franklin MS & Schooler JW (2012) Inspired by distraction: Mind wandering facilitates creative incubation, *Psychological Science*, Vol. 23, No. 10, pp. 1117–1122

Bowers KS, Regehr G, Balthazard CG & Parker K (1990) Intuition in the context of discovery. *Cognitive Psychology*, Vol. 22, pp. 72–110

Breslin D (2014) *The Routinization of Group Behavior and the Evolution of Ideas*, 14th European Academy of Management Conference, Valencia, Spain, June

Breslin D (2018a) Off-task breaks and group creativity, *The Journal of Creative Behavior*, DOI: 10.1002/jocb.229

Breslin D (2018b) Group creativity and the time of the day, *Studies in Higher Education*, DOI: 10.1080/03075079.2017.1413082

Camacho LM & Paulus PB (1995) The role of social anxiousness in group brainstorming, *Journal of Personality and Social Psychology*, Vol. 68, 1071–1080

Currey M (2013) *Daily Rituals: How Great Minds Make Time, Find Inspiration, and Get to Work*, London: Palgrave Macmillan

DeYoung CG, Hasher L, Djikic M, Criger B & Peterson JB (2007) Morning people are stable people: Circadian rhythm and the higher-order factors of the Big Five, *Personality and Individual Differences*, Vol. 43, No. 2, pp. 267–276

Díaz-Morales JF (2007) Morning and evening-types: Exploring their personality styles, *Personality and Individual Differences*, Vol. 43, No. 4, pp. 769–778

Diaz-Morales JF & Sanchez-Lopez MP (2008) Morningness-eveningness and anxiety among adults: A matter of sex/gender? *Personality and Individual Differences*, Vol. 44, pp. 1391–1401

Dijksterhuis A (2004) Think different: The merits of unconscious thought in preference development and decision making, *Journal of Personality and Social Psychology*, Vol. 87, No. 5, pp. 586–598

Dijksterhuis A & Nordgren LF (2006) A theory of unconscious thought, *Perspectives on Psychological Science*, Vol. 1, pp. 95–109

Dugosh KL & Paulus PB (2005) Cognitive and social comparison processes in brainstorming, *Journal of Experimental Social Psychology*, Vol. 41, No. 3, pp. 313–320

Dugosh KL, Paulus PB, Roland EJ & Yang HC (2000) Cognitive stimulation in brainstorming, *Journal of Personality and Social Psychology*, Vol. 79, pp. 722–735

Fabbri M, Antonietti A, Giorgetti M, Tonetti L & Natale V (2007) Circadian typology and style of thinking differences, *Learning and Individual Differences*, Vol. 17, No. 2, pp. 175–180

Giambra LM (1995) A laboratory based method for investigating influences on switching attention to task unrelated imagery and thought, *Consciousness and Cognition*, Vol. 4, pp. 1–21

Giampietro M & Cavallera GM (2007) Morning and evening types and creative thinking, *Personality and Individual Differences*, Vol. 42, No. 3, pp. 453–463

Harinck F & De Dreu CK (2008) Take a break! or not? The impact of mindsets during breaks on negotiation processes and outcomes, *Journal of Experimental Social Psychology*, Vol. 44, No. 2, pp. 397–404

Harvey S (2013) A different perspective: The multiple effects of deep level diversity on group creativity, *Journal of Experimental Social Psychology*, Vol. 49, pp. 822–832

Hasher L, Zacks RT & May CP (1999) Inhibitory control, circadian arousal, and age, in Gopher D & Koriat A (Eds.), *Attention and Performance XVII: Cognitive Regulation of Performance: Interaction of Theory and Application*. Cambridge, MA: MIT Press

Hasler BP, Mehl MR, Bootzin RR & Vazire S (2008) Preliminary evidence of diurnal rhythms in everyday behaviors associated with positive affect, *Journal of Research in Personality*, Vol. 42, No. 6, pp. 1537–1546

Intons-Peterson MJ, Rocchi P, West T, McLellan K & Hackney A (1998) Aging, optimal testing times, and negative priming, *Journal of Experimental Psychology*, Vol. 24, No. 2, pp. 362–376

Jackson LA & Gerard DA (1996) Diurnal types, the "Big Five" personality factors, and other personal characteristics, *Journal of Social Behavior & Personality*, Vol. 11, pp. 273–283

Karau SJ & Williams KD (1993) Social loafing: A meta-analytic review and theoretical integration, *Journal of Personality and Social Psychology*, Vol. 65, pp. 681–706

Kim S, Dueker GL, Hasher L & Goldstein D (2002) Children's time of day preference: Age, gender and ethnic differences, *Personality and Individual Differences*, Vol. 33, No. 7, pp. 1083–1090

Koestler A (1964) *The Act of Creation*, London: Penguin

May CP, Hasher L & Foong N (2005) Implicit memory, age, and time of day: paradoxical priming effects, *Psychological Science*, Vol. 16, No. 2, pp. 96–100

May CP (1999) Synchrony effects in cognition: The costs and a benefit, *Psychology Bulletin & Review*, Vol. 6, No. 1, pp. 142–147

May CP & Hasher L (1998) Synchrony effects in inhibitory control over thought and action, *Journal of Experimental Psychology*, Vol. 24, No. 2, pp. 363–379

Mecacci L & Rocchetti G (1998) Morning and evening types: Stress-related personality aspects, *Personality and Individual Differences*, Vol. 25, No. 3, pp. 537–542

Nijstad BA & De Dreu CKW (2002) Creativity and group innovation, *Applied Psychology*, Vol. 51, No. 3, pp. 400–406

Nijstad BA, Stroebe W & Lodewijkx HFM (2002) Cognitive stimulation and interference in groups: Exposure effects in an idea generation task, *Journal of Experimental Social Psychology*, Vol. 38, pp. 535–544

Okhuysen GA (2001) Structuring change: Familiarity and formal Interventions in Problem-Solving Groups, *Academy of Management Journal*, Vol. 44, No. 4, pp. 794–808

Paulus PB (2000) Groups, teams, and creativity: The creative potential of idea-generating groups, *Applied Psychology: An International Review*, Vol. 49, pp. 237–262

Paulus PB & Brown VR (2007) Toward more creative and innovative group idea generation: A cognitive-social-motivational perspective of brainstorming, *Social and Personality Psychology Compass*, Vol. 1, No. 1, pp. 248–265

Paulus PB, Larey TS & Dzindolet MT (2000) *Creativity in groups and teams*, in Turner M (Ed.), *Groups at Work: Advances in Theory and Research* (pp. 319–338), Hillsdale, NJ: Hampton.

Paulus PB, Larey TS, Putman VL, Leggett KL & Roland EJ (1996) Social influence processes in computer brainstorming, *Basic and Applied Social Psychology*, Vol. 18, pp. 3–14

Paulus PB & Yang H (2000) Idea generation in groups: A basis for creativity in organizations, *Organizational Behavior and Human Decision Processes*, Vol. 82, pp. 76–87

Randler C (2009) Proactive people are morning people, *Journal of Applied Social Psychology*, Vol. 39, No. 12, pp. 2787–2797

Rietzschel EF, Nijstad BA & Stroebe W (2006) Productivity is not enough: A comparison of interactive and nominal brainstorming groups on idea generation and selection, *Journal of Experimental Social Psychology*, Vol. 42, pp. 244–251

Roenneberg T, Kuehnle T, Pramstaller PP, Ricken J, Havel M, Guth A, et al. (2004) A marker for the end of adolescence, *Current Biology*, Vol. 14, No. 24, pp. 1038–1039

Simon HA (1996) Scientific discovery and the psychology of problem solving, in Colodny RD (Ed.), *Mind and Cosmos: Essays in Contemporary Science and Philosophy* (pp. 22–40), Pittsburgh, PA: University of Pittsburg Press

Sio UN & Ormerod TC (2009) Does incubation enhance problem solving? A meta-analytic review, *Psychological Bulletin*, Vol. 135, No. 1, pp. 94–120

Smallwood J, Obonsawin MC & Heim SD (2003) Task-unrelated thought: The role of distributed processing, *Consciousness and Cognition*, Vol. 12, pp. 169–189

Smallwood J, O'Connor RC, Sudberry MV & Ballantyre C (2004) The consequences of encoding information on the maintenance of internally generated images and thoughts: The role of meaning complexes, *Consciousness and Cognition*, Vol. 4, pp. 789–820

Smallwood J & Schooler JW (2006) The restless mind, *Psychological Bulletin*, Vol. 132, No. 6, pp. 946–958

Smith SM (1995) Fixation, incubation, and insight in memory and creative thinking, in Smith SM, Ward TB & Finke RA (Eds.), *The Creative Cognition Approach* (pp. 135–156), Cambridge, MA: MIT Press

Smith SM & Blankenship SE (1989) Incubation effects, *Bulletin of the Psychonomic Society*, Vol. 27, pp. 311–314

Staudenmayer N, Tyre M & Perlow L (2002) Time to change: Temporal shifts as enablers of organizational change, *Organization Science*, Vol. 13, No. 5, pp. 583–597

Van Oortmerssen LA, van Woerkum CMJ & Aarts N (2015) When interaction flows: An exploration of collective creative processes on a collaborative governance board, *Group & Organization Management*, Vol. 40, No. 4, pp. 500–528

Volk S, Pearsall MJ, Christian MS & Becker WJ (2017) Chronotype diversity in teams: Toward a theory of team energetic asynchrony, *Academy of Management Review*, Vol. 42, No. 4, pp. 683–702

Vollmer C & Randler C (2012) Circadian preferences and personality values: Morning types prefer social values, evening types prefer individual values, *Personality and Individual Differences*, Vol. 52, No. 6, pp. 738–743

Wallas G (1926) *The Art of Thought*, London: Cape

Webster A, Campbell C & Jane B (2006) Enhancing the creative process for learning in primary technology education, *International Journal of Technology and Design Education*, Vol. 16, pp. 221–235

Wieth MB & Zacks RT (2011) Time of day effects on problem solving: When the non-optimal is optimal, *Thinking & Reasoning*, Vol. 17, No. 4, pp. 387–401

Wittmann M & Merrow M (2006) Social Jetlag: Misalignment of Biological and Social Time, *Chronobiology International*, Vol. 23, No. 1–2, pp. 497–509

Zellmer-Bruhn M, Waller MJ & Ancona D (2004) The effect of temporal entrainment on the ability of teams to change their routines, *Research on Managing Groups and Teams*, Vol. 6, pp. 135–158

Zhong CB, Dijksterhuis A & Galinsky A (2008) The merits of unconscious thought in creativity, *Psychological Science*, Vol. 19, pp. 912–918

Part 5

Concluding remarks
The way ahead

We have endeavoured to take a look into the future of engineering education and in doing so we have concluded that it will be interdisciplinary. We have also posited that teaching and learning in engineering has to undergo some radical changes through breaking boundaries.

The world is complex, interconnected, and in constant turmoil. This constantly, rapidly changing, unrelenting flux can be scary, but it can also be exciting. It is a challenge, but also an opportunity. In this 'liquid world' those who are 'good swimmers' will thrive. Employability attributes such as positive attitudes, confidence, competence, self-promotional and career management skills, the willingness to learn, keep on learning, and reflect on learning will help our future engineers to deal with perpetual change.

This will require a holistic approach in integrating knowledge with practical experience, technical, and non-technical interactive skills, achievable through an interdisciplinary approach and the breaking down of existing boundaries and barriers. It will involve flexibility and an open approach by all stakeholders and a change of ethos.

We should not aspire to create experts full of facts but to assist our future engineers to become complete individuals with the know-how to use these facts, and confidence in their abilities to do so, as well as the flexibility of mind to adapt to whatever particular challenges they will face.

However, apart from the substantial body of knowledge our future engineers will have to acquire in the particular disciplinary field of their choice, they must also possess a thirst for knowledge which they will have to maintain, keep up-to-date, and improve throughout their careers.

In order to be fit-for-purpose, our educational systems must be able to rekindle in our students the spirit of curiosity, creativity, and enterprise we all have as children. In parallel, we need to expose them to critical and constructive thinking, and enable them to develop original ideas and turn them into ideas of value. Such ideas always benefit when they are exposed and examined through different perspectives. Ideas have to be communicated across boundaries, and in doing so, the personal and professional communication skills of our engineers will be strengthened. At the same time, we must be able to build their confidence so they can balance a competitive spirit with a spirit of collaboration.

Confidence is built on self-esteem and self-belief, so the educational voyages of our students must allow time for self-discovery and self-reflection. Multidisciplinary projects, flipped classes, interactive laboratory work, and liberal studies, such as discussed in the earlier pages of this book, all provide for a diverse communication of ideas, collaborating, and real-world experiences across disciplines. Such approaches contribute to our future graduate engineers in learning to work in partnership across disciplines and cultures, learning to constructively criticize and at the same time be tolerant of the ideas and opinions of others.

Approaches such as these are of course not without risks. However, when they are carefully designed and implemented in a supportive environment, they allow our students to become more comfortable in understanding the realities of working in teams, under real time pressures, in order to manage and deliver complex and, at times, not clearly defined goals.

The various proposals we have advocated provide our future engineers with rich hands-on experiences for putting their ideas and knowledge into practice for 'real' clients well before they graduate. Dealing with messy, vague, not cleanly defined, open-ended problems forces the students to ask questions in order to clarify what is intended, further embedding their communication, team working, networking, and other interpersonal skills.

Such engaged learning gives students more accountability and sets them on the way to becoming independent learners, and typically has the extra benefit of acting as the starting point of a positive motivating cycle.

Through exposure to influences from the increased cultural connectivity, as one by-product of globalization, there is a growing awareness of how and what other people learn, and we see the influence of non-Western educational thinking that is slowly being amalgamated into our own approaches to education.

We are talking about liberal studies, renaissance engineers, transformative learning, educating the complete person, holistic approaches to learning, etc. These perspectives are much more attuned to the social communal nature of learning traditionally accepted in non-Western societies, where one learns for the benefit of society rather than individual personal gain.

Moving into the 21st century, we are stepping out from the cognitive domain that dominated education of the recent past by integrating all four domains. The cognitive, the affective, the conative, and the psychomotor domains involve not only the capacity to think but also the mind, body, and emotions, recognizing that there is no separation between body and mind.

Of course, this is nothing new. Greeks were lauding education and the pursuit of knowledge from the time of the 5th century BC; Consider ἀνεξέταστος βίος οὐ βιωτὸς ἀνθρώπῳ, "The unexamined life is not worth living," the learning of mathematics and science, and the sign Μηδείς ἀγεωμέτρητος εἰσίτω, "Let no one ignorant of Geometry enter" printed at the entrance of Plato's Academy, as well as the Socratic espousing of self-awareness, γνῶθι σεαυτόν, "Know thyself." In Socrates, Plato, and Aristotle we find skills such as logic, critical thinking, problem solving, and resilience are highly valued.

The idea of signature pedagogies used as a vehicle for the scholarship of teaching and learning in engineering education and their alignment is argued to be a good methodology to be adopted. This approach sets quality teaching and learning upon three fundamental dimensions, developing within our students the habits of heart, mind, and hands appropriate for enterprising behaviour, in the context of engineering education. Achieving such integration is aimed at initiating our students into the best values and behaviours through which to participate more fully in their potential futures, a fundamental aim of scholarly teaching.

It is plainly clear that the challenges facing us are global and as such they have to be approached in a joined holistic way if we are to make any headway in facing them. We have set out our ideas for the need to develop a holistic and interdisciplinary approach to the education of our future engineers on a model of student-based learning. This approach has many implications for all key stakeholders, and requires the active contribution of all participants in order to break down discipline-based norms and planning procedures.

As described in this collection of ideas about teaching and learning, educators are stepping up to the challenge, and although allowances have to be made, what is stopping us is only the limits of our own imagination. It is well worth remembering what Lee Shulman said in his "Signature pedagogies in the professions," in *Daedalus*, summer 2005, that "the way we teach will shape how professionals behave – and in a society dependent on the quality of its professionals, that is no small matter."

We looked into the future of engineering education, and anyone foolhardy enough to put their head above the parapet knows, as Niels Bohr succinctly stated, that "prediction is difficult, especially about the future."

However, there is nothing preventing us from imagining the future we want for ourselves, our children, and our children's children, and then expending our efforts to create that future for ourselves and them; this way we can be masters of our future, and not simple bystanders of it.

Index

AAU *see* Alborg University
ABET 20, 24, 50, 97, 134
abilities 63, 74, 97, 117, 118, 121, 152, 154, 165, 169, 191
Academogy 157
active interviews 63
active learning 25, 29, 77, 78, 79, 82, 83, 84, 86, 88, 89
activity theory 171, 172, 173
aesthetics 15, 29, 49, 56
agreeableness 183
Alborg University 21
A levels 10
alumni 61, 65, 66, 68, 69, 70
andragogy 156, 173
ANOVA 97
appreciation for beauty 121
apprenticeships 10, 11
aptitudes 53, 116
architecture 20, 29, 53, 56
artificial intelligence 153
ASIIN 97
assessment framework 97, 98, 103, 106
assessment models 152
attendance monitoring 44, 45
attitudes 52, 90, 113, 114, 115, 116, 117, 120, 121, 122, 126, 128, 135, 191
authenticity 91, 123
authentic signature pedagogy 169

basic skills 115
Behaviour in Teams: BIT 71
Bildung 124
blogs 57
Bloom's cognitive taxonomy 81
Bologna recommendations 96

capstone 138
carefulness 91, 123

cascade teaching 61, 63, 67, 73
case studies 27, 82, 83, 86, 88, 128
CDIO 24, 25, 52
charging models 35
charity 56
Chartered Engineers 50, 51
chronotypes 182, 186
circadian rhythms 182, 183, 184
in class quizzes 81
cognitive performance 182
collaborative online tools 66
commitment 49, 50, 91
communicating and defending ideas 62
competencies 39, 90, 95, 96, 101, 109, 111, 114, 117, 119, 125, 144, 147, 152, 161, 166
complex problems 70, 83, 157
conformance 183
conformist personality 183
conscientiousness 183
conscious competence 119
conscious incompetence 119
constructive alignment 123, 170, 171
continual reflection 122
continuous reflection 91, 123, 124
core skills 60, 119
costing models 35, 45
co-teaching 144
courage 91, 123, 160
creativity 1, 14, 62, 72, 90, 128, 129, 142, 147, 148, 152, 153, 154, 155, 160, 161, 177, 178, 179, 180, 181, 182, 183, 185, 186, 191
creativity crisis 152
critical skills 11, 119
cross-cutting skills 116, 119
cross-disciplinary working 29, 59
cultural collectivism 183
cultural individualism 183

cultural values 135, 137
curiosity 1, 12, 121, 159, 160, 166, 191
curriculum 28, 37, 39, 40, 49, 52, 59, 60, 61, 90, 120, 123, 135, 142, 144, 147, 153, 156, 172

death by PowerPoint 73
decision-making methodology 97, 103
declarative knowledge 117
Delft University of Technology 144
demonstrator recruitment and payment 44
design of the teaching spaces 38
design thinking 138, 154, 166
desire 90, 118, 121, 128, 166, 169
dispositions 90, 91, 113, 120, 123, 128
distance learning 1, 2, 17, 18, 19, 20, 24
divergent thinking 28, 153, 154, 181

Education for Capability 20, 25
efficiency gains 33, 42, 44
e-learning enabled delivery 98
emotional engagement 154
Emotional Intelligence 117
Employment-related skills 116, 119
Engagement Teaching Methods for Engineers 85
Engineering Council, The 23, 50, 69
engineering design process 12, 62, 63, 72
Engineering Habits of Mind 2, 15
engineering lite 135, 137
engineering practice 98, 99, 133, 134, 135, 136, 126
engineering problems 61
engineering skills challenge 11, 15
engineering skills shortage 2, 8
Engineers Australia 97
engineer's habits of mind 166
enjoyment 122, 123, 124
enterprise education 147, 165, 166, 167, 168, 169, 170, 171, 172, 173, 174
enthusiasm 21, 91, 123
entrepreneurial learning 152
entrepreneurship 101, 137, 154, 167, 90, 96, 127, 142, 154, 156, 159
entrepreneurship education 166, 170
essays 57, 122
ethics 29, 49, 50, 56, 83
examination strategies 152
experiential learning 122, 124, 165
experimental activities 47

face-to-face promotive interaction 70
facilitators 61, 62, 63, 66, 67, 70, 73, 74
failure 25, 40, 59, 78, 83, 91, 123, 124

feedback 2, 45, 57, 62, 66, 67, 71, 76, 80, 91, 120, 121, 123, 126
finance 29, 33, 50, 56
Finniston Report 20
flipped class 78, 80, 82, 192
flipped class method 80
Flipped Learning Network 81
framework development and testing 97, 103
freedom 91, 122, 123, 124, 141, 168, 173
freeloading 70, 73

GCSEs 8, 9, 10
generic skills 119
generosity 91, 123
Global Engineering Challenge 29, 59
grade data input 44
graduate teaching assistants: GTAs 44
Grand challenges for Engineering 6
group cohesion 180
group creativity 177, 179, 180, 181, 183, 186
Group processing 70
growth mindsets 152
GTAs *see* graduate teaching assistants
guide-on-the-side 1, 29, 57, 155

habits of mind 2, 12, 15, 166, 167
Harvey Mudd College 51
Health and Safety 41, 42, 43, 44, 55, 114
Health and Safety compliance 44
heutagogy 156, 157, 173
higher education 10, 20, 60, 95, 96, 114, 135, 142
holiploigy 120, 121
Humanitarian Engineering 52

IChemE 95, 97
implementation 67, 95, 98, 103, 128, 142, 147, 152
In-class Reflections 84
incubation 177, 178, 179, 180, 185, 186, 187
incubation breaks 177
incubation periods 187
individual accountability 70
induction labs 41
innovation 5, 17, 31, 74, 91, 126, 127, 133, 135, 142, 147, 148, 151, 152, 153, 154, 155, 160, 161, 165, 166, 177
Innovation and Ideas Creation 74
innovation educator 155
instrumental reasoning 143
integrity 91, 123, 139
intellectual humility 91, 123
Intellectual Property 114
interactive-engagement methods 78

interdisciplinary programmes 33, 37, 40
interdisciplinary teams 59
interpersonal 50, 70, 117, 127, 192
Intersections of Technology, Social Justice, and Conflict 138
intrapersonal intelligence 117
intrinsic goals 144
iTeach European project consortium 95

key competencies 119
knowing student 128

lab books 43
laboratories 18, 19, 22, 33, 34, 36, 37, 38, 43, 44, 45, 91, 135
laboratory space provision 35
large class sizes 38
Lassonde School of Engineering 51
Laurentian University 51
leadership experience 66
learning activities 77, 78, 123, 170, 171
learning objectives 79, 80, 83
learning outcomes 22, 25, 39, 53, 54, 55, 95, 96, 98, 99, 110, 125, 151, 156, 170, 172
learning to be 120, 154, 160
learning unit 79, 80, 86
lecture-centric modules 77, 78
liberal arts enriched 137
Liberal Engineering 29, 49, 50, 51, 52
Liberal Science 49, 51
Liberal Studies in Engineering 133, 135, 136, 137, 138, 139, 142, 143, 144
liquid knowledge 169
'liquid' world 119, 120, 191
LSD 97

marketing 29, 50, 56, 63
marking 45, 62, 66, 72
mathematical habits of mind 13
meddler-in-the-middle 155, 156, 158
MEE *see* Multidisciplinary Engineering Education
memory 156, 158, 159, 178, 179, 185
mind-wandering 185
MIT 18, 21, 24, 143, 133
module design 79, 82, 85, 86, 88
MOOC 18
morality 137
motivation 68, 114, 121, 123, 133, 144, 154, 156, 157, 180, 184, 186
multi-disciplinary, multi-cultural team working 62

multidisciplinary approach 28, 33, 34, 35, 37, 38, 44, 47
Multidisciplinary Engineering Education 34, 35, 37, 39, 40, 41, 42, 43, 44, 45
multi-objective optimization 97, 103
mutual learning 145

Narrow Demographic 136
National Science Foundation 133
negotiation processes 180
networking 70, 114, 116, 126, 157, 192
neuroticism 183
Nipissing University 51
NMiTE 29, 49, 50, 51, 52, 57
noise pollution 29, 56
nurturing team working 66

off-task breaks 148, 177, 178, 179, 180, 181, 182, 184, 185, 186, 187
Olin College 51
online marking 66
online quizzes 80, 81
openness 91, 123, 135, 142, 183
Open Resources 18
Open University 17, 18, 19

passion 121, 170, 171
PBL 21, 60, 82, 83, 114
pedagogical advantages 33
pedagogical options 123
pedagogy 12, 29, 56, 77, 82, 83, 123, 156, 166, 167, 169, 174
peer assessment 63, 73
performative student 128
Personal & Professional Skills 113, 124, 128
personal and professional development 69
personal development 59, 117, 125, 167, 172
personality characteristics 117
philosophy 133, 137
plasticity 154, 159
'plasticity' of the brain 154
politics and political protest 29, 56
pooling resources 38
positive interdependence 70
Post-16 education pathways 9
practical skills 23, 41, 98
practical teaching 28, 33, 34, 35, 37, 38, 39, 40, 42, 44, 47, 66
present-show-try 82
problem-based learning 21, 60, 67, 82, 85, 88, 114
problem-based learning 23, 80
problem identification 12, 166

problem solving and creativity 62
problem solving skills 99, 119, 144
procedural knowledge 117
procurement 44
productivity gap 177
professional development 69, 99, 117, 125
professional identity 137
professionalism 40, 114, 116
professional skills 95, 113, 119, 124, 125, 128
profit motive 29, 56
progressive practical curriculum 39
public health 29, 56
public presentations 57
Purdue Polytechnic 138, 139

QAA 114, 123, 152, 165, 167
Quest University 51

readiness for employment 116
reasonable adventurer, the 122, 167
reflecting on learning and articulating knowledge 62
reflection 41, 53, 61, 66, 75, 84, 88, 117, 118, 121, 122, 123, 124, 126, 134, 140, 143, 158, 166, 167, 168, 169, 192
reports 57, 62, 71, 84, 114, 116, 136
Researcher Development Framework 116, 124
resilience 91, 123, 166, 192
respect for others 91, 123
restraint 91, 123
rigid structures 135
role model 69, 156
Royal Academy of Engineering 11, 12, 28, 59

sage-on-the-stage 1, 155
scientific habits of mind 13
self-assessment skills 119
self-belief 91, 120, 123, 192
self-confidence 91, 120, 123
self determination theory 157
self-discipline 24, 91, 123, 192
self-exploration 122, 124
self-motivation 91, 120, 123
self-reflection 120, 192
service teaching 34, 35
skilled student 128
skills development 60, 67, 68, 69, 74, 75
Smith College 138, 139
social-cognitive factors 179
socialization processes 180, 181, 183, 186
social jetlag 183

sociology 29, 56, 143
soft skills 60, 119
space utilization 45
spiral curriculum 60
SPSS 97
staff time 35, 44, 45, 63
STEM 77, 78, 136, 137
sticky learning 158
student cantered experiential learning 122, 124
student motivation 68
subconscious competence 119
subconscious incompetence 119
sustainability 61, 68, 72, 144
sustainable design 62
Sustainable Development Goals 1, 7
synthesis 154, 158

TDU *see* Technical Univeristy of Denmark
Teaching and Learning International Survey: TALIS 160
teaching sandwich 41
team reflection/review 66
Technical University of Denmark 21
think-pair-share 84
timeliness of activity 38
time-of-day effect 182
timetabling 20, 36, 38, 44
tolerance of ambiguity 167, 183
transferable skills 74, 99, 114, 119, 124, 127
transformative learning 166, 168, 169, 192
tutorials 77, 81, 82
two I 147, 151, 160, 161

UCL 51
unconscious moments 187
unconscious problem-solving 177
underpinning skills 119
Univ California 143
University of Portland 143

values 117, 121, 122, 135, 137, 141, 167, 174, 183, 193
virtual learning environment: VLE 62
visioning skills 28, 153
vocational and technical pathways 10
voting systems 66

Wakeham Review 60, 75
web sites 57
Wellesley College 138, 139
willingness to speak 91, 123
Working in Groups 84, 88

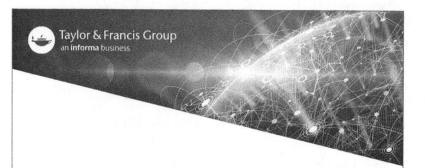